A HISTORY OF MARKSMANSHIP

CHARLES CHENEVIX TRENCH

LONGMAN

Printed in Great Britain by Jarrold & Sons Ltd, Norwich

A HISTORY OF MARKSMANSHIP

Contents

Acknowledgements   7

1   Primitive Missile Weapons and Marksmanship   9

2   Bowman's Glory   23

3   Modern Archery   77

4   Villainous Saltpetre   103

5   Shooting Flying   126

6   Musket and Rifle   193

7   Pistols and Revolvers   226

8   Modern Rifle Shooting   251

Index   317

ACKNOWLEDGEMENTS

The author and publishers wish to thank the following for permission to reproduce the many paintings, drawings, photographs, illustrations from books, etc. with which their book is illustrated.

Messrs V. Alinari
Basil Boothroyd, Esq.
Kelvin Brodie, Esq.
Bibliothèque Nationale, Paris
Bibliothèque Royale, Bruxelles
Bodleian Library, Oxford
The Trustees of the British Museum
Bürgerbibliothek, Bern
The Chester Beatty Library, Dublin
Deutsche Jägerverein
Mrs Mary Farnell
Freer Gallery of Art, Washington
Germanisches Nationalmuseum
Messrs Stephen Grant and Joseph Lang Ltd
Haddon Library, Cambridge
Mr Karel Hajek
Messrs Hämmerli, Switzerland
E. G. Heath, Esq.,
Max Hirmer
Hermitage Museum, Leningrad
Mr J. Holecek
Messrs Holland and Holland Ltd
Mr C. O. v. Kienbusch
Lehnert & Landrock
Mr Jaroslav Lugs
John Marchington, Esq.
L. MacNally, Esq.
McCord Museum, Montreal
Metropolitan Museum of Art, New York
Ministério de Educação Nacional – Direcção-Geral do Ensino Superior e das Belas Artes – Museu Nacional de Arte Antiga, Lisboa
Musée Crozatier, Puy-en-Velay
Musée Royal des Beaux-Arts de Belgique

Museo Nacional del Prado, Madrid
Museum of Fine Arts, Boston
National Gallery, London
Nationalmuseet, Copenhagen
Verlag J. Neumann-Neudamm
New York Public Library
Novosti Press Agency
Nyt Nordisk Forlag – Arnold Busck A/S, Copenhagen
Messrs Parker-Hale Ltd
The Earl of Pembroke
Axel Poignant, Esq.
J. and M. Ribière
Rijksmuseum, Amsterdam
Roy Shaw, Esq.
School of Infantry Small Arms Museum, Warminster
Messrs Singlepoint Ltd
Staatliche Graphische Sammlung, Munich
Staatliche Museen Preussischer Kulturbesitz, Berlin
Schweizerische Landesmuseum, Zürich
Mr Ivor Silis
Topkapi Saray Museum
Transworld Feature Syndicate
University Museum of Archaeology and Ethnology, Cambridge
Victoria and Albert Museum, London
Wallace Collection, London
West Point Museum, New York
Roger Wood, Esq.
Messrs Carl Zeiss, Oberkochen
Zentral Bibliothek, Zürich

1

Primitive Missile Weapons and Marksmanship

It is sometimes said, by those who wish to shock their audience and to disparage the wisdom of the ages, that man is simply an animal who cooks his food. It might equally well be said that man is an animal, the only animal, who uses missile weapons. There are rather dubious accounts of monkeys tossing twigs and dirt. Denham and Clapperton, nineteenth-century explorers of Lake Chad, were 'gently pelted' by apes. But there are no authentic accounts of apes throwing things as weapons. So the first man to hurl a stone at a wild beast or at another man took an enormous step forward in the development of the human race, a step at least as important as the discovery of fire.

Weaker and slower than many animals, less well armed with tooth and claw, by devising a means of killing his meat or defending himself from a distance, he moved out from among them, established a special position for himself, a superiority which over millions of years was steadily to increase with the invention of one missile weapon after another. From among the brute creation, man stands out as a marksman.

No doubt men got the idea from seeing animals felled by stones falling down a cliff. From that it would be an easy step to push stones down, and then to throw them. It has been surmised, though there is no evidence, that in the history of man's aggression and self-defence stone-throwing preceded the use of hand-to-hand weapons: even the crudest club or spear needs some artificial shaping, while a stone can be hurled in its natural shape. The great apes seem to be nearer the use of stones than of clubs. Spears, with fire-hardened points, were in use about 400,000 B.C. so the stone as a missile weapon is of unimaginable antiquity.

But from it man learned the basic principles of ballistics and marksmanship. There is an ideal weight of stone, just as there is of arrow or bullet, for every job, varying mainly according to the range at which it is to be used. A stone weighing, say, 10 lb may deliver a crushing blow at a few yards, but cannot be thrown far. Nor can a stone which is too light; besides, it has little striking-energy. The best stone for all purposes is about the size of a cricket-ball, or baseball, perhaps a bit heavier. Up to an angle of forty-five degrees with the horizontal, the higher the stone's trajectory, the further it will go: but above forty-five degrees, the higher the trajectory, the shorter the range. All this, which we take for granted, primitive man had to learn from trial and error. The only basic problem of marksmanship with which he was not concerned was the effect of wind. A cross-wind has a very marked effect on the flight of arrow or bullet, but virtually none on a stone's cast.

The stone has always been man's commonest weapon, the first that came to hand.

9

The heroes of the *Iliad* opened a battle by stone-throwing. Hector,

> stooping to the ground
> With his broad hand a ponderous rock he seized
> That lay upon the plain, dark, jagged and huge,
> And hurled it against the sevenfold shield.

It is a formidable weapon up to some 50 yards. Australian aborigines, leaping from side to side to present a difficult target, could throw stones as fast and nearly as accurately, over a short range, as a magazine-rifle. From Jericho to Badajoz, stones hurled down at the storming-parties have been among the garrison's most fearsome weapons. Swiss mercenaries were formidable stone-throwers, going into battle with several stones each. As late as the Battle of Kappel (1531) their stone-throwing broke up the ranks and checked the impetus of an enemy cavalry charge.

Stoning to death is a very horrid form of execution, still used in some Moslem countries as the traditional punishment for a woman taken in adultery. A mob armed with nothing but stones is still something to fear, as any policeman in Paris or Belfast knows.

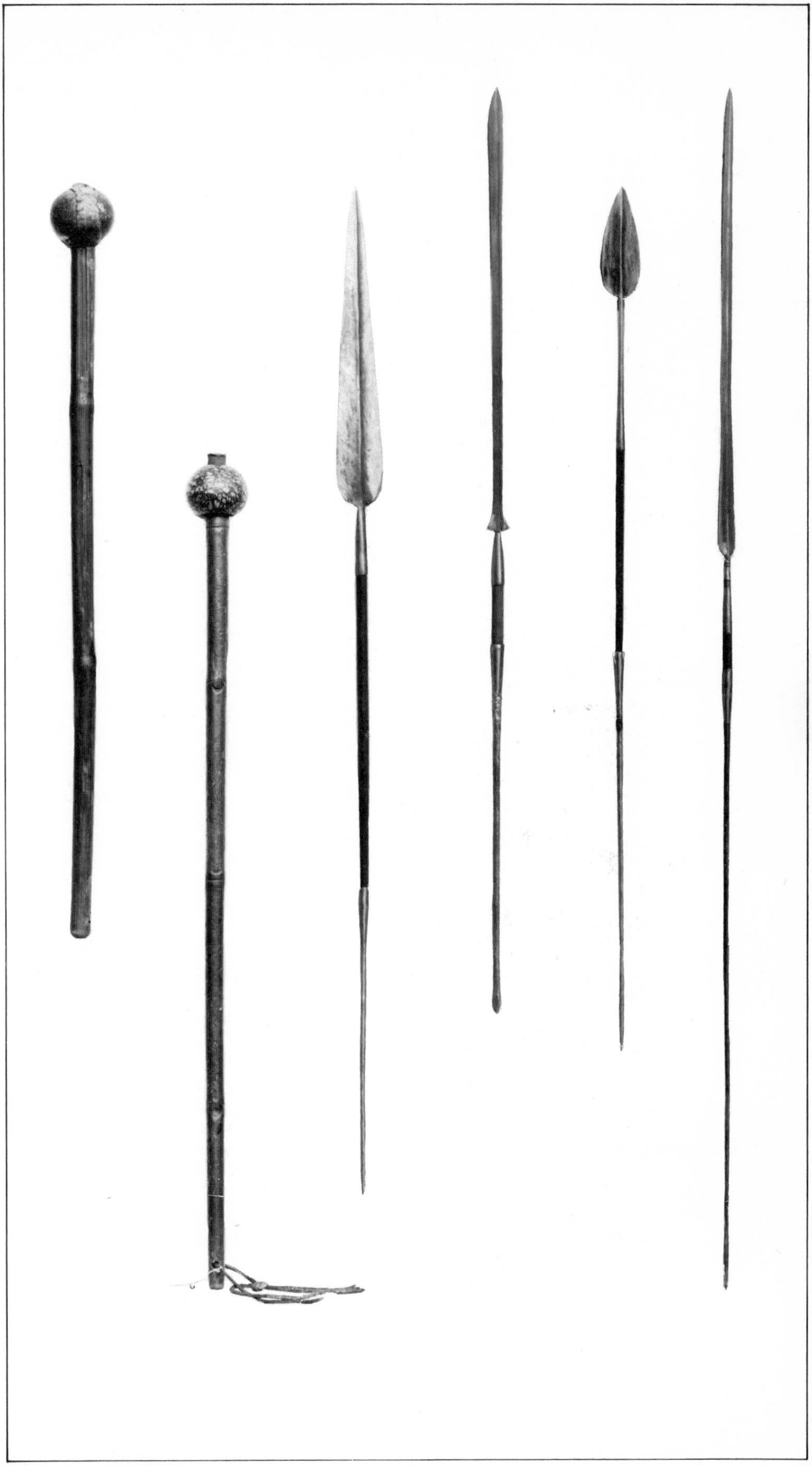

Knob-kiris –
Masai throwing-
spears

Opposite page
To pick up a stone
and throw it was
probably the first
act of missile man,
as it may well be
his last. The last
recorded use of
stone-throwing as
a military weapon
is the Battle of
Kappel in 1531.
Here they are
being used for
defence in 1476

The Ownep. New Caledonian version of the amentum: a separate looped cord with a knot at one end fastened to the shaft with a half-hitch

Opposite page, top
Portion of Upper Palaeolithic (Magdalenian) spear-thrower. Note the low relief carving of an ibex

Bottom
A spear-launcher on the same principle as the Magdalenian thrower

If a man is threatened by a bad-tempered dog, his first reaction is to reach for a stone. Raising a stick, or turning to run, may provoke an attack: the threat of a stone will deter one. In many parts of Asia and Africa crops are protected against pig and deer by a night-watchman on a high platform, armed with a bagful of stones.

Even against really dangerous animals a stone may be the answer. In Maralal, in the Samburu district of Kenya, at certain times of the year elephants used to invade our garden, making havoc of the herbaceous border, young trees, and vegetables. I used to keep a box of heavy stones on the veranda and, when elephants woke me up, hurry out in my dressing-gown to hurl these, with appropriate objurgations, at the huge dark shapes. A thump as a stone hit a ponderous barrel, a sudden silence – and they were gone.

We used to do a lot of safari on horseback, and lions are partial to horseflesh. Since a lion will always stalk upwind, lest his quarry scent him, the horses and camels were always tethered to trees with two or three fires downwind of them, the askaris sleeping in pairs near the fires. Unable to approach, lions used to circle the camp, hoping to stampede the horses: the first sign of one coming would be a restiveness among our animals, as they stood up, fidgeted uneasily, and stared into the darkness. Then the lions would start demonstrating – deep-bellied, grumbling grunts at first, working up to a full-throated roar – *Aaar-unh! Aaar-unh-unh-unh-unh-unh!* diminuendo.

It was impossible not to feel anxious, though reason argued that we were in no danger. The askaris and I had rifles, but would be mad to use one, as the chance of a kill was remote while a wounded lion is something no one likes to have round a camp. So if a lion could be located, crouching under a bush, say, 20 or 30 yards away, we would hurl volleys of stones at him. A thump as one hit the target, an indignant grunt, and he would go ambling away. So must our remote ancestors have driven away lions from their camp-fires and sheepfolds.

A swiftly moving snake is a difficult target, particularly if it is moving towards you. Fortunately, snakes seldom do. An exception is the hamadryad or king-cobra, which has a very aggressive nature. Jim Corbett, famous hunter of man-eating tigers, was attacked by a hamadryad just as he was closing on the man-eater he had been hunting for weeks, and did not wish to alarm her by a rifle-shot. Obeying the instinct of a million years, he stooped down for a good stone, hurled it at the snake and broke its back. He was a *very* good shot, with any missile weapon from stone to high-velocity rifle.

There is an ancient, atavistic thrill in a well-aimed stone's throw. The cruel sport, now illegal, of stoning a cock, modern games such as cricket and baseball are all founded on this. Throwing stones at a target is probably man's oldest competitive sport. What seaside holiday-maker can resist pelting a piece of floating driftwood or a groyne sticking out of the sea? A woman does not feel the same compulsion: aeons ago she stayed in the cave, while man fought and hunted for her.

The next missile weapon was the throwing-stick. Men discovered that a stone attached to a slender 18-inch or 2-foot handle which, so to speak, lengthened the thrower's arm, could be hurled with much more force than from the hand. From this developed a short stick, heavily weighted at one end. Known by a thousand names – *widda*, *rungu*, knobkerrie are common – it is still a favourite weapon of Australian and African tribes, a weapon to brain an enemy, bruise or smash his bones. Lighter throwing-sticks are used against birds. Modern European man is not very good at throwing: but H. S. Cowper* and a friend found it not difficult, with a little practice, to bring down a bird on the wing with throwing-sticks. The technique is to walk

* Author of *The Art of Attack* (1906).

13

The javelin

through the fields side by side and, when a bird is put up, for one hunter to aim above and one below it: avoiding one stick, the bird often flies into the path of the other. Many a beater has brought down a running hare with a whirling, well-thrown stick.

Some throwing-sticks are carved of a single piece of wood: others have a weight fixed to one end. There are in museums Australian aborigines' throwing-sticks to the end of which a heavy weight is fixed with a vegetable gum. Incredibly long ago the weight from a throwing-stick came off and, unimpeded by the shaft, flew fast and far. The sling was born, man's first precision weapon. The principle of the sling is the same as that of the throwing-stick. Within certain limitations imposed by the strength of his muscles, the longer a man's throwing-arm, the greater the force of his throw. The sling artificially lengthens his arm.

The earliest slings seem to have been solid. Two have been found in Spain, dating back to before 30,000 B.C.* They are made of stags' antlers, carved in the shape of a horse's head. The stone must have been wedged in the jaw, and discharged by a quick overarm jerk of the hand and arm. But it could hardly have been an accurate weapon, for the moment of discharge could not easily be regulated, so its

---

* Although described by archaeologists as slings, I wonder if they were, rather, spear-throwers.

14

trajectory must have been very unpredictable. Something better was needed, an extension to the thrower's arm which would release the stone at exactly the right point.

Man's answer to the problem – we have no idea when he found it – was to make a sling from a doubled strip of leather (or a pouch with a cord tied to each end of it). The stone is placed in the fold (or pouch), the loose ends of the sling are held in the thrower's hand, one perhaps tied to finger or thumb. He whirls the sling and, at the moment of projection, lets go the loose end of the sling to release the stone. It flies with great force and velocity.

The bola, which is essentially a stone fixed to the end of a cord, is a similar device, also of great antiquity. It is probably easier to use than the sling, but less efficient, since the cord flies off with the stone and is lost to the thrower. The bola survives as the gaucho's tool, instead of the lariat, in South America. Three stones, attached by cords to a central point (like a starfish) are hurled at the legs of a steer and, swinging round to secure them, bring him down. South American Indians, on horseback, used to hunt ostrich-like rhea with the bola.

The difficulty with the sling or bola lies in throwing with accuracy, in picking the precise moment to release the cord and let fly the stone. It is a skill developed only by endless practice. David, confronting Goliath, had no doubt that, with five smooth stones, he could hit a target the size of a man's (admittedly a giant's) forehead. At what range? We do not know, but further than Goliath could hurl his

Man's second composite weapon, the sling, in action.
From an early MS.

Aboriginal man's equipment: spears, spear-thrower,
boomerangs, club and digging stick

spear. If the latter was indeed like a weaver's beam, its head weighing 600 shekels of
iron, giant as he was, he could not have thrown it far.

In the days recorded by the Old Testament, the sling was a common weapon,
and the Hebrews, as became a people living in mountainous, stony country, very
skilled with it. Were there not, in the tribe of Benjamin alone, 'seven hundred chosen
men left-handed; every one could sling stones at an hairbreadth, and not miss'?
In David's tent too there were 'mighty men, helpers of war', who could use both the
right hand and the left in hurling stones – presumably with a sling.

Slingers (*petraboli*) were sometimes used on the flanks of Greek armies; but the
Greeks thought little of them, and despised this gadget as a servile weapon. However,
until the end of the Middle Ages, slingers from the Balearic Islands were employed
as mercenaries in the armies of southern Europe, so they must have been useful
soldiers. A heavy stone slung with force might stun a man even though he wore a
helmet, or crack his ribs or limbs though protected by mail. The sling was last used
in Europe for military purposes at the Battle of Sancerre in 1572.

Almost as old a weapon as the stone is the spear, and it is a very short step from
thrusting overhead with a spear to throwing it. The earliest spears were of wood, the
points sharpened and hardened by fire. Later, man made points of bone, flint and,
finally, of iron.

16

The throwing-spear or javelin was used in every continent and is still the most common weapon over the greater part of Africa: in many remote regions a man is seldom seen without one. There are two main types. The heavy spear, made mainly of iron, can be used either for stabbing or for throwing a short distance. It is a very powerful weapon, able by its weight to penetrate a shield or a rhinoceros's hide. In the ancient world it was exemplified by the Roman legionary's *pilum*, and nowadays a good example is the spear of the Masai *moran*. This has a double-edged, sword-like iron blade some 3 feet long; and an iron spike, of similar length, as its butt. Only the handle, a foot or so in length, is of wood. It has great penetrative power: not long ago a Masai *moran*, in a fit of temper, hurled his spear into the back of a District Officer. It passed clean through him, killing him on the spot, and stuck deep into a fence post beyond him. It is by no means unusual for a *moran* to kill a lion, a rhinoceros, or an elephant with this weapon. As the wounded animal dashes off, the protruding shaft is banged about by trees and bushes, and the sharp-edged spearhead makes a terrible wound inside, quickly bringing the poor beast down.

The other type is the throwing-spear proper, exemplified by the assegai of southern Africa. It is a light, slender weapon, which can be thrown much further than the Masai spear, effectively up to 40 or 50 yards, but does not have nearly such penetration or shock-effect. Recognizing this, Zulu warriors used to prove their valour and determination to get to close quarters by breaking their assegais off short, so that they were no use for throwing and could be used only to stab. When a Zulu impi broke its assegais, its enemies were in for trouble.

The ancient Persian javelin was only $2\frac{1}{2}$ or 3 feet long. So, too, must have been the javelin which poor old Saul threw, in one of his evil moods, at the unbearably successful, sly, and sychophantic David, since it was by implication an indoor weapon, kept at hand while he sat crosslegged upon the cushions of his throne. Belisarius, the great Byzantine general, devised a missile even shorter, only about 18 inches long, heavy and feathered at the butt like modern toy-darts. The troopers of his horse-guards carried two or three in clips inside each shield, and hurled them overhand at the enemies' faces in combat. Some short throwing-spears are pointed at both ends and thrown so as to turn in the air like a throwing-stick. The usual javelin is, however, at least 6 feet long and is thrown overhand so as to spin, like a rifle-bullet, on its own axis. The warriors of some African tribes vibrate the spear in the hand before throwing it, so that in flight the head describes the arc of a 6-inch circle. This, they believe, adds to its efficiency, but it is difficult to say why. One would have thought that a spear thrown true, so as to spin but fly quite straight, would gain both range and accuracy.

There have been various gadgets to lengthen the range of a javelin, all based on the principle of the sling, that a man can throw further if his arm is lengthened. The best known is the Australian spear-thrower or throwing-stick. This is elliptical in shape and about $2\frac{1}{2}$ feet long. At one end is the handle; at the other, a stud pointing back towards the handle. The spearman grasps the handle, the instrument held back over his shoulder, the stud uppermost. The spear rests on the flat surface of the spear-thrower, held lightly between the spearman's finger and thumb, the stud inserted into a hole in the spear-butt. As the cast is made, the effect is as though the

Bladder-float and Eskimo harpoon

spearman's arm is lengthened by 2 feet or more, and the spear is hurled to a pro-digious distance, it is claimed as far as 150 yards, though I personally take this figure with a pinch of salt.

The Australian aboriginal was not the only Stone Age man to use the rigid spear-thrower. In the Upper Palaeolithic (Magdalenian) deposits in southern France so many spear-throwers have been found, operating on exactly the principle just described, as to suggest that men 50,000 years ago hunted the reindeer princi-pally by these means. One is here illustrated, carved from horn with an ibex ram in low-relief.

A less effective device is a sling, some 9 inches long, attached to the spear-shaft at the point of balance. Throwing overhand, one holds the end of the sling and the effect is, again, to lengthen the arm. So a longer range is achieved, probably at some cost in accuracy.

Spearheads have been made in infinite variety, of many materials but principally flint and iron. Some are made narrow to penetrate deep, others broad to make a wider wound; some are barbed, so that they cannot be withdrawn without tearing the victim most hideously; others are detachable, so that the head remains embedded in the flesh when the shaft is pulled away.

In the ancient Mediterranean world the javelin was the horseman's favourite weapon. Riding bareback, he could not sit firm enough for shock-action or to wield sword or spear in a mêlée, but was used rather for reconnaissance, skirmishing, and pursuit. The horseman's favourite tactic was to canter up to some 15 yards of the enemy, hurl a javelin, wheel round and withdraw. It is not surprising that he was less feared and less valued than the heavily armed hoplite or legionary fighting blade to blade on foot. These feeble tactics survived in Spain, a military backwater, until the Late Middle Ages; and the *jerid*, a sort of mounted chase and mock combat fought with blunted javelins, was founded on them. But in northern Europe the javelin was not much used: the spear became the infantryman's pike or the horse-man's lance. Right up to the eighteenth century, however, the javelin was used in display and in sport, being one of the weapons – with sword, lance, and pistol, used in riding-school displays and practices. From the *Iliad* we learn that javelin-throwing as a sport dates back at least as far as the siege of Troy.

18

Stone, throwing-stick, sling, and javelin – these were the earliest missile weapons of primitive man, and all survive, as weapons, for sport and war, to our day. Before going on to the far more sophisticated bow, we may examine some other missile weapons which, though extremely simple, cannot be positively traced back to Neolithic man. Among the most interesting is the boomerang.

There is in a drawing from ancient Egypt a man holding something which looks very like a boomerang, and the Bhils and Marawas, Indian jungle tribes, may have used this weapon in the past. But so far as is positively known, the boomerang was developed and used only by the aboriginal tribes of Australia, whose culture 200 years ago was more primitive than that of Neolithic man.

The heavy type, used for war and for hunting animals, is simply a form of throwing-stick, with a sharp, cutting edge and two rounded points. Thrown so as to spin rapidly as it flies through the air, it can cut into flesh or break bone up to a considerable distance. A hundred and fifty yards has been quoted as its maximum effective range, though frankly this sounds incredible. It does not return to the thrower.

Head of a harpoon

The returning boomerang is a light model, used only for hunting birds, or as a toy. It is made of wood, angled in shape, flattish in section – one side being convex and the other flat or slightly concave. It is gripped at one end, the other end pointing towards the target, the convex side uppermost, and thrown with a violent jerk so as to spin rapidly, like a plate, as it flies through the air. If it is thrown into a slight breeze, and is still spinning fast when the forward momentum is lost, then it will rise in the air and, still spinning, return to the thrower. I cannot do the trick, but I can well understand that, given a strong wrist and forearm, one could eventually learn it. To achieve a simple return is said to be comparatively easy, but I am told (though I have never seen it) that the real aboriginal expert can make the boomerang loop the loop and perform a pirouette before starting on its return journey. The practical value of the returning boomerang is that, without being lost, it can be thrown at a bird over water or thick bush. Of course, it only returns if it misses: if it hits the target or anything else, it drops. Stories of a boomerang decapitating a foe and returning, all bloody, to the hand which threw it are products of some travellers' exotic imaginations – or perhaps of the Australian addiction to pulling legs.

There is no evidence of prehistoric man using the blow-pipe as a weapon, though the Stone Age artist did use a short one to spray paint on cave walls. Of course, the blow-pipe is a common weapon only where materials for it can easily be found, long hollow tubes such as the bamboo provides. It is, therefore, a weapon of tropical jungle, notably of South-East Asia and South America. Perhaps it was brought to Europe by Arab traders; it is mentioned as a fowler's weapon in Pietro de Crescenti's *Opus Ruralium Commodorum* (1425). Eighteenth-century fishing-tackle and sporting-goods dealers advertise 'trunks', which seem to have been blow-pipes used for shooting darts and pellets at small birds. It was known also in France, Italy, and Germany; and today it survives precariously as the pea-shooter. If men used these weapons many thousands of years ago, we have no proof of it: but our knowledge of prehistoric man comes mainly from countries with drier climates where their art and some of their weapons can still be found.

Used as a weapon, the blow-pipe is a small-bore, hollow tube, usually from 6 to 10 feet long. The missile is a light dart, some 9 inches long, with a cone or ball of cotton at the butt end to prevent any escape of air when the blower blows. Its maximum range is said to be, if the blower has lungs of leather and a really good puff, no more than 140 feet, its effective range, with any degree of accuracy, about half that. The muzzle velocity of the blow-pipe is obviously low, the missile light, so it has very little penetration. Its efficacy depends on its being poisoned. Depending on the strength of the poison, it can be lethal for birds, quite large animals, or man.

There are various multiple-bladed, or multiple-beaked throwing weapons, the principle of which is that they are thrown overarm and made to spin so that one

The aerodynamic boomerang designed by Dr Brenning James. Probably the first weapon of this kind to be really effective

The sampit of the Sunda Islands. 6–8 feet long, it was
shod with a piece of iron like a bayonet, enabling it to
be used as a lance as well

blade is bound to penetrate. They could be so easily deflected that they cannot have
been very efficient weapons.

Finally, there is the *chakra*, the war quoit of the Sikhs. Made of steel, this can never
have been used by primitive man, and no one has found anything like it of stone, so
one can assume that it is not a device of great antiquity. It has been suggested that the
ancient Greek discus was originally a weapon similar to the *chakra*, but so far as I
know there is neither archaeological nor literary evidence to support this theory.
Until the eighteenth century the Akali Sikh used to go to battle with two or three
chakra, of some 7 inches internal diameter, carried, like coronets, round his high,
conical turban. The weapon was, apparently, spun round the forefinger and hurled
spinning with great force but, one suspects, little accuracy. Heavy and razor-edged,
it could cut through neck or arm. Being the target for a succession of *chakra* hurled by
an expert must have been an alarming experience, but it was not so useful a weapon
as to survive into modern times.

From a gunsmith's catalogue of 1928

of negro archers marching
from the tomb of an officer
... in on one side and
...he

2
Bowman's Glory

None of these primitive weapons could compare in range or accuracy with the bow, which is man's first 'device in which energy can be accumulated slowly, stored temporarily and released suddenly under control and direction'.*

It is an invention of extraordinarily ingenuity, devised, so far as one can see, from nothing. One can readily trace from stone and club the ancestry of the throwing-stick, bola, sling, and javelin; but one cannot see how the bow could have evolved gradually from previous inventions. That it originated from a game-trap made of a bent tree is the only positive suggestion I have seen, and I find it singularly unconvincing.

It is very remarkable that the bow should have been in use in prehistoric times in every continent except Australasia. One can see how its use could have spread rapidly over Europe, Asia, and Africa: the first tribe armed with the bow would have an immeasurable advantage, in hunting and in war, over its neighbours, so that by conquest and imitation this wonderful invention would spread rapidly. But in the Americas the bow must surely have had another inventor, an origin independent of Eurasia. Of this, however, we have no positive proof: archaeological evidence of the earliest bows has been found only in Europe and North Africa.

Japanese
throwing arrows

Opposite page
Models of Negro
bowmen from the
tomb of Masabili
(Middle Kingdom)

It used to be thought that the bow was a Post-Glacial Mesolithic invention, dating from about 12,000 B.C. But the discovery in south-east Spain and north-west Africa of large numbers of flint arrow-heads dating back to Glacial, Upper Palaeolithic times, between 50,000 and 30,000 B.C., proves that the bow is a much older invention. It may even precede these arrow-heads: for arrows can be, and still are,

---

* *Encyclopaedia Britannica*, 'Archery'.

tipped with bone, or simply made of pointed wood. So we really have no evidence of how old the bow is, but it was certainly invented over 30,000 years ago.

Whether or not man used the bow, with plain wooden or bone-tipped arrows, before he learned the art of flaking arrows from flint, there is no doubt that the flint arrow-head, sharp-edged and pointed, tanged so that it could be easily fitted to a shaft and barbed so that it could not easily be withdrawn, greatly increased the efficiency of the bow. A flint arrow-head is not a toy: modern experiments have proved that it has just as good a penetration through hide, muscle, and flesh as a steel arrow-head. Its drawback is that it is brittle, and snaps if it strikes bone.

The first arrows, as we can see from cave-paintings, were fletched. The multiplicity of eagle remains found in Stone Age settlements suggests that the eagle's feathers were most used for fletching. The shaft was straightened and smoothed by grooved stone arrow-straighteners. By the year 1200 B.C., if not before, man was protecting his wrist against the bowstring with a stone wrist-guard. The bowstring must have been made of animal tendons, chewed until soft and pliable, then twisted into a cord.

The bow and the flint-tipped arrow greatly increased man's hunting powers at a time when, as the ice slowly receded, Eurasia swarmed with game. It also added small animals and birds to his diet. In the Glacial Age man grew no crops and kept

24

no domestic animals to milk. But meat alone was bad for him, he needed vegetables too. The collection of edible fruit and berries was slow and laborious at the best of times, in winter impossible; his digestion could not cope with grass and lichens. But the reindeer's could. So by far the easiest way to supplement and vary his meat diet was to shoot a reindeer and eat the sour, half-digested stomach contents, mainly lichens and other plants which are rich in iodine and vitamins, just what man needed. In the autumn this unappetizing but nutritious mess could be frozen hard and, during the next six or eight months, sliced like salami to provide winter vegetables.

With the more plentiful and more varied diet provided by the bow, man must have increased and multiplied. He also had time off from food-procuring to cultivate the arts of gracious living, to develop his spiritual potentialities, and to contemplate the immaterial world. Sculpture and cave-painting followed the invention of the bow.

Man did not practise art for art's sake, he did not paint or carve simply to give pleasure to himself and others: this is proved by the fact that many cave-paintings are in deep, dark caverns where they could hardly be seen save obscurely by torch-light, and are superimposed on one another so that it is difficult to make them out. Man's art was a form of magic, of wish-fulfilment. By carving, with remarkable skill, the rich, voluptuous lines of the pregnant Venus of Laussel, he assured that more women of his tribe would attain that happy state. He painted bowmen slaying ibex or deer in order to make it so. Once he had depicted an animal being shot, that animal was already half-dead. His painting was a trap in which game had to go.

Blame for failure or honour for success went less to the hunters than to the artist. With his magical powers, he was a professional man, privileged, exempt from the food-procuring duties enjoined upon others. An even earlier professional was the arrow-head-flaker. Palaeolithic, and later Mesolithic, flint arrow-heads are wonderful works of art, turned out as regularly almost as a factory model. Indeed they were, in a sense, factory models: the concentrations in which they are found suggests that they were turned out, not by any Tom, Dick, or Harry, but in regular workshops by specialist artificers.

Agreeing roughly on when the bow was invented – at any rate in Europe and North Africa, where they have chiefly investigated – archaeologists differ strongly on who invented it. The general consensus seems to be that it was invented south of the Alps and the Pyrenees, either by the Solutreans of south-east Spain, or by the Aterians who inhabited what is now Morocco. It is unnecessary for us to get involved in these learned controversies. What is most interesting to us is the type of bow they used.

The simplest form is a 'self-bow', made of a single stave of wood, bent into a plain arc. Obviously this was the earliest bow. The oldest bow yet discovered is of this type, found in a Mesolithic settlement at Holmegaard in Denmark, made between 8000 and 7000 B.C. The dig provided one complete bow, and fragments of two or three more. They have no 'string follow', that is to say no bend caused by remaining strung, which suggests that they are unfinished, or at least unused weapons in a workshop. They all seem to be of the same type.

The complete bow is 152 centimetres or about 5 feet long. (One of the fragmentary

Reconstruction
made in the
laboratory
of the Cambridge
Museum of
Archaeology

Opposite page
A 20th-century
Vedda using a
simple bow and an
iron-tipped arrow

bows seems to have been between 160 and 170 centimetres.) It is no mere stave, but properly fashioned, of elm. The back (the side furthest from the archer) is smoothed flat, the belly rounded as in the English longbow, to give the maximum elasticity and power. One end has a shoulder, the other a notch to hold the string. The handle is properly shaped, cut away on each side so that it can be easily gripped, in the manner now known as 'centre shot'.

27

Spear-throwing bow – a Dahomey brass in traditional design

Opposite page
Top: East African bow – *Middle*: Japanese bow and quiver packed for travelling – *Bottom*: South African bow and arrows

Bows like this were used in western Europe for the next 8,000 or 9,000 years, until the development of the longbow. The only improvement was the provision of a nock, instead of a mere notch, at the end of the bow to hold the string. With a notch, a bow must remain permanently strung, which soon produces a permanent curve and weakens the bow's cast. A nock enables it to be strung and unstrung with ease. It is curious, and perhaps significant in considering racial characteristics, that some African tribes have not yet discovered the advantages of the nocked bow: archery there – and the bow is still widely used – is still in roughly the stage reached elsewhere in Mesolithic times, except that the arrow-head is now of iron.

28

The Badarian period (about 4000 B.C.) is the earliest in Pre-dynastic Egypt of which anything much is known. As one would expect, the flint arrow-head was then common. The Badarians probably used a self-bow made of acacia wood, such as were found in Egyptian remains of some 1,500 years later. Similar bows are still used over most of tropical Africa, their effect increased by many tribes by smearing a poisonous paste on the shaft of the arrow-head which, when fresh, is said to bring down a large animal in some fifteen minutes. North American Indians, too, used a bow of this kind, but strengthened by deer-sinews stretched along the back.

There is, therefore, quite a lot of evidence on the probable performance of the prehistoric bow: it was probably rather better than the very short, weak bow of the South African Bushman, who relied more on poison than on the penetration of his arrow; and rather worse than the sinew-backed bow of the Apache, Sioux, and other North American tribes. Gordon Grimley, author of *The Book of the Bow*, estimates its effective range against game as no more than 30 yards. Experiments with North American Indian and Eskimo bows show that they had a cast or maximum range varying from 90 to 153 yards. (They were, unlike the Holmegaard bow, strengthened by a sinew backing, but experiments have shown that the effect of backing is to prevent the bow breaking when fully drawn, not to increase the cast.) African bows, subjected to the same tests, had much shorter casts.

The efficiency of a bow depends, of course, not only on its cast, but on its accuracy and its ability to shoot a heavy arrow with great penetration. Badly made bows are harsh to draw, twist in the hand, kick when released, and are quite useless for accurate shooting. No doubt bad prehistoric bows had all these faults, while good ones were smooth, sweet, and joyful to use. But of this we know nothing, except what we can learn from comparable bows in America and Africa. There is no reason to doubt Mr Grimley's estimate of an effective range of some 30 yards, to which one might add a cast of about 100. In battle, not really aimed at an individual

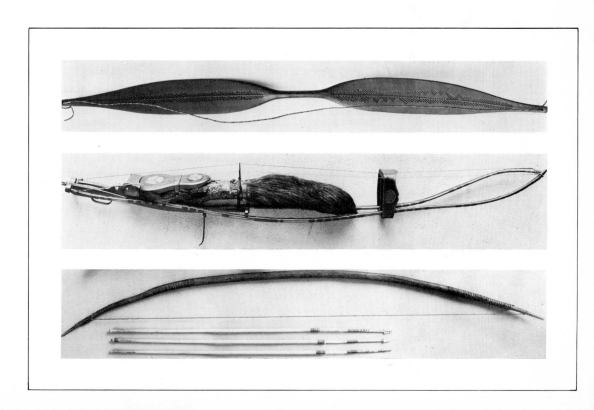

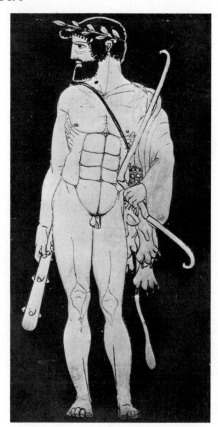

Hercules with a composite bow as depicted on a Greek vase

Opposite page
A Spanish rock drawing (Stone Age) showing that even then recurved bows were in use

but shot at an elevation of forty-five degrees so as to drop into a closely packed enemy, they might be reasonably effective up to the limit of their cast. The skill of the prehistoric bowman – and, indeed, of the European bowman of the Dark Ages, which followed the fall of Rome – lay not so much in long-range accuracy with his weapon, as in stalking, like the Bushmen, to within a range at which he could hardly miss. Provided it did not strike a bone, the flint-pointed arrow would then do all that was required of it, bringing down an animal on the spot if it hit a vital organ, or within a few minutes by haemorrhage.

The Plains Indian, hunting bison on horseback, used to drive his arrow in right to the feather, or even clean through the huge animal – provided, of course, it did not strike any heavy bone. But this is less impressive than it sounds, for he was shooting at a range only of a few feet, and there is nothing much in the belly or chest cavity of a bison to stop an arrow.

Thirty thousand years ago or today, a bowman must practise to attain any accuracy, and practice leads inevitably to informal competition. We can be quite certain that Stone Age archers held archery competitions of some kind or another. But they were not, of course, competition-shooters, nor was their military organization and tactics so advanced as to require the regular training of English long-bowmen. Their archery must have been very similar to that of African hunters today,

31

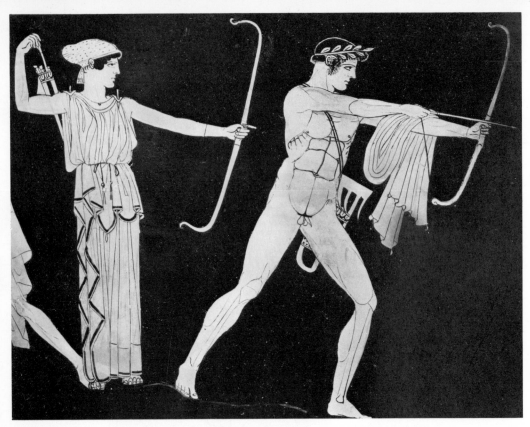

Bows in action – Artemis and Apollo at work. (Note the latter's short draw)

Opposite page
The shaped throwing-stick was probably man's second missile. It is a reasonably accurate weapon. Here it is being used to knock down wild fowl in the reed beds of the Nile

or American Indian forest-dwellers a century ago. Of this we have precise details, for the famous American bowman Saxton Pope found in 1911 in California one who has been described as the last primitive Indian, Ishi, of the Yana tribe, completely untouched by civilization. Pope, a doctor by profession, observed him as under a microscope and recorded meticulously all he saw as Ishi made his bow, his arrows, and his kills.

The bow was of juniper wood, backed with deer's sinew, 42 inches long. His arrows varied: he, like other archers, experimented. Many were in two pieces, a shaft of witch hazel and a foreshaft of birch or some heavier wood. Into the foreshaft was fitted with resin and bound with sinew the arrow-head, of obsidian, chipped glass, steel, or anything he could get hold of. They were fletched with three turkey, buzzard, or hawk feathers, not glued but bound on with sinew. They varied in length from 25 to 30 inches.

The bow and arrows of Stone Age man were probably very like Ishi's, except that the arrows were of a single, simple shaft – not composed of a shaft and a heavier foreshaft. Arrows made by Ishi flew remarkably well, better than most of those which Saxton Pope tried. So we may take it that Ishi's performance and method were comparable with those of the Stone Age hunter, but somewhat better. There is another example, scientifically observed, in a Seminole chief, Charlie Snow, with whom another expert American bowman hunted for several years. From this we know pretty well how good an archer the Stone Age bowman was.

At short ranges, constant practice and the fact that he was shooting for his supper made him quick and accurate: he seldom missed a target even as small as a squirrel at 20 yards and often hit at 50. At longer ranges he was not so good: the high trajectory of his arrows made it difficult for him to shoot with any accuracy, and he missed a wild cat with several successive shots at 60 yards. Red Indian archers competing against white archers at target-shooting put up a very poor performance: it was not their game; but at twenty paces a good Indian marksman could hit a 10 cent piece or a button three times out of five, 'and be rewarded with it and a small piece of tobacco'. So the Stone Age hunter must have been a first-class stalker and a dead shot up to about 30 yards, with an arrow which would certainly kill ibex, reindeer, or any smaller animal. It was enough to establish his mastery over the brute creation, to ensure that he would inherit the earth.

It is in man's nature always to seek improvement, and the short self-bow was by no means a powerful weapon. Greater power and a longer cast can be obtained in what is called the 'recurved', or 'reflex', bow.

Assyrian mounted archers

The ordinary or straight-ended bow, short or long, is (or should be) a straight stave when unstrung and a plain arc when strung. But the recurved bow is an arc, plain or flattened, when unstrung, the back of the bow being the concave side. When it is strung the curve is reversed, so that the belly of the bow is concave, the back convex. This makes a more powerful weapon than a self-bow of the same length and weight.

Since it is not easy to find wood with the natural curve required for such a bow, it is generally of composite construction, made of strips of wood, horn, and sinews glued together. The earliest models of which we have any detailed description, in the *Iliad*, were made basically of two ibex horns, joined at the handle. A pair of buffalo or long cattle horns also gives the required shape, and were common in central Asia where the recurved bow was normally used and best developed.

Such an ingenious improvement on the simple bow, requiring such skilled and complicated manufacture, one would expect to find rather late in human history, so it is extraordinary to find the recurved bow shown indubitably in Mesolithic and perhaps in Upper Palaeolithic cave-paintings. In some paintings, recurved and straight-ended bows are shown in the same picture. A recurved bow is shown on a bas-relief from Uruk in Mesopotamia, dating from about 5000 B.C., and another on a palette from Pre-dynastic Egypt. A particularly well-shaped one, almost certainly composite, is carved on the slab of a Late Bronze Age tomb in north Germany.

In ancient Greece the bow was not held in high esteem: the image of the archer is of a cunning, unvalorous fellow skulking round the edge of the battlefield and, himself in safety, picking off the better men at a distance. The bow was held to be the weapon of Scythians and Persians. However, Ulysses used a bow – a recurved, composite bow based on ibex horn – to dispose of his wife's suitors. Menelaos was slain by an arrow which penetrated the buckle of his belt and the double breastplate beneath. Teucor and Menian competed in what is the first recorded archery contest, shooting at a dove tied to the top of a high mast. The Amazons, who may have been a legendary version of the Sauromatian tribe, the women of which were forbidden to marry until they had killed a man, were reputed to cut off their right breasts so that it did not get in the way of their draw. They must have been more generously developed than modern female archers, who find their curves no impediment. Greek archers drew only to the chest, shooting a very weak arrow.

In the rival civilization of Persia it was considered that a boy of good family needed to learn only three things – to ride, to shoot, and to tell the truth.

We do not know what these ancient recurved bows were made of, but taking such evidence as there is, in the *Iliad* and from later bows still existing, we can assume that they were of wood, horn, and sinew all glued and bound together. A Turkish recurved composite bow examined by Sir Ralph Payne-Gallwey had a wooden core in three pieces, a handle, and two arms, each nocked at the end. This is a mere lathe, in places only one-eighth of an inch thick, adding nothing to the strength or elasticity of the bow.

The belly is of two strips of buffalo or antelope horn, joined at the handle. The back is made of the great neck tendon of an ox or a stag, a very powerful and elastic tendon which contracts and expands as the animal raises and lowers its head. It is glued together and covered with cherry-tree bark (skin or thin leather covers were also used) to preserve it from damp. The cover is painted and lacquered.

The strength of this bow, that is to say the weight required to draw it to the full length of its 25½-inch arrow, is 118 lb. (Really strong Turkish bows required a pull of 150 to 160 lb. The old English longbow probably had a pull of 75 to 100 lb; a powerful modern target-bow has a pull of 50 to 60 lb, a hunting-bow one of 60 to 75 lb.)

The recurved composite bow had an extraordinary strong strength-length ratio. This did not in itself mean that it had a long cast. Saxton Pope's brother, Major B. H. Pope, found that a strong Tartar recurved bow, pulling 98 lb, had a cast of only 100 yards. But a well-designed Turkish bow had a terrific cast. In 1795 Mahmoud Effendi, Secretary to the Turkish Ambassador in London, who did not claim to be a great bowman and was out of practice, at a meeting of the Toxophilite Society shot an arrow 480 yards. At Istanbul there were marble columns recording exceptionally long shots; the shortest of them was 625 yards, the longest 838 yards. There are many authentic examples of 600-yard shots by Turkish bows. The longest known shot, by the Sultan Selim in 1798, witnessed by the British Ambassador, was a prodigious 972 yards 2¾ inches. This did not in itself make it a better weapon than the best form of self-bow, the English longbow: their relative efficiency is discussed later. But the Oriental bow certainly shot much further.

Making such a bow was, of course, the work of an expert. So honourable was the bowyer's craft that the Sultans of Turkey, obliged by custom to learn and become proficient in a trade, always chose that of a bowmaker.

Not least of the bowman's art lay in stringing this short, very powerful bow. Both arms, both legs, and all the strength of a man's back were required for this: indeed some recurved bows could not be strung by a single man. Two pictures, of a Scythian about 600 B.C. and a Turk some 2,000 years later, show the only way this could be done. To do it properly requires great strength of wrist: if the wrist weakens, a twist is given to the limb of the bow and it is irretrievably ruined.

The long cast is achieved by the combination of a powerful bow and a short (25 inches), light arrow, the military value of which is discussed later. But an arrow

The method of speeding a spear with a spear-thrower has not changed basically since these were introduced in Magdalenian times (see page 13. Here an Australian aboriginal is poised prior to the throw

Opposite page
The sling is one of man's earliest missile launchers. Here incendiaries are being dispatched by sling and arrow, early 13th century

can be drawn, normally, only to its head, in this case some 23 inches, which is not exploiting the full power of the bow. To get over this difficulty, and to facilitate drawing a very stiff bow, the Turks had by the eighteenth century (perhaps long before) developed two gadgets peculiar to their archery. One was a horn groove in which the arrow-head rested when it was drawn back until no longer resting on the left hand, and the other a thumb-ring.

Here a digression is necessary into the different 'locks' or positions of the archer's fingers as he draws. The instinctive method of drawing is to grip the arrow between finger and thumb and with it pull the string. That is what every untaught beginner does. So do many primitive archers – Bushmen, for instance, and the natives of New Guinea and the Solomon Islands. American bowmen call this method the 'savage loose'. This simple thumb-lock has no strength, and can be used only with the weakest bows. Ishi, and presumably many other American Indians, used a better thumb-lock in which the thumb was hooked round the string, so a rather stronger draw was possible. European archers use the Mediterranean loose in which three fingers act as hooks to draw back the string, the forefinger above the arrow, the second and third fingers below it. By this method the most powerful bows can be drawn. Equally effective is the Mongolian loose, used by Turks and other horse-archers of Asia, in which the first joint of the thumb (like Ishi's) is locked round the string, but the thumb is helped bear the terrific strain by the first or second finger

36

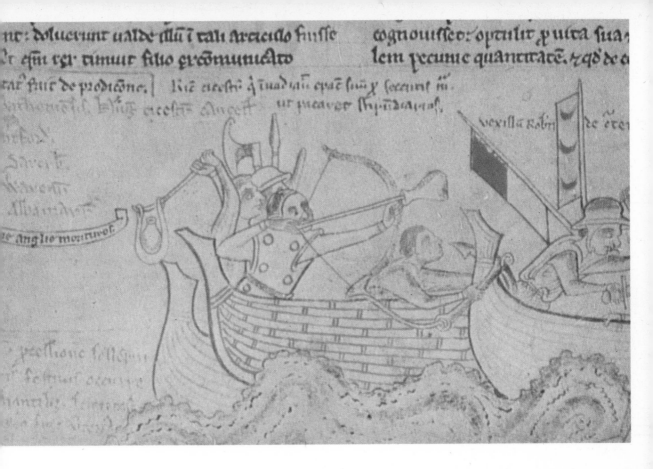

supporting it. It is necessary, apparently, when loosing to spring the finger first; springing the thumb first endangers the nail.

So the second gadget peculiar to Turkish and other Asiatic horse-archers was a ring of ivory, or other hard substance, protecting the ball of the thumb against the pull of the string. The arrow was shot from the right side of the bow – not the left as with the Mediterranean loose – provided the bowman drew with his right hand, and the arrow-groove was fitted on to the top of the left thumb. Another Turkish device was the arrow-nock made of horn with narrow-sprung jaws which admitted the string and then closed on it. This enabled an arrow to be carried strung, ready for instant use, even by a galloping horseman.

The great virtue in the recurved bow lay not only in its power, but in its shortness. For from about the year 1000 B.C., the bowman of the great steppes, of Mesopotamia, Anatolia, and wherever the Turks conquered, be he Scythian, Assyrian, Mongol, Hun, Persian, Tatar, or Turk was essentially a mounted archer. (In the infancy of horsemanship, the Assyrian archer had a companion to lead his horse so that he could concentrate on the bow.) A horseman's bow *must* be short. I doubt if the most powerful reflex bows were in fact used by mounted men: I doubt if a man on horseback could draw a 100-lb bow, and I am sure he could never string it. But the recurved, composite bow of moderate power became the Asiatic horseman's weapon. Another reason for the prevalence there of the composite bow was the shortage in the

Stringing the bow
(*top*) Scythian;
(*middle*) Egyptian;
(*bottom*) Assyrian

Opposite page
The different ways
of drawing the
bow.

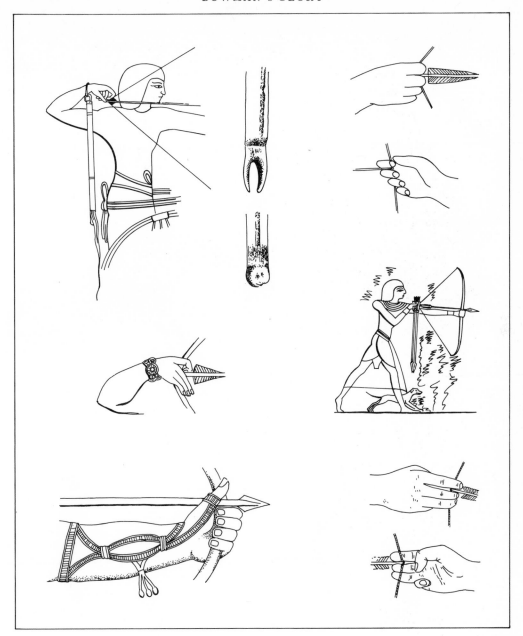

steppes, deserts, and great plains of timber suitable for good self-bows.

Western Europe never took to the recurved bow. Reasons for this are discussed later. Belisarius, whose Byzantine cavalry regiments contained many Huns, armed his best regiments with it. As a test of equitation and skill at arms each trooper had to string his bow at a gallop, shoot an arrow at one target, throw a dart at another, and attack the third and fourth with lance and sword.

A rock drawing of Bushmen with their weapons,
spears and a simple bow

Setting out for the hunt in the early centuries A.D.
Note the recurved bow

Much has been written of the marvellous shots of superhuman accuracy made by Turkish and other Asiatic archers. Let us subject some of these to critical examination.

When hunting, as is proved by innumerable pictures, the mounted Turk or Persian, like the Red Indian bison-hunter, shot at a very short range, seldom more than 10 yards, generally much less. Thomas Herbert, travelling through Persia in the seventeenth century, reported, 'they can in full career cleave an orange which is hung athwart the hippodrome, and [when past the mark] with another hit the rest, turning [in his short stirrups and Morocco saddle] backwards'.

We can, I think, assume that the shot was taken at not more than 7 yards. Assuming an orange of 3 inch diameter, the arrow could be $1\frac{1}{2}$ inches away from the centre of the target and still 'cleave' it. An error of $1\frac{1}{2}$ inches at 7 yards is roughly the equivalent of an error of 21 inches at 100 yards. The modern target 'gold' is a circle of $9\frac{3}{5}$ inches diameter, allowing an error of just over $4\frac{1}{2}$ inches.

'Ah,' one may object, 'but this was from a galloping horse.'

True, but this makes surprisingly little difference, particularly if the horse has, like most Arabs, a smooth gallop. I am a poor polo-player, but I do not expect to miss a stationary or even a rolling ball at full gallop – at least, not often. As a cavalry-man I practised at the gallop (though not often, for my regiment was soon mechanized) with sword and lance: although an indifferent performer, I could hit the tent-peg or the centre of the dummy as often as not. Later I used to practise on horseback

41

The longbow
being used by
Pisans in the naval
attack on Jaffa.
From the 15th-
century *Anciennes
Chroniques de Pisa*

with a revolver: at short ranges it is not much more difficult than shooting on foot:
the only time I needed it in earnest, I brought my man down at full gallop, with my
third shot, at about 20 yards. Now I am not a particularly good horseman, nor a
particularly good shot: so if I can do these things, I regard the reputed feats of real
Turkish experts with admiration, but with neither scepticism nor undue amazement.

As for Arab tricks of shooting out a candle, or splitting an arrow on the edge of a sword-blade stuck in the ground, these were performed with a light bow such as modern archers sometimes use for indoor darts shooting, so the implication is that the range was very short.

There must, of course, have been exceptionally skilful archers among the Parthians who massacred the Roman legion at Carrhae, or the Seljuk Turks who from time to time, in overwhelming numbers and when they could evade the charge of the more heavily mounted and armoured lancers, defeated the Crusaders. But such victories were won not by individual marksmanship, but by hundreds of arrows, shot by horsemen circling round safe from retaliation, dropping into the tightly packed ranks of the legion or the 'press of knights'. The Parthian army of 10,000 horse-archers was accompanied by 1,000 camels carrying nothing but spare arrows, which indicates a fantastic consumption of ammunition.

While on the steppes and plains of central Asia and Anatolia this extraordinarily effective weapon was being developed, a weapon which very nearly enabled the Mongols to overrun all Christendom, in the West archery stagnated. The ordinary short self-bow used by both sides (but principally by the Normans) at Hastings in 1066 was little better than the Holmegaard bow of 9,000 years earlier.

Bowmen were consequently regarded, as they had been at Troy, as of very little worth. Mastery of the battlefield was disputed between heavy mailed infantry, wielding sword, spear, and axe, and heavy mailed cavalry, wielding lance and sword. The best examples of the former were the Franks who saved Europe by beating the Moors at Poitiers, the Vikings, and the English; cavalry were best exemplified by the Normans, descendants of the Norsemen who had minds flexible enough to adopt a style of fighting quite new to them. Which was to prevail was decided by the Normans at Hastings against Harold's Housecarles, and at Dyrrachium against the Varangian Guard, mainly Vikings, of the Byzantine Emperor. For the next two and a half centuries the mailed mounted knight was master. It is, however, possible that the Norman victory at Hastings was won partly by Duke William's intelligent use of his despised archers, though the story of King Harold being slain by a high-trajectory arrow dropping over the shield-wall into his eye, has, apparently, no contemporary foundation.

Western Europe first acquired a better missile weapon not by improving the short self-bow, but by inventing, or rediscovering, the crossbow.

Although it was not in common use, and is not mentioned in Classical literature, the crossbow seems to have been known to Roman hunters: there are in the Musée Crozatier in Puy-en-Velay two bas-reliefs of the first and second century A.D., in which this weapon is depicted: the arms of the crossbow are so short as to suggest that it was made of steel, which at that time was produced locally.* The crossbow was more common in China: the British Museum has bronze trigger mechanisms of crossbows dating from the third century A.D., and many more are in existence. Then the crossbow seems to have been forgotten for a few hundred years, to reappear in the West during the eleventh century. William of Poitiers, the Conqueror's Chaplain,

---

* For this interesting information and speculation I am indebted to Monsieur R. Gounot, Curator of the Musée Crozatier.

The shooting lesson.
A young prince is
taught how to use
the bow.

says it was used at Hastings, but he wrote from six to eight years after the battle and is not considered an absolutely reliable historian: no other chronicler mentions it at Hastings and it is not shown on the Bayeux Tapestry. The implication is, then, that the crossbow was reinvented in western Europe between 1066 and 1072. It was certainly taken by the men of the First Crusade to Constantinople in 1098; and was surely not introduced from the East but reinvented by Frenchmen, Normans, or Germans, for Anna Comnena, the prim little Byzantine princess, seeing it for the first time described it as a terrible weapon, *unknown* to Greeks and Barbarians. But Moslems soon adopted it and perhaps improved upon crude early models. King John's Crossbow-maker was named Peter the Saracen.

The principle behind the crossbow is perfectly simple, and had probably been exploited already in the ballista, a siege-engine which was a gigantic crossbow throwing a ponderous dart. A bow far too stiff and strong to be drawn in the normal manner, can be drawn if the archer uses both arms, all the strength of his back, and his two legs. If, fully drawn, it can be held back mechanically with no fatigue or trouble to the archer, he can release it when he wills with deadly accuracy and devastating force.

The simple, early crossbow consisted of a very stiff wooden bar fitted to a wooden stock some 3 feet long. The two were lashed together by a 'bridle' of sinew, put on

46

The Turkish bow
in action

wet and tightening as it dried, to make a very rigid joint. Along the top of the stock
ran a shallow groove to hold the bolt or quarrel, which was shorter, thicker, and
heavier than an arrow. The cord was thick and strong. To bend this weapon the
crossbowman put both feet on the bow, on either side of the stock, to hold it down.
Then he pulled the cord with both hands until, with the bow fully bent, it engaged
with and was held by a sear protruding from the groove of the stock. To shoot, all he
had to do was to place a bolt in the groove, aim, and lower the sear by a lever-like
trigger under the stock. This model was improved by fitting an iron stirrup to the
stock, through which the archer put one or both feet instead of actually on the bow.

The 'arbalista ad unum pedem' and the 'arbalista ad duos pedes', bent respectively with one and both feet, were far more powerful than the ordinary short-bow,
for the heavy bolt smashed through mail at a range further than the arrow of an
eleventh-century bow could carry. So dreaded was the crossbow that repeated Papal
edicts vainly forbade its use against Christians. It was soon adopted, by all who could
afford it, for hunting, for not only did it strike a deer more accurately and harder
than an arrow, but it could be carried all ready for use by a horseman and shot at a
gallop. It was also the ideal weapon of the highwayman and murderer. William
Rufus in 1100 was killed in mysterious circumstances, while hunting in the New
Forest, by a bolt from a companion's crossbow. Such a mishap was a recurring theme.

47

The recurved
composite bow
in action against
lion

Sultan Murad II
shooting at the
Qabaq, from a
late 16th-century
MS.

Although the Chinese used crossbows to repel the invasions of the nomads for several centuries B.C., it had been thought that they were not used in western Europe until just before Hastings; however, the evidence of 1st or 2nd century A.D. bas-reliefs from Solignac and Puy-en-Velay proves that they were known and used during the Roman period at least. Here is a Roman crossbow and quiver, with the hunter's knife in its sheath with a sling

Opposite page
The goat's-foot lever bending a small crossbow

Five centuries later the Archbishop of Canterbury, a man of sedentary habit, was ordered by his doctor to take light exercise, so went a-hunting. Aiming a crossbow at a stag – he was not a very good shot – he had the misfortune to slay instead one Peter Hawkins. As James I remarked sympathetically, 'An angel might have miscarried in this way.'

As a weapon of war the crossbow made its mark in the First Crusade, for with its longer range than the bow, it could keep the Turkish horse-archers at a distance until the chance came for the mailed knights to charge. Unfortunately, the Franks had too few of them. But among the leaders of the Third Crusade was Richard Cœur de Lion, who combined with his courage, his great physical strength, and less amiable qualities, considerable military talent: he could *think* about war. He saw the potential of the crossbow, saw that in combination with the mounted arm it could beat the Turks. He took to the Holy Land an adequate force of foot-soldiers armed with this weapon, and at Arsouf triumphantly put his theories into practice. Throughout the history of that Crusade one finds that the combination of the cross-bowmen and the mounted knights was the key to Richard's tactics – the crossbow-men in defence and to secure a firm base, the knights for attack.

The King was himself an expert with the crossbow, and even when laid low with malaria at Acre, had his bed placed within range of the walls and picked off any Saracens who appeared above the battlements. Eventually he was himself mortally wounded by a bolt shot from Chaluz Castle which he was besieging. Dying, he forgave the man who had killed him. But his officers knew better: they had the saucy fellow flayed alive. The pious attributed the King's death to the vengeance of Heaven for his encouraging the use of this weapon.

The crude eleventh-century crossbow was greatly improved over the next 400 years. The stiff wooden bow was replaced – perhaps after Crusaders had seen the Turkish composite bows – with an even stiffer one. This had a core made of some twenty strips of whalebone, glued together, the edges towards the back and belly of the bow. The back and belly were of yew, strengthened with the neck-ligament of horse or ox. In the late fourteenth century a steel bow, more powerful still, was introduced.

As the crossbow was made even stronger, the archer required mechanical help

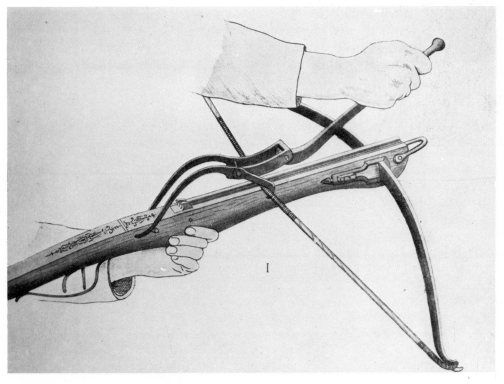

I

Aiming the crossbow
from G. Lopez *Martyrdom
of St Sebastian*

Crossbowman cocking his bow by
pulley from Pollaiuolo's *Martyrdom of
St Sebastian*

53

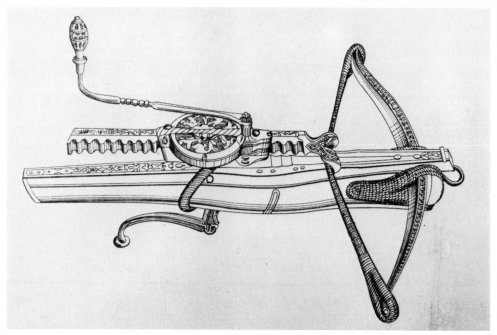

The crannikin

to string it. The first device, which appeared in the twelfth century, was a strong leather thong fixed at one end to the crossbow-butt, passing through a pulley attached to the cord, and tied at the other end to a claw hanging from the archer's belt. This gave him, in drawing the bow, a two to one mechanical advantage, twice the strength of the direct pull with his hands.

In the early fourteenth century there was invented an ingenious and even more powerful device, the goat's-foot lever. This was particularly useful as it enabled a crossbow to be bent quickly, even by a mounted man. It was accordingly much favoured by hunters.

But the goat's-foot lever could not bend the steel crossbow of the fourteenth century, for which there was invented a screwed rod, passing through a screwed eye on the butt, hooked at the bottom and over the cord and tightened by turning, like some modern car-jacks. This was immensely powerful, but very, very slow.

Finally, in the fifteenth century, there were invented the crannequin and the moulinet, two engines which would draw the strongest steel bow far quicker than the simple screw and handle. The crannequin consisted of a toothed steel rod, moved up and down by a toothed wheel fitted to the stock and turned by a handle. The moulinet consisted of two cords, each passing through two pulleys (this giving a four to one mechanical advantage) tightened by a windlass.

There were, in general terms, by the fourteenth century, three types of crossbow. The most powerful was the siege crossbow, weighing some 18 lb, with a range, at 45 per cent elevation, of about 450 yards. This was rather heavy and slow to draw

54

for field-work, for which a lighter model was preferred, weighing about 16 lb with a maximum range of 380 to 390 yards. The sporting model was lighter still, often used by ladies.

To shoot, one either held the butt under the arm-pit, or rested it on the shoulder. The left hand supported the weight of the bow. The fingers of the right hand held the long trigger, the thumb lay in a groove cut obliquely on top of the butt. The tip of the thumb served as a backsight, the upper edge of the bolt as a foresight. Thumb-grooves were cut at two or three different depths for different ranges – the longer the range, the shallower the groove. This was the first adjustable backsight. But the field-crossbow had a very flat trajectory: at 50 yards the drop of the bolt was only from forehead to chin.

On the Continent the crossbow remained the favourite missile weapon until the development of firearms. But in England it was generally replaced, as a military weapon, during the fourteenth century by the longbow. The crossbow, however, was highly prized for hunting and target-shooting until well into the seventeenth century. Ladies in particular liked it because it was easier to manage than the long-bow and, unlike guns, had no bruising recoil. Queen Elizabeth's crossbow-shooting was much praised. (Good or bad, courtiers were well advised to praise it.)

Among other advantages, discussed later, it required no strength to draw and not much skill to shoot, so it appealed to those whose age, clerical status, embonpoint, sex, or exalted social position precluded prolonged practice at the butts.

The crossbow which was bent by
a screw and handle

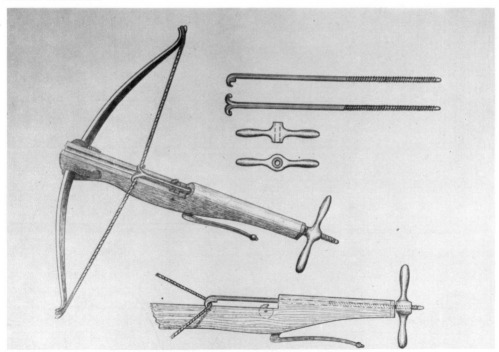

55

Detail of crossbow and crannikin from *Basle Chronicle*,
1478

Opposite page
The simple bow still in use in the 19th century

But it was not, like the longbow, officially encouraged; on the contrary, an Act
of Parliament in the reign of Richard II made it illegal for anyone even to own a
crossbow unless he was a substantial property-owner. This was, of course, because
it was the ideal hunting weapon, deadly to the King's deer.

Only in Spain was the power of the crossbow reinforced by poison. The juice of
a white hellebore root was boiled and tested first, with a needle, on a chicken, which
should become drowsy and die 'before one could say a Credo'. Smeared on bolt-

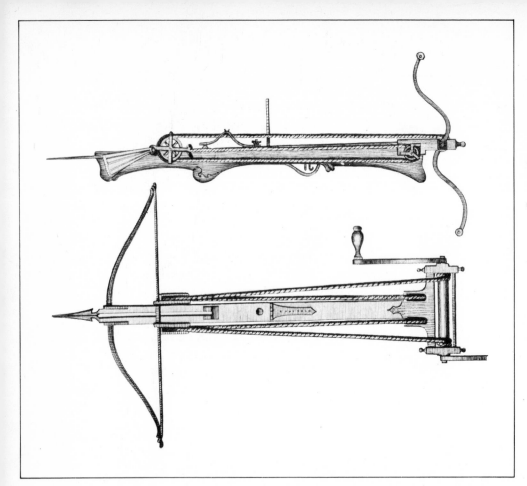

heads, it was used for hunting. A stag hit anywhere by a poisoned bolt would run no more than 100 yards, stop, cough, and die.

For birds, a light, blunt bolt was used. In the Late Middle Ages a 'stonebow' was developed, a crossbow shooting a round pebble or bullet at birds and rabbits.

Since the longbow became the favourite national weapon of the English, winning a succession of staggering victories, its origins have been described in a hundred English history books.

Before ever the longbow began to dominate the battlefield, there was a revival of interest in archery. The Danes and Vikings were, by the poor standards of their day, good archers. They even used a longish bow, though it was of poor wood, and could not compare with the longbow proper. William the Conqueror made intelligent use of archery at Hastings, and his son, Henry I, did likewise at Tenchebrai and Beaumont, early in the twelfth century.

It was, perhaps, in the latter's reign that Englishmen began to practise seriously, though not yet with the longbow. Perhaps the crossbow was such a weapon as to encourage practice. At all events, Henry I passed a Statute to the effect that accidents in archery practice should not be punishable by the law.

It seems that the longbow did not appear until the late twelfth century, and it was the Welsh mountaineers who invented it. In their rough hills foot-soldiers could hold their own against mounted men provided they had a good missile weapon. The recurved composite bow was perfectly well known in western Europe since the Crusades, but it must have been very expensive and difficult to make, it shot too light an arrow, and it deteriorated in a damp climate. The short self-bow was not much good. Either it was too weak, having but a short cast; or, if stiff enough, it fractured when a 25-inch arrow – the shortest that was any use for war or hunting – was drawn to the head. The remedy was either to back the short self-bow with sinew, which would allow it to be fully drawn, or to lengthen it. The Welsh chose to lengthen it.

We have very full details of this development from Giraldus Cambrensis, a historian who travelled through Wales in 1188. He found that the bowmen of Gwent and Morganwg were the best. 'The bows used by these people are not made of horn, ivory or yew' (an indication that he knew about the composite bow), 'but of elm, ugly, unfinished-looking weapons, but astonishingly stiff, large and strong.' It did not have a particularly long cast: presumably bowyers took time to learn the secrets of the perfect bow. But it had great penetration. 'William de Braose testifies that one of his soldiers, in a conflict with the Welsh, was wounded by an arrow which, passing through his thigh and the armour with which it was cased on both sides, and,

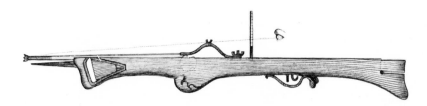

through that front of the saddle which is called the *alva*, mortally wounded the horse. Another soldier had his hip, equally sheaved in armour, penetrated by an arrow quite to the saddle, and on turning his horse round, received a similar wound in the opposite hip, which fixed him on both sides to the seat. What more could be expected from a ballista?'

It was Welsh archers, 300 of them, 'the flower of the young men of Wales', who with 90 knights set off in 1171 to conquer Ireland. (Walsh is now one of the commonest Irish surnames.) Early in the twelfth century, in a poaching affray in Rockingham Forest, a forester was grievously wounded by a *Welsh* arrow. In 1266 Henry III ordered 500 archers to be raised from the Weald: in his writ these are described as 'Welshmen, foresters and others'. The history or legend of Robin Hood, closely associated with the longbow, seems to date from this period, and his reputed tombstone bore an epitaph, no longer legible but still remembered at the end of the eighteenth century, stating that he died on Christmas Eve 1247.

The longbow was spreading, though one cannot be sure that the King had this specific weapon in mind when in 1251 he ordered all freemen whose revenue in land

Trigger mechanism of a Chinese crossbow of the 2nd/3rd century B.C.

Opposite page
Stand of the crossbowmen at the great shooting tournament held at Zürich in 1504

was less than 100*d.* a year to provide themselves with a bow and arrows. Thirty years later a crossbowman was still considered to be worth more than an archer – 4*d.* and 2*d.* a day respectively. However, at Falkirk in 1298 the longbow indubitably won its first great victory.

Thereafter, for 130 years, constantly at war in Scotland, France, Spain, and Italy, English armies were only once defeated – at Bannockburn, when proper use was not made of the bowmen.

This is not the place for a recital of the battles of Crécy, Poitiers, Agincourt, and all the rest. Suffice it to say that every victory was won by professional commanders who learned how to combine archers and men-at-arms. The tactics were always defensive. Apart from a small reserve, the whole army dismounted for battle. The knights and men-at-arms were arranged in a thin line, the archers in 'harrows' or wedges, protruding from the line like the teeth of a saw, so that they could enfilade an enemy, on horse or foot, assaulting the line. Where they had time, they protected themselves against cavalry by sharp stakes, driven into the ground and pointed towards the enemy at such a height as to take a horse in the chest.

The English armies consisted mainly of bowmen – about 5,000 out of 9,000 at Crécy, 5,000 out of 6,000 at Agincourt. No doubt these included many artists with the bow, the medieval equivalent of the sniper; but they could hardly have shot with extreme accuracy save with their own arrows of a fletching, weight and spine which they knew. When these were shot, the expert would be reduced to using issue-arrows handed out in bundles from the baggage-carts, or arrows tugged out of dead or

61

wounded enemy. The real value of the bow was as a weapon of mass destruction. Capable each of shooting at least six arrows a minute, their shooting controlled and directed by veteran officers, the bowmen could create a beaten zone in which, before the development of plate-armour, neither man nor horse could live. When the French knights covered themselves with plate-armour, their horses continued to be slaughtered or rendered quite unmanageable with fear and pain by the terrible arrow-hail. When the horses were armoured too, they became totally immobile from the 30 stone or so they had to carry. When the French attacked on foot they reached the English position – those who had not taken a cloth-yard shaft through a joint in their armour or in some part unprotected by plate – utterly exhausted, to meet there the defender fresh and eagerly awaiting them.

Such was the pattern of one battle after another. What of the men who won them?

During the Hundred Years War they were not feudal levies, but long-term

The Hunt
by Blazzo Mantua

Taking aim

professional soldiers serving under contract for what was then the handsome wage of 3*d*. or 4*d*. a day, plus good prospects of plunder. Their principal weapon was no longer the rough elm-stave of Gwent, but the product of skilled artificers with a century's experience in making longbows. It could be hazel, ash, or elm, but was preferably of yew, and Spanish mountain yew at that, for English yew was generally too quick-growing and knotty to be of much use. It was a self-bow, constructed with a convex belly and a flat back. The stave had to consist of a proper proportion of white sapwood and red heartwood. The sapwood, which is resistant to stretch, formed the back and about one-quarter of the bow's thickness: the remainder was of heartwood which is resistant to compression. It was, of course, nocked, so that it could be unstrung. Its length varied, but as a rough rule of thumb the bowstring was as long as the man using it.

Its weight – that is to say the weight of the pull necessary to draw it to the full length of the arrow – varied also according to the man using it, from about 75 to 100 lb.* Of course, weight alone did not produce a powerful bow with a long cast: it needed resiliency also. (To take an exaggerated example, it might require a 150-lb pull to bend an iron bar, but it will not send an arrow far because it has no resiliency.) The limbs had to be carefully shaped by the bowyer so that the action was properly

---

* Approximately twice that of the modern target-bow.

distributed from one end to the other: otherwise it would recoil unevenly, kick, be unpleasant to use, and certainly inaccurate.

The longbowman's arrows also varied in length: the term 'cloth-yard shaft' can be interpreted in several ways. Again as a rough rule of thumb, they were supposed to be half the length of the string. A bowman of 5 feet 6 inches, therefore, perhaps the average in those days, would have a bow, when bent, of that length, and arrows of 33 inches. A 6-foot giant would use a 6-foot bow, with a 90-lb draw, and yard-long arrows. Presumably issue-arrows on service were of a standard size, perhaps 36 inches, and each man cut them down to the size which suited him. They were fletched with three feathers. Goose feathers were supposed to be best, peacock feathers the smartest but somewhat too stiff – and surely expensive? The head was socketed, which made the shaft less liable to split on impact than the Turkish arrow, of which the head was tanged. There were two main types of head, no doubt with many variations. The broad head was designed mainly for hunting, for it made a terrible

Red Indians using deerskins for stalking

Opposite page
The stalking horse in the 16th century. One of Edward
Pierce's painted panels in the hunting room at Wilton House

wound from which the victim, if not struck in a vital spot, soon died of haemorrhage.
The bodkin-head, a thin square-sectioned spike of steel, was designed to penetrate
mail or the chinks of plate-armour. The 'sheaf-arrow' used in battle, weighed from
2½ to 3 ounces. The bowman also carried a few lighter 'flight-arrows' for long-range
shooting. It took Saxton Pope an hour to make a good arrow and it probably took a
medieval bowman or fletcher just as long. One of Pope's pupils remarked that he
found it took four hours to make a bad one.

In 1341 the price of a longbow was 1s. 6d. painted, 1s. unpainted; and twenty-
four arrows cost 1s. 2d. So a bowman could provide himself with his basic weapons
for eight days' pay. Besides these he needed, to be fully equipped, a bracer to protect
his left forearm against the string, a glove for the drawing hand, sword, dagger, maul
for hammering in stakes, iron helm, and mail or leather jerkin.

Modern tests with replicas of old English longbows and arrows confirm the tales
of Giraldus Cambrensis. Saxton Pope with a 75-lb longbow, shot a bodkin-headed
arrow at a suit of chain-mail hung on a dummy man constructed of a pine box and
burlap. The head struck 'with such force that a shower of sparks flew from it, and the
arrow drove through the centre of the back penetrating 8 inches, piercing one side

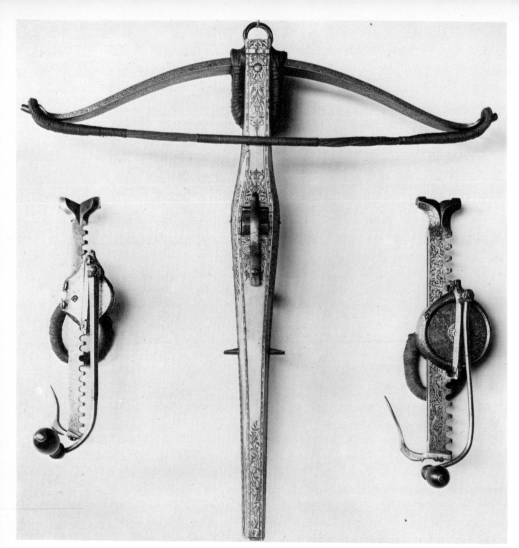

The crossbow
and its
mechanism seen
from either side

Opposite page
Combined
crossbow and
firearm

of the shirt and two sides of the box'. His broad-head arrow, shot at a charging grizzly bear at 40 yards, 'severed two ribs and buried itself in the heart wall, causing a tremendous flooding of the entire chest cavity with blood'.

The bowman attained his skill from constant practice from boyhood into middle age. The law, from the Assize of Arms in 1252 and the Statute of Winchester in 1285, compelled every freeman, from fifteen to sixty, to keep bow and arrows; and subsequent enactments compelled him to practise archery every Sunday and holiday. The butts at Finsbury, outside London, were so crowded that it was inadvisable to shoot more than one arrow at a time lest it disappear, and the ground was so scarred with arrows that no turf grew. (Who organized the shoots and saw to safety precautions?) It was not under such conditions that the bowman could learn his trade, and learn in particular to shoot so fast that he could have three arrows in the air at once. But no doubt in the market-towns and villages, whence most bowmen came, conditions in the butts were more conducive to steady practice, and of course the professional would practise far more than once a week.

66

In 1545, when the bowman's glory was fading, Roger Ascham wrote his famous manual of archery, *Toxophilus*. From this we know pretty well how men shot in his day; and how 'you cunning archers, being very Englishmen, never cease piddling about your bows and shafts when they be well' – in other words, could not leave well alone but must always be messing about with their tackle, a trait not unknown today. Whether or not archery had changed much in the 350 years since Giraldus Cambrensis first described the longbow, we do not know: for, as Ascham observed, 'Men that used shooting most and knew it best were not learned. Men that were learned used little shooting.'

He described caustically manifold errors in style. 'One shooteth, his head forward as though he would bite the mark. . . . Another winketh with one eye and looketh with the other. Some make a face with writhing their mouth and countenance so, as though they were doing you wot what; another blereth out his tongue; another biteth his lips; another holdeth his neck awry . . . others heave their hand now up now down, that a man cannot discern whereat they would shoot, another waggeth the upper end of his bow one way, the nether end another way. Another draweth his bow low at the breast. . . . Another maketh a wrenching at his back, as though a man pinched him behind. And another cowereth down, and layeth out his buttocks as though he would shoot at crows. . . . Once I saw a man which used a bracer on his cheek, he had scratched all the skin off the one side of his face. . . . Another I saw which at every shoot, after the loose, lifted up his right leg so far that he was ever in jeopardy of falling. . . . Some stamp forward and some leap backward. . . . Now afterwards when the shaft is gone, men have every fault which evil custom hath brought them to, and especially in crying after the shaft, and speaking words scarce honest for such an honest pastime. Such words be very token of an ill mind.'

All these imperfections must be avoided, and 'a man shall . . . take such footing and standing as shall be both comely to the eye and profitable to his use . . . that both all his strength may be employed to his own most advantage. . . . One foot must not stand too far from the other, lest he stoop too much which is unseemly, nor yet too near together, lest he stand straight up, for so a man shall neither use his strength well, nor yet stand steadfastly. The mean betwixt both must be kept, a thing more pleasant to behold when it is done than easy to be taught how it should be done.

'To nock well is the easiest point of all. . . . Nock the cock feather upmost. . . .

'Drawing well is the best part of shooting. Men in old time used other method of drawing than we do. They used to draw low at the breast, to the right pap and no further. . . . Drawing to the ear [is best], whereby men shoot both stronger and longer; drawing to the ear is better than to draw at the breast. . . .

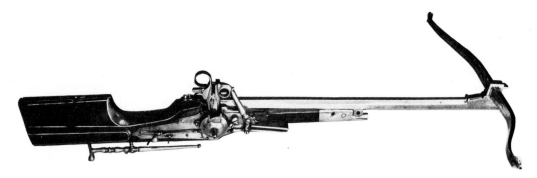

'Holding must not be long, for it both putteth a bow in jeopardy and also marreth a man's shoot. It must be so little that it may be perceived better in a man's mind when it is done, than seen in a man's eyes when it is in doing.

'Loosing must be much like. So quick and hard that it be without all girds, so soft and gentle that the shaft fly not as it were sent out of a bow-case. The mean betwixt both which is perfect loosing is not so hard to be followed in shooting as it is to be described in teaching. . .

'And these precepts I am sure if you follow in standing, nocking, drawing, holding and loosing shall bring you at last to excellent fair shooting.'

Curiously enough Ascham does not recommend any particular loose. Nowadays Western bowmen all use the 'Mediterranean loose', drawing with three fingers. An alternative is the 'Flemish loose', using only two fingers (in either case the arrow is held lightly, not gripped, between first and second fingers). One would have thought that, for drawing a powerful war-bow three fingers would be better than two. But medieval pictures of English bowmen show both methods in use. As for *how* to loose, Ascham is not the only writer to despair of describing it.

Nor does Ascham describe in any detail how to draw. For this, we must turn to Bishop Latimer, who enlarged on the subject during the course of a sermon. Carping critics may protest that archery is hardly relevant to Christianity; the good bishop knew better. 'Men of England, in times past, when they would exercise themselves (for we must needs have some recreation, our bodies cannot endure without some exercise) they were wont to go abroad in the fields a-shooting, but now it is turned into glossing, gulling and whoring within the house. The art of shooting hath been in times past much esteemed in this realm, it is a gift of God that he hath given us to excel all other nations withal, it hath been God's instrument whereby he hath given us many victories against our enemies. But now we have taken up whoring in towns, instead of shooting in the field. A wondrous thing, that so excellent a gift of God be so little esteemed. . . . In my time my poor father was as diligent to teach me to shoot as to learn me any other thing, and so I think other men did their children. He taught me how to draw, how to lay my body to my bow, and not to draw with strength of arms as other nations do, but with strength of the body. I had my bows bought me according to my age and strength: as I increased in them, so my bows were made bigger and bigger: for men shall never shoot well, except they be brought up in it.'

Richard Nicols, writing in 1616, well after the bow had ceased to be a national weapon but while there were still alive men who had drawn it in battle, describes an archer

> Not stooping, nor yet standing straight upright;
> Then with his left hand, little above his sight,
> Stretching his arm out with an easy strength
> To draw an arrow of a yard in length.

'Laying the body to the bow, not drawing it with the strength of the arms'; 'stretching his arm out with an easy strength' – better than Ascham, but still rather imprecise, and to some extent mutually contradictory. However, that is all we have on how our ancestors drew and loosed. It is not very much, to be sure: although they

One of the prizes of marksmanship, the 'king's' collar of the Brotherhood of Chimay, one of the many associations of marksmen in France and other countries

wrote thousands of words on bows, arrows, strings, braces, gloves, and archery in the ancient world, a description of how to draw and loose seems to have eluded them. Ascham did, however, stress that the draw and the loose must be exactly the same for every shot; this was the very essence of consistent shooting.

On aiming Ascham had a good deal more to say. The main point was that 'a man cannot shoot straight perfectly unless he look at the mark. . . . The chief cause why men cannot shoot straight is because they look at the shaft. Having a man's eye always on the mark is the only way to shoot straight.' In short, they shot like a man walking up snipe, or snap-shooting with a pistol – more by instinct than by conscious aiming. This, of course, was the product of long practice, probably more practice than any modern archer gets.

'The greatest enemy of shooting is the wind and the weather, whereby keeping a true length is chiefly hindered.' To the rifleman only a side wind is of any importance: a head or tail wind makes virtually no difference to the flight of a bullet. But the archer saw things very differently. 'It is no marvel if the poor little shaft being sent alone so high into the air, into a great rage of weather, one wind tossing it that way, another this way, it is no marvel, I say, though it lose the length and miss that place where the shooter had thought to have found it.' So you must not merely judge the wind, but judge how your bow will cast with it, for every bow reacts differently to the wind. 'Weak bows and light shafts cannot stand in a round wind. . . . A good archer will first learn to know the nature of the wind, and with wisdom will measure in his mind how much it will alter his shoot, either in length keeping, or else in straight shooting, and so with changing his standing, or taking another shaft the which he knoweth perfectly to fit his purpose either because it is lower feathered, or else because it is of a better wing, will so handle with discretion his shoot that he will seem rather to have the weather under his rule . . . than the weather to rule his shaft.'

69

The wind could best be tested by 'casting up a handful of light grass'. A favourable wind could be a decisive advantage in battle.

Heat and cold, damp and dry, could also affect a bow's cast and a self-bow is particularly apt to tire during the course of a long shoot.

The longbow never had a cast to compare with the recurved composite bow or the crossbow. This is most convincingly proved by the fact that Carnarvon Castle was built in the days of the longbow 330 yards from a high hill overlooking the courtyard. A Statute of Henry VIII laid down that no one should practise at less than 140 yards with sheaf-arrows and 220 yards with flight-arrows. Justice Shallow says of old Dorble, 'Jesu! Jesu! Dead! a'drew a good bow; and dead! a'shot a fine shoot. John a Gaunt loved him well, and betted much money on his head. Dead! a'would have clapped i' the clout at twelve score; and carried you a forehand shaft [flight-arrow?] at fourteen and a half, that it would have done a man's heart good to see.'

This kind of evidence, of which there is plenty, together with that of experiments conducted by Saxton Pope and others, indicates that on a windless day on level ground a good bowman might shoot a flight-arrow 300 yards, and a sheaf-arrow some 30 yards less. But at that distance he could not expect much accuracy: the effective range against any individual target, man or deer, would be hardly 200 yards for the best archer in the best conditions.

Butts were like modern rifle-butts, banks of earth grassed-over. Up to about 140 yards the target was a white disc; beyond that it was a 'clout', a canvas-covered, straw-stuffed disc of some 18 inches diameter. 'Rovers' meant shooting at a variety

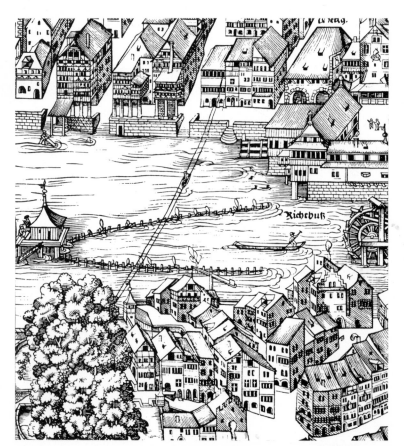

Aerial conveyor for returning crossbow bolts to the firing stand across the river at Zürich

Ryffli's 'masterly shot', when this Swiss hero sent his bolt straight into his opponent's temple

of targets at unknown distances. The skill of medieval bowmen was, I suppose, roughly equal to that of the best archers of the nineteenth century, before the introduction of bow-sights, precisely manufactured arrows, and bows made of steel, fibre-glass, and other materials more consistent in performance than any wooden self-bow. The greatest English archer of the Victorian Age was H. A. Ford. One of his performances was in shooting a Single York Round (six dozen at 100 yards, four dozen at 80 yards, two dozen at 40 yards) at a standard target*and scoring:

100 yd	80 yd	60 yd
69 hits, score 371	48 hits, score 274	24 hits, score 154

'Mettez cela dans votre pipe,' he told a friend and fellow archer, 'et smokez le.'

The 'gold' on a standard target has a diameter of $9\frac{3}{5}$ inches. Ford often made three golds in succession at 100 yards, and on at least two occasions, backed himself to do so.

His American contemporary, Maurice Thompson, excelled more in field- than in target-archery. Badly wounded in the Civil War, finding his house and plantation destroyed by 'Sherman's dashing Yankee boys' on their march through Georgia, he and his brother for some time lived by their bows in the great pine forests round their old plantation. He abhorred the use of any target: all his practice was in 'rovers'. At 10 yards he could hit a pencil, the equivalent of a Saracen archer splitting an arrow on a sword-blade: on one occasion he shot nine out of eleven arrows, at 80 yards, through a gourd 8 inches in diameter. He once broke thirty-seven out of fifty glass balls, tennis-ball size, thrown towards him at 12 yards.

This was the sort of standard probably attained by good medieval bowmen. Having practised since childhood, whereas Ford took up archery as a young man,

---

* Of 48 inches diameter, not much bigger than a man on foot and much smaller than a horse and rider.

they might have done a bit better, but it is doubtful if any bow then made could (to use a term of musketry) 'group' closer than 9 inches at 100 yards. What about all those stories of Robin Hood and others splitting a willow wand and performing such improbable feats? Were they possible? Well, why not? He would not do it every time; but if I, a moderate Bisley shot, could with a rifle that grouped to 4 inches at 200 yards, from time to time hit a 1-inch 'egg' and thereby win a few shillings on the 'Egg Pool', why should not a really fine archer from time to time split a willow wand? Taking into account the grouping capacity of his bow, I should expect him to do it, at 100 yards, about once in a dozen shots. But no doubt veteran archers from time to time remembered their feats with advantage, and 'drew the longbow' in more senses than one.

The English tactics in the Hundred Years War were purely defensive. So long as the French obliged by making frontal attacks on the English line, they were invariably beaten. But when they declined to fight the battle so carefully prepared for them, when they began to manœuvre and bring up field-cannon to enfilade the English line, then they started to win. The tide turned with Patay in 1429, and by the middle of the century all France except Calais was cleared of the invader.

The last battle dominated by the longbow was Flodden (1513): for, although most of the Scots were slain by English bills, it was the bowmen who first broke up the dense, stubborn schiltrons of spearmen, to let the billmen in.

Henry VIII was himself a noted archer, shooting as 'strong and as great a length as any of his Guard'. Exhibiting his skill at the Field of the Cloth of Gold, he moved Paulus Jovius to remark, 'No man in the dominions drew the English bow more vigorously than Henry himself; no man shot further or with a more unerring aim.'

He tried hard to preserve English archery, but for various reasons, discussed in the next chapter, it steadily declined. Having been fully occupied for two generations

Charles II shooting at
Finsbury Fields

Opposite page
Archery practice in France.
Note the archer's peculiar
stance and draw. Five yards
would be about his maximum
range. The French were not
great archers

with the Wars of the Roses and the Tudor reforms, when they again began inter-
fering in European affairs, the English found that their national weapon was almost
obsolete, and their own skill with it sadly diminished.

Indeed, according to Raphael Holinshed (1520–81), 'Certes, the Frenchmen and
Rutters [German cavalry], deriding our new archery in respect to their corselets,
will not let in open skirmish [if any occasion serve] to turn up their tails and cry,
"Shoot, English"; and all because our strong shooting is decayed and laid in bed:
but if some of our Englishmen now lived, that served King Edward III, the breech of
such a varlet would have been nailed to his bum with one arrow; and another
feathered in his bowels, before he should have turned about to see who shot the first.'

In the English Civil War a company of bowmen offered their services to Charles I,
but do not seem to have accomplished anything. The only record of the bow being
used in battle was in Montrose's campaign in the Highlands.

The respective merits of crossbow, recurved bow, and longbow are constantly
argued. The English, remembering Crécy, Poitiers, and Agincourt, assume that
only the longbow had any virtue at all, but each had its advantages and its drawbacks.

The crossbow threw a heavy bolt to a considerable range with remarkable
accuracy. This is not to say that the expert shot better with this weapon than with
the others, but a fair standard of accuracy was more easily obtained with the crossbow. To bend it required no physical strength. Once bent, it stayed bent, with no
effort by the user, until ready to shoot. The arbalister did not have to worry about
the intricacies of the 'sharp loose', bugbear of other bowmen, but aimed and shot

73

Shooting at the popinjay

almost as easily as with a musket and with no recoil. The bolt, being heavy (about $2\frac{1}{2}$ ounces) and projected with a high velocity, had great 'striking energy'.

There were special circumstances in which the crossbow was the best missile weapon. One was hunting. Many Englishmen hunted, legitimately or otherwise, with the longbow, just as Turks and Persians hunted always with the recurved bow: it was the national weapon, the weapon they kept in their cottages, with which they practised every Sunday. But those who could afford it hunted, legitimately or otherwise, with the crossbow. (Poaching was not only or mainly a poor man's crime. The Norman and Plantagenet Game Laws, which preserved deer for the King, were bitterly resented by all classes: nobles, knights, and even bishops rejoiced in defying them. Nor were poachers, in post-Norman times, hanged, flogged, or mutilated: they were simply fined according to their means, not very heavily.) In hunting the arrow-hail was irrelevant: what was needed was a weapon which would shoot accurately, possibly from a cramped position in a hide or from the back of a galloping horse, a single heavy missile which would bring the deer down. That it took a long time to bend and loose the crossbow did not matter: there were other hunters, or an attendant was ready with a spare crossbow, ready bent.

Only an arbalister could shoot from a cramped position, crouching or even lying down. In defence of a castle he could shoot more easily through an arrow-slit or loop-hole, over the battlements without unduly exposing himself, or from a room so low-ceilinged that the archer would have no room to draw. Consider a longbowman and an archer waiting, just within range of the walls, for a defender momentarily to appear. When a head pops up, the archer must draw and loose: the crossbowman, his weapon already bent and perhaps on the aim, resting on a breastwork, need only

74

shoot, and will surely send off his shaft first. Finally, the crossbow was an excellent weapon for ambush and assassination.

The insuperable drawback of the crossbow was, of course, that it took a long time to load: hence the expression, 'he has shot his bolt', the implication being that he is for some time helpless. The Chinese invented a repeating crossbow, with bolts falling in turn from a magazine into position for shooting; but this did not help much, for the time taken was in bending the stiff bow, not placing the bolt in position.

While the arbalister was laboriously winding up his crannequin or moulinet, the bowman could loose five or six arrows. Nevertheless, even in the hey-day of the longbow, English armies continued to include some crossbowmen. In the ill-fated Bannockburn campaign, well after the longbow's first great victory at Falkirk, Edward II employed almost as many arbalisters, presumably English, as archers. Thereafter, on the Continent, they were generally Gascon levies or foreign mercenaries.

The recurved composite bow seems at first sight to have everything a bow needed – long cast, high rate of shooting, accuracy. The weakness lay in the arrow. It shot the arrow far, but partly because the arrow was so light, no more on average than 17 drachms, the weight of two shillings and a sixpence, and moreover, tanged, not socketed, compared to a bolt or an arrow from a longbow, it did little damage. The Sieur de Joinville at the Battle of Damietta was wounded by five Turkish arrows, his horse by fifteen. Neither were incapacitated nor even, it seems, greatly incommoded. The Sieur Bertrandon de la Brocquière observed that the light tanged Turkish arrow split rather than penetrated if it hit anything hard. So the wonderful Turkish bow had its drawbacks: yet it was perfectly adapted for the harassing tactics of mounted archers, who could on horseback have used neither a longbow nor a powerful crossbow.

Howard Hill, the American big-game hunting archer, tried all types of bow, both for target-archery and hunting. He found the recurved bow excellent for target-archery, but too 'sensitive' for hunting: that is to say, it exaggerates the archer's errors. In target-shooting that does not matter: all the conditions are such as to eliminate error. But in hunting, when shots are often taken in haste, from cramped positions, in brushwood and perhaps at a moving target, it matters a great deal. So for hunting he always used a longbow, and heavy arrows. Much the same conditions would have applied to war-archery.

There were, perhaps, two other reasons why the composite bow was not adopted by English and French archers who must have become perfectly familiar with it on the Crusades. The first was expense: compared with the longbow it must have been very costly. The second was climate. It is said that a composite bow will not stand a damp climate. (But what, one may ask, of the composite crossbow? Perhaps whalebone is different.)

The longbow had a shorter cast than either of its rivals, but it shot a heavier and far more deadly arrow than the recurved bow, and had a far faster rate of fire (to use an inappropriate term) than the crossbow. It was very cheap, the common man's weapon. In the field, because of its ability to pour down upon an enemy a hail of arrows which could pierce mail, kill man and horse, it was by far the deadliest weapon yet invented.

One of the more intriguing 'ifs' of history is, 'What would have happened if the English longbowmen had encountered the Turkish horse-archer?' They never met, except perhaps in isolated cases: the great Crusades ended before the longbow came into its own. One who gave considerable thought to the question was the Sieur Bertrandon de la Brocquière, Knight and First Esquire Carver to the Duke of Burgundy, who during the early fifteenth century made the pilgrimage to Jerusalem and then performed the extraordinary and hazardous feat of returning home overland, in disguise, via Syria, Anatolia, and Constantinople. An experienced soldier, familiar with French, English, and German fighting men, he wrote a report of his journey which he regarded as a military reconnaissance for yet another attempt to recover the Holy Sepulchre. He was convinced that this could be done, by a balanced force of French, English, and Burgundian knights, English longbowmen and German arbalisters. He was sure that the longbowmen would outshoot the Turkish horse-archers, adding to the familiar and obvious reasons the rather recondite detail that the Turkish bowstring, and therefore the Turkish arrow-nock, was much wider than the English, so that if the longbowmen were running short of arrows, they could at a pinch recover and use the Turkish arrows which had been shot at them, but the Turks could never use the English arrows. It was a curious detail, but it showed he kept his eyes and ears open.

The longbow had almost as great an effect as the Black Death in undermining the feudal system.

In the twelfth century the foot-soldier had been regarded as a mere encumbrance on the battlefield, useful perhaps for camp fatigues and pioneer duties, but for nothing else. If defeated, he was slaughtered casually, with neither rancour nor remorse, as not worth a ransom. But 200 years later he was a highly skilled, well-paid, respected and, indeed, feared, professional, master of a weapon which was the arbiter of battles.

Moreover, the longbow, and to a lesser extent the cannon, added a new element to war – the professional general. To command in battle and administer a force of all arms was a task far beyond a mere feudal lord. Of course, many of the professional commanders were also feudal lords and aristocrats – men like the Black Prince, the Earl of Lancaster, Sir John Chandos, Sir Thomas Erpingham, Bertrand de Guesclin, and the Sieur Dunois. But they owed their position to professional expertise, not to their status in the feudal society. And, to take only one example, Sir Robert Knollys, famous leader of the Free Companies, was of very humble origin.

Just as the relations between the classes changed in war, so it did in peace. The freeman in feudal society had always had his rights, but had not always been able to obtain them. Now he had an argument more potent than the manorial parchments – the longbow. By the fourteenth century a Peasants' Revolt was something to be taken very seriously.

3

Modern Archery

From the reign of Charles II to that of Victoria the English kept archery barely alive as an elegant social accomplishment. Archery clubs and societies, with names like the Woodmen of Arden, suggestive of Sir Walter Scott's romances, practised a little with the bow, but do not seem to have displayed any outstanding expertise. Indeed, the emphasis was on the convivial aspects of archery rather than on marksmanship. Toxophilists met together and were not altogether displeased when:

> Whene'er without a wind or rain
> Forbids us to touch a feather
> Then snug within we all remain
> Unruffled by blust'ring weather
> For blest with a convivial set
> Howe'er it blow
> Or overflow
> No pastime we regret
> Spite of the day
> We feast away
> And nectar crowns the board
> We bumper it up
> With a chirping cup
> To the lass by each adored. . . .
> So we laugh a little
> And quaff a little
> And joke a little
> And shoot a little
> And fiddle a little
> And fool it a little
> And sing ourselves home in a crack.

Detail of the handle of the Holmegaard bow shaped according to the same principle as that of the best modern bow today

Manhood by
Lancret

They prided themselves on the therapeutic and moral value of their pastime, which they praised in songs replete with analogies drawn from Ascham:

In the circle of Fashion if Vanity leads
    Carol it, carol it, hey to the ditty;
Extravagance loosens and Folly succeeds
    Carol it, carol it, hey to the ditty;
But in Archery's circle Economy guides
We have Health to reward us and Vigour presides,
      With derry down derry,
      We're lively and merry,
        Sing derry down, derry down, hey down derry.

In 1840 there were about forty-five archery clubs and societies in Britain, nearly all in England, but precious few real archers. But a solicitor named Horace Arthur Ford

78

Archery 1790

applied not only his powerful body, but his mind to the matter, and in his classic book, *Archery, Its Theory and Practice* (1856) set out the principles of modern archery. Ford used the traditional English longbow and wooden arrows, but his methods of shooting were much closer to those of today, than to those of 1350. He, if any one man can be so called, is the father of modern archery.

Between medieval and modern archery are basic differences. The fact is that the bowman of Crécy was armed with what was primarily a weapon of mass destruction, not a precision weapon. There were, of course, degrees of skill: no doubt a master bowman could hit a very small target at a long range: but to produce an annihilating arrow-hail meticulous accuracy was not necessary: what was necessary was rapidity of shooting and drilled, schooled, practised strength to increase the range of the hail and to drive a bodkin-pointed arrow through a knight's mail at close range. But to the vast majority of modern archers accuracy is far more important than the strength of the shot: only the very few who hunt big game with the bow need shoot

79

Archery 1818

a strong arrow. This difference is reflected both in the modern archer's equipment –
he seldom uses a bow more powerful than 50 lb – and in his methods.

The second great difference has been brought about by the application to an
ancient art of modern science and methods of manufacture. Bows can now be made
of materials which are faster and more consistent in performance than the best yew,
yet at the same time are easier to draw; factory-made arrows, generally of aluminium
alloy tubing, can be manufactured to precise degrees of weight and 'spine',* so they
are far more consistent in performance than handmade wooden arrows, however
skilful the maker. Bow-sights simplify aiming.

The third new factor is the habit of and facilities for scientific inquiry into the
mechanics of shooting an arrow, which are far more complicated than at first sight
appears.

Consider the case of an archer drawing, as beginners instinctively draw, by
holding the arrow between finger and thumb and loosing it with 'the primitive
loose'. The string flies straight forward to its final position as a straight line between

* The technical term for 'stiffness'.

the two nocks of the bow. But the arrow must diverge from that line: it cannot fly straight forward as impelled by the string, but must fly at an angle, to the left of the bow-handle. It has, in fact, been proved by photography that the arrow-shaft, when loosed, curves away at first to the left, the convex side pressing against the bow. Then the arrow's vibration produces a reactive curve to the right, with the concave side in contact with the bow. The next vibration takes the butt of the arrow, released now from the string, to the left, out of contact altogether with the bow. Finally, the arrow departs on its flight, a serpentine flight at first which, disciplined by the fletching, straightens out until it is flying true.

This divergence between the arrow's first course and the course taken by the bowstring, is complicated enough when the ineffective 'primitive loose' is employed. With any other loose further complications arise. Take, for instance, the three-fingered Mediterranean loose used by the medieval longbowmen and most modern archers. Here the string does not simply fly forward when released from the pressure of finger and thumb: it must, on release, slide to the left over the first joint of the three fingers before it is clear of the finger-tips and free to fly forward. When it does fly forward, it must move appreciably to the right, away from the arrow's course, exaggerating the arrow's curve. However sharp the loose, this distortion is bound to occur in some degree.

It must now be obvious why two arrows differing in 'spine' or whippiness will, though shot with identical stance, draw, aim, and loose, fly on different courses. No doubt the master bowman of Crécy or Agincourt knew this, and selected or made his arrows as nearly alike in spine as possible, but they could not possibly be as consistent in performance as modern arrows factory-made of aluminium tubing. When his favourite arrows were shot, he had to make do with any arrows, issued by the armful from carts in the rear or tugged from corpses of writhing bodies of the wounded. This in itself proves that the bow in battle was not a precision weapon.

It must also be obvious why two arrows, precisely similar in spine, shot with the same stance, aim, and loose, will, if one is drawn further back than the other, differ

Shooting bison

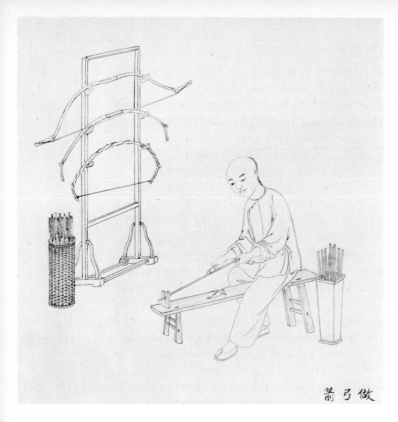

箭弓做

Chinese bow- and
arrow-maker

Opposite page
Irvine Toxo-
pholite Society
shooting at the
high target

not only in elevation but in direction. Of course, the archer whose loose varies from one shot to another cannot hope to shoot consistently.

All this may well have been familiar in practice, if not in theory, 9,000 or 10,000 years ago when the Holmegaard bow was made with a handle so shaped as to make the arrow's course coincide as nearly as possible with that of the string. Some modern composite bows have a deep-cut groove or channel along which the arrow flies almost through the centre of the bow. But it is still impossible to eliminate completely the ancient difficulty known as the 'archer's paradox': it is only possible, by perfecting the loose, to reduce its effects.

H. A. Ford's bow and arrows would not have seemed strange to the bowmen of the White Company. If his technique differed from theirs, it was because his object was different – to hit the gold, not to drive a cloth-yard shaft through mail or send a stream of arrows into a press of knights 200 yards away. Ford, and all archers of his and the next two or three generations, used self-bows. By far the best were of mountain yew, though lemonwood, osage orange, and lancewood, all products of North America, run it close. But good yew is extremely difficult to obtain, and in the 1930s bows of tubular steel were tried. Most modern bows are composed of layers of plastic and fibre-glass glued to a maple frame. Even the self-bow has, under meticulous scientific examination, changed its form, and is no longer round or elliptical, but rectangular in section: its main advantage nowadays is, however, that it is cheap. For reasons which only a physicist will appreciate, the modern bow, composite or made of tubular steel, is more efficient than the old English longbow: that is to say, its shooting strength is greater in relation to the weight of its draw. It is more consistent in performance: with the same length of draw, it stores an equal amount of energy for dozens of successive shots: it does not 'tire' nearly as much as even the best traditional longbow. Nor is it affected by heat or humidity. Matched with arrows of the proper spine and weight for that particular bow, it almost certainly shoots straighter and more consistently than the medieval longbow.

It is no good having bow and arrows properly matched for consistent shooting if the archer himself does not shoot consistently. The very essence of archery is the exact replication by the archer, for each shot, of all the movements of standing, nocking, drawing, aiming, and loosing. Whether the target is far or near, whether it is a windless day or half a gale is blowing, the archer's movements must not vary: the only thing he changes is the point of aim.

He stands like his ancestors, feet flat, heels some 9 inches apart, weight evenly distributed, sideways on to the target so that a straight line from the target would pass through his two heels.

There are various methods of nocking, the traditional one, still the most common, being to hold the bow horizontally across the body with the left hand, and the arrow between finger and thumb of the right. The arrow is slid forward on top of the bow until the nock is level with the string, then securely nocked. Three fingers are then hooked round the string, the first and second fingers on either side of the arrow and in light contact with it. The bow is turned to a fore-and-aft position, about forty-five degrees to the ground, with the arrow resting in the groove between the bow and the joint of the forefinger (or, in some bows, in an artificial arrow-rest which reduces friction), and the archer is ready to draw.

There are now, as there were in Roger Ascham's time, various methods of holding the bow and of drawing. Some archers grip the bow tightly in the left hand, others hold it very loosely; some hold the string in the top joint of the fingers, others between the joint and the finger-tips. Some begin to draw before they raise the bow to an aiming position, others while raising it, others after raising it. On some points, however, all are agreed. The fingers during the draw are mere hooks: they do not move. The draw is made by pushing the bow forward with the left arm and pulling the string back with the right, employing all the muscles of wrists, forearms, upper arms, shoulders, and back. This is what Bishop Latimer meant by 'laying the body to the bow', and it is still necessary when the bow has only half the strength of the great war-bow.

At this point the bowman of Crécy would make a pungent criticism of his twentieth-century successor. He drew right back to the ear: the modern archer draws only until the string touches the point of his chin and his drawing hand is locked under the angle of the jaw, a position known as the 'anchor-point'. The ancient method of drawing to the ear was necessary when the range and the penetration of the arrow were all-important; but it was not easy to shoot accurately by that method. Using the modern anchor-point, it is easier for the archer to be sure of the direction of his aim because he can look straight along the shaft (though in target-shooting he generally uses a sight); he can be sure of the elevation of his aim,

Archery 1880

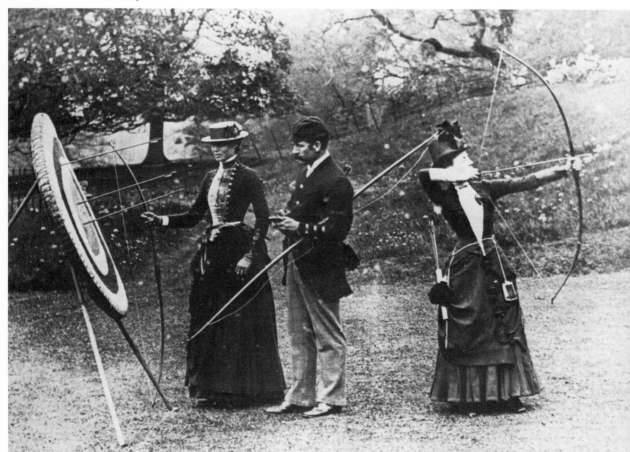

Monpelier Gardens 1890

because his drawing hand is, for every shot, locked under the angle of his jaw which is a more definite, exact anchor-point than any other. Finally, his loose is easier, because his hand so locked is not so liable to creep forward as when it is free. On all these points the archer drawing to the ear is at a disadvantage: his only gain is in the strength of his shot, which nowadays is hardly relevant. Apart from improvements in his equipment, it is this draw to the anchor-point of the chin which most sharply distinguishes the modern archer from his ancestor who drew to the ear. But Howard Hill, the big-game hunting archer, drew to an anchor-point on the cheek-bone, almost as far back as the ear.

In aiming too there are differences between ancient and modern archery. The bowman of old made allowance for range, wind, even for his own idiosyncrasies of style by picking an aiming point above, below, or to either side of his target and aligning the arrow-head on that. Most modern target-archers (though not hunters or field-archers) use a simple bow-sight, which performs the function of the fore-sight of a rifle and can be moved up and down the upper limb of the bow – up for a close shot to depress the pile of the arrow, down for a long shot to elevate it: lateral adjustments make allowance for a side wind. So now, in target-shooting, the bow-sight is aligned on the gold, and its adjustment provides the necessary aim-off.

As in Ascham's day, some archers keep the eye undeviatingly on the aiming-point, raise the left hand as they draw, come to the aim just as the draw is complete and instantly loose. This is the instinctive method of shooting, necessary when the

Lady champion of the world –
1936

Opposite page
Olympic Games 1908

target is a fleeting one which may disappear. It is now used mainly in field-archery or hunting. When, however, the principal need is for meticulous accuracy at a stationary target at a known range, rather more time can be taken over the aim: the draw completed, the archer pauses momentarily to check his position, his aim, his anchor-point before loosing.

Then comes the supreme moment, the most difficult thing in the whole art of archery. It is perfectly simple: all you have to do is, without disturbing your aim, to straighten the fingers and allow the string to fly forward. But 'When you have perfected your loose,' wrote A. E. Hodgkin in *The Art of Archery*, 'you will have done what no archer has ever done before.'

There are two principal errors in loosing. The first is to allow the string, as it slides over the finger-tips, to shift too far off its proper alignment to the left.* This, as had already been explained, will accentuate the errors in direction which are the result of the 'archer's paradox'. The second is to allow the string, just before the moment of release, to creep slightly forward.

* It is assumed throughout that the archer is a right-handed man, holding the bow with his left hand and drawing with his right.

86

Roger Ascham, it will be recalled, frankly admitted that he could not in writing describe the perfect loose.

H. A. Ford was perhaps the first to make the attempt, and his is the classic description. 'The *modus operandi*, like so many other things connected with archery, is extremely difficult to describe, if not altogether impossible; but the great characteristic with regard to it is, that *the fingers do not go forward one hair's breadth with the string*, but that their action be, as it were, *a continuance of the draw* rather than an independent movement, yet accompanied with just sufficient additional muscular action in a direction away from the bow, and simultaneous expansion of the fingers at the final instant of quitting the string, as to admit of its instantaneous freedom from all and each of them, at the same identical moment of time; for should the string but leave one finger the minutest moment before its fellow, or all or any of them follow forward with it in the slightest degree, the loose will be bad, and the shot in all probability a failure. So slight, however, is this muscular movement that, though a distinct and appreciable fact to the mind of the shooter, it is hardly, if at all, perceptible to the looker-on; yet, though apparently of so slight a character so important is it, that the goodness of the loose, and the consequent accurate flight of the arrow mainly depend on it.'

A 'dead' loose is one in which the fingers are just relaxed. This is comparatively easily done, but inevitably the string creeps slightly forward before release, so strength is lost and the arrow, if it is to hit the gold, must fly in a high trajectory. Still, simply for target-archery at known ranges, a dead loose, if consistent for every shot, produces reasonably good results especially at the shorter ranges.

In a 'sharp' loose there is no creep, for the archer momentarily increases the pull as he relaxes his fingers and allows the string to roll smoothly off them. Saxton Pope thus described it: 'The arrow is released by drawing the right hand further backward at the same time the fingers slip off the string. This must be done so firmly, yet deftly, that no loss of power results, and the releasing hand does not draw the arrow out of line. Two great faults appear at this point: one is to permit the arrow to creep forward just before release, and the other is to draw the fingers away from the face in the act of releasing.'

A modern archer, E. G. Heath, writes, 'If the fingers are relaxed and at the same time there is a slight movement in the direction of the draw by the shaft hand, as it were in continuance of the draw, the string, being under extreme tension, will release itself from the fingers, at the same time throwing the fingers clear.'

The sharp loose, so described, is the bowman's ideal. But most target-archers settle for something between a sharp and a dead loose.

Finally, in clout-shooting or hunting where power is more important than pinpoint accuracy, there is the snatch or slip loose, in which the string is quickly drawn back the last inch and at the same time the fingers by a conscious effort are straightened.

Since this book does not set out to tell anyone how to shoot, but merely relates how people have shot and why they have shot so, no advice will be proffered on this extremely abstruse subject. But once again it must be repeated that for consistent, accurate shooting the stance, nocking, draw, anchor-point, and loose must never vary; all that varies from one shot to another is the aim. The whole operation of

According to Joseph Acerbi, an Italian who travelled in Scandinavia in 1799, the Finlanders were still using this early form of crossbow in shooting squirrels

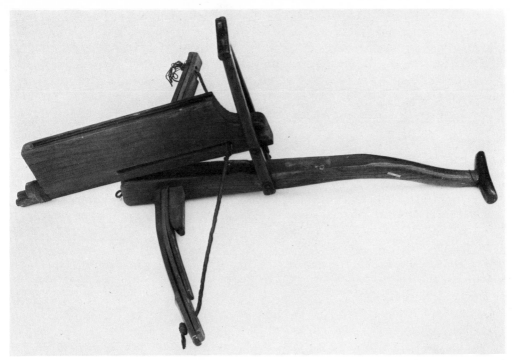

A Chinese repeating crossbow captured in the early 1900s

shooting an arrow should flow from start to finish in a smooth, regular rhythm. And the arrow having been loosed, the archer should remain motionless, watching its flight until it hits, or misses, the target.

The phenomenon known as 'freezing' or 'target shyness' is perhaps peculiar to the modern target-archer, since it is the product of a search for perfection in aim at a very small mark. The archer seems frozen, unable to move his bow-hand that last inch which will align his sight with the gold or the arrow-pile with the aiming-point. The bow-hand shakes, the string creeps forward under the strain – try as he will he cannot get the right aim. Finally, he lets go in a weak, wild arrow which probably buries itself in the ground yards in front of the target. Certainly that was not how Crécy and Agincourt were won.

In 1844 the sport of archery in England, which had degenerated into a mere garden-party pastime, received a powerful stimulant in the shape of the first Grand National Archery Meeting, thereafter held annually, at which archers competed in standard rounds – at first the Double York, then (for ladies) the Hereford and others. The Grand National Archery Society, formed in 1861, took over the running from that year.

With the example of H. A. Ford before them, English archers began to study the art and improved greatly in performance. Similarly in the United States the formation in 1879 of the National Archery Association co-ordinated the efforts of several clubs and stimulated the development there of target-archery. But although American archers are second to none in the target sport, and have held more than

A 20th-century Siamese crossbow

their share of world records, it is in field-archery and hunting with the bow that they have contributed most to the sport. This is discussed later in the chapter.

The modern archery target is said to have been devised by the Prince Regent, although his embonpoint, even before he discarded his stays and 'let his belly down', was surely such as to preclude any great prowess with the bow. It is circular. In the centre is the bull's eye, known to archers as the 'gold', of $9\frac{3}{5}$ inches diameter. Surrounding this are rings of red, blue, black, and white, each $4\frac{4}{5}$ inches wide. The exact centre of the gold is known as the 'pinhole'. Hits score 9 points in the gold; 7, 5, 3, and 1 in the red, blue, black, and white respectively.

A list of scores at various rounds would make dull reading, but some examples should be given of modern skill. The Double York Round, for instance, longest and hardest round of all, consists of twelve dozen shots at 100 yards, eight dozen at 80 yards, and four dozen at 60 yards. The highest possible score for a Double York Round would, therefore, be 2,592. For over a century Ford held the British public record with a score of 1,251 at an open meeting.* Indeed, it was doubted for many years whether anyone else would ever score over 1,000 points in a Double York: Ford's performance with the traditional longbow, which he always used, has in fact never been beaten. Now, however, with improved bows and arrows, the current British record, made in 1970 by R. D. Matthews, is 2,138; while in the same year J. I. Dixon scored 1,097 with half as many shots in a Single York Round. It is safe to say that no medieval bowman could have made anything like these scores.

Clout-shooting is still practised – not, to be sure, at 'twelve score' but generally at a distance of 180 yards for men and 120 for women. The clout itself is a small flag stuck in the ground. Five points are scored if the arrow lands within 18 inches of this; 4, 3, 2, and 1 points if it lands within 3, 6, 9, and 12 feet respectively. The principles of clout-shooting, combined with those of golf, have produced a variant known as 'archery golf'. Flight-shooting, too, survives, the record flight being that of the American archer, Harry Drake, in 1969 – 856 yards. This is a far longer flight than any whose authenticity is beyond doubt, though still not as long as the 972 yards $2\frac{3}{4}$ inches credited to the Sultan Selim, with a Turkish composite bow in 1798. (Using his feet to bend the bow, that is by turning himself into a crossbow, Harry Drake shot an arrow 1,861 yards.)

Popinjay-shooting was never popular in England or America, but it is still practised quite a lot in France and Belgium. A series of coloured model birds, each carrying its value in points, are attached to an 85-foot mast. Archers standing at the foot of the mast try to knock down these birds with blunt arrows shot vertically. Oddly enough there was a similar contest at Kilwinning in Scotland, competitors shooting at a single bird on top of a 100-foot pole. The year's winner had the title, 'Captain of the Papingo'.

Far more interesting is 'field-archery', practised most in the United States. It is a sort of artificial hunting. Targets in the form of deer, rabbits, or other animals are placed half hidden in several acres of woodland, with scoring rings on the vital parts. The archer moves slowly through the wood, searching and shooting at any target he sees, at ranges which he must estimate. Because the ranges are not known, field-archers generally use a faster bow with a flatter trajectory than target-archers. Shots may be uphill, downhill, or on the level: targets small or large, near or far: to simulate the conditions of real hunting, not more than two shots may be made at each target. In most competitions bow-sights and other artificial aids to aiming are banned: aiming must be quick and instinctive, all the archer's attention is concentrated on the target. It is a sport, or an art, very different from modern target-archery with its sights, standard targets, and fixed ranges – something much more like the archery of our ancestors.

It was a splendid, defiant gesture which made the British archer, Jack Churchill, take to France in 1939 a 100-lb yew bow and some hunting-arrows. On the retreat to Dunkirk in May 1940, he saw through a gap in a wall three German soldiers some 40 yards away. He drew his mighty bow, aimed, loosed – and one fell with an arrow through his chest.

---

* In a private match he once scored 1,414.

On various occasions during the years 1939–45 the bow was contemplated as a means of silently slaying sentries, or for other stealthy operations of war. So far as I know, however, Churchill was the only bowman in that war to slay an enemy with an arrow. But in the beginning of the Mau Mau Rebellion the Christian missions in Kikuyuland had to defend themselves and their converts from murderous attacks by day or night: firearms were at first scarce, and for some months the Kikuyu Home Guard, first formed by the missions, was armed with two very ancient weapons, the spear and the bow. Bishop Latimer would have approved.

Finally, let us return to the oldest of all forms of bowmanship, hunting with bow and arrow.

It is still widely practised by primitive bush- and jungle-dwellers in Africa, South America, and parts of Asia. Their bows are, by European standards, weak and in-

H. A. Ford

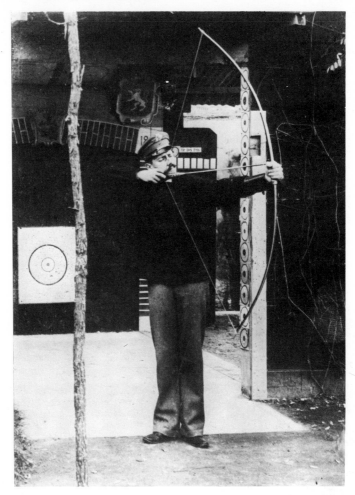

A Belgian
champion

efficient weapons, and their arrows have not much penetration.* But at the range at
which they shoot – seldom more than 30 yards – they are very accurate, and the shafts
of their arrows are often smeared with some quick-acting poison which brings down
an animal as large as a giraffe within ten or fifteen minutes.† These men are hunting
for food, for clothing, for giraffe-hide with which to make water-buckets. Modern
Western man has revived hunting with the bow as the greatest and most difficult of
non-equestrian field-sports.

It is natural that hunting with the bow should flourish most in the United States
and Canada, where there are plenty of archers, plenty of game, and plenty of space.
Indeed, some hunting-grounds are reserved for the bow.

---

* The Waboni and the Waliangulu, elephant-hunting tribes of north-east Kenya, are exceptional in that they
use powerful, long self-bows.

† The poison must, however, be fresh: I have seen a Somali tribal policeman hit in the thigh by a poisoned arrow.
He naturally resigned himself to a quick death, for we had no antidote: but because the poison was old, he lived,
and took little harm for what was a mere flesh-wound.

The Royal Company of Archers

Opposite page
Shooting gallery of the Guild of St Sebastian, Bruges

The Thompson brothers, Maurice and Will, were the first modern men to specialize in hunting with the bow, living by it for some years after the Civil War.

The best-known modern big-game hunting archer is Howard Hill, who has shot with the bow every species of American animal, and many in Africa. In hunting buffalo he deliberately handicapped himself by hunting as the Plains Indians have done, that is riding bareback, with only a hackamore to control his pony at full gallop, screaming like a Sioux to get the herd too into a gallop. 'We were going fast. During all the years I had dreamed of such a chase as this. I had vastly under-estimated the thrill it would be. . . . For a moment I was truly a wild man. I was yelling one whoop after another.' They passed through the stragglers of the herd and came up alongside a big bull. 'In a few strides the horse and the fleeing bull were cantering in time with each other. I quickly drew my arrow to the head as my horse came off the ground. As she and the big bull hit the ground, I let go, aiming behind the fore shoulder and well up into the lung region. I reasoned that the buffalo was hot, and a lung shot would bring quicker death than a heart one.

94

'Not more than thirty feet separated the horse and the ton of buffalo. The arrow flew straight to its mark and slipped through the carcase as though it had been so much cheese. Half the feather were out of sight before the shaft stopped.

'The bull seemed to buckle for a second, then he straightened out again. My pony stayed right alongside, keeping even strides with the speeding beast. I whipped a second arrow out of my quiver, nocked it, looked at my target and started to draw.

'Then it happened. The bull faltered, his front legs buckled, and he went over and over and pulled up in a heap, dead.'

Among other remarkable feats of Howard Hill was killing a bull elk at 185 yards. The first arrow was too high, the second too low; but the third hit him in the chest and killed him stone dead. He is – or was at the time he did it – the only white man who ever killed a bighorn ram, wariest of wild animals and most difficult to approach, with the bow. There can be no doubt that hunting with the bow demands far more field-craft, knowledge of the habits of game and stalking skill than hunting with the rifle.

Howard Hill took to East Africa a 100-lb bow made of split bamboo, and heavy, steel-tipped dural arrows. With this in one safari he killed three elephants. He found that an arrow, shot into the forehead of a charging elephant, had neither the penetration to cut through some 14 inches of hide, muscle and bone to reach the brain, nor the shock-effect of a bullet. It did not in the least deter or check the bull, who had to be shot with a rifle. But fired into the chest cavity or behind the shoulder, where there are no heavy bones to stop or deflect it, the arrow kills as well as the

bullet for it produces a much faster haemorrhage. Lesser animals are easily killed with the bow. At 25 yards a broad-headed arrow drove straight through the chest of a crocodile, and another through the head into the brain.

Another shot at an elephant provided, however, an interesting example of the arrow's erratic flight before, disciplined by the feather, it straightens out. In this case a hunting-arrow, shot at about 20 yards, was deflected by a vine which was not in the line of sight and, instead of driving into the chest, cut through the lower jaw. The animal promptly charged, unsuccessfully, and was later seen pulling out the arrow with his trunk.

Howard Hill's narrowest escape came not from any animal in Africa, but from a wild boar in California. 'As I eased forward foot by foot, with bow half-drawn and arrow in position for a shot. I kept my eye glued to the small opening out of which I knew the hog would come at any second. I could hear the threatening noise of the wild boar as he sharpened his rapier-like tusks, upper against the lower. The sound made by this action is like a scraping stick, not too loud, but those who have heard it will agree it is not pleasing to hear. While the seconds ticked past I thought of many other times I had stalked cornered tuskers, none of which had ever been so formidable as this. . . .

'Every muscle in my body was tingling, but was not taut. Tautness would be fatal, I knew: at such a time one wants to be alert, with each muscle ready for action but not tied up. Only the muscles pulling my bowstring partially drawn were under a strain.

'. . . I could not see the boar but I prayed for a chance to shoot before he could charge. I was no more than thirty feet away when the tusker shot out of the thicket between the dogs at top speed and bore down upon me.

The modern bow being used at Grand National Archery Meeting at Oxford

Opposite page
The range of the Guild of St Sebastian, Bruges

'When yet ten feet from me he made a powerful leap, much like a lion makes, and came hurtling through the air shoulder high. His mouth was wide open and the noise that escaped his throat was simply blood-curdling.

'I drew quickly and loosed an arrow. It struck him in the lower jaw, passed down his neck and embedded in the point of his shoulder. The arrow did not even slow him down.

'As the missile left the bow I had leaped from the right. I felt the boar's tusks rip through the top of my trousers near the small of my back. His shoulder hit me a glancing blow that spun me half-around, but I was able to keep on my feet . . . he whirled and charged for me again, but this time he was coming at me low and I shot a second arrow that caught him just forward of the shoulder blade bones. It cut through the tusker's body, partially severing the spinal cord, and passing through the lungs . . . he slumped forward and lay still.'

On another occasion he was charged by a wounded boar. 'At thirty feet I could see the red eyes of the angry beast . . . I realized that only a brain or spinal shot would stop him. He was a scant fifteen feet away now. . . . He was coming in for the kill.

'In one smooth motion I raised and drew the heavy bow, aimed for the flat of his head just above the eyes and let go. The arrow struck him a little too low. It cut through the upper part of the nose just under the right eye, penetrated the jowl, came out and buried in his right shoulder.' But it did not stop him. Hill dodged the charge, drew and nocked another arrow as the boar turned to come for him again.

97

The broadhead struck a couple of inches above the eyes and exactly in the middle of the head. There was a distinct crack as the steel head cut through the hard skull. The tusker froze in his tracks, then slowly toppled and rolled over.'

Howard Hill claims that there is no better measure for game preservation than the use of the bow in hunting. One can see his point.

The crossbow has a rather different appeal, to those interested in mechanical ingenuity rather than manual dexterity. Perhaps for historical reasons, it has retained its popularity far more on the Continent than in Britain. In Switzerland the Brotherhood of St Sebastian, of Schaffhausen, and the Guild of Crossbowmen of Zürich have held tournaments since the thirteenth and fourteenth centuries. Until recently they used ancient bows dating back to the seventeenth century; now they use Bollinger crossbows, first manufactured in 1880 or later patterns. Traditionally the range at which they shoot is one hundred paces, or 85 metres.

There is now an International Armbrust Union, holding international competitions, usually at 30 metres. The modern Winseler crossbow is a very powerful weapon, with a 150-kilogram (over 300 lb) draw, shooting a heavy bolt weighing 32 grams, and fitted with a spirit-level to help in aiming. In England a small but dedicated band of crossbowmen compete at ranges similar to those of ordinary archery; but the targets are half the size, for the crossbow is a very accurate weapon.

As in the Middle Ages the crossbow was undoubtedly the best weapon for hunt-

Members of the Guild of St Sebastian, Bruges, shooting at the popinjay

Opposite page
Modern crossbow with a collimator sight (Singlepoint)

ing, so in the last twenty years hunting with the crossbow has had an interesting, exotic revival.

This sprung from the invention by veterinary surgeons of a self-injecting syringe for use in treating dangerous or excited animals, who will not stand quietly while the vet slowly presses home the plunger. Dr John King, called upon to immobilize an Aberdeen Angus cow which had gone completely berserk, succeeded in doing so with a self-injecting syringe attached to an arrow shot from a longbow. Someone then had the bright idea of similarly immobilizing wild animals for transport from where they are a nuisance to where they are wanted, for example from farms or settlement schemes to National Parks or game reserves.

The first problem was, how to deliver the dart? A longbow was not really satisfactory, for comparatively few vets and game wardens are expert archers, and a syringe upset the delicate balance of an arrow. Ordinary firearms had too high a velocity: either the animal was badly wounded; or the syringe was smashed on

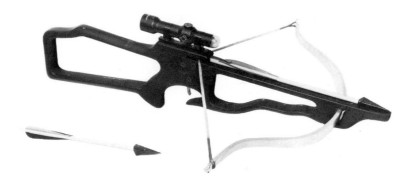

impact; or the needle penetrated, but the thicker syringe, striking too hard, pressed in skin and flesh and caused a rebound which bounced the syringe off, leaving the needle still embedded. One solution is a special low-velocity gun, using black powder. Another is a crossbow.

The crossbow used in Kenya is a medium powered, hand-drawn weapon with a draw weight of about 110 lb. More powerful bows were tried, but they were not found any better in performance because in order not to smash the business part of the dart, impact must occur near the end of a flattish trajectory, while the missile is losing its velocity: the stiffer the bow, the further off this point must be; but the available trigger mechanism was heavy and not conducive to accuracy. In South Africa, however, a more powerful bow is used successfully, with a mechanical loading device.

The barbed dart is of stainless steel, mounted in a drilled aluminium bolt about 9 inches long. Inside the bolt is the syringe, holding up to 1 ml of the drug, which on impact is injected by a spring-actuated plunger. The complete missile is very light, weighing only some 10 grams.

The 110-lb bow and a bolt, sighted for 30 yards, make about a 9-inch group:

at 50 yards the drop in elevation is about 11 inches, and at 60 yards, about 27 inches. Accurate range-judging is, therefore, of great importance.

Drugs used may be tranquillizers, paralysers or 'neurolept-analgesic' drugs which cause disorientation, sedation and eventually anaesthesia. The drug most commonly used, entorphine (M99), is of the last type. The size of the dose can be determined only by experiment and experience, and has little to do with the size of the animal. Buffaloes, for instance, react surprisingly quickly to quite a small dose. Animals in parks and game reserves, accustomed to men and vehicles, need only about half the dose of those in hunting blocks. They are easily tranquillized, a purely mental state almost impossible to achieve in truly wild animals.

In Kenya, where much has been done on these lines, all kinds of antelopes, giraffes, zebras, buffaloes, rhinos, lions, and even elephants have been successfully 'darted', usually with the object of moving them from places where they are a nuisance and liable to persecution into National Parks where they will be an economic asset in the sacred cause of tourism. In effect, however, darting an elephant is labour in vain because, even when he is down and out, you cannot move him; buffaloes are so common that they are not worth the trouble of darting; lions cannot easily be tracked at speed when they make off after first being 'darted', so by the time the darting party catches up with a lion, the effect of the drug may have worn off. The animal most commonly darted is the rhino, because he is a dangerous nuisance on farms and settlement schemes, easily killed by poachers who will sell his horn as an aphrodisiac, and believed, unless protected, to be in danger of extinction.

Although the rhino is a very large animal, the target for the dart is pretty small, about the size of a soup-plate. The dart must penetrate a muscle-mass in the brisket, the shoulder or the hindquarters – preferably the last, as it is less likely to be knocked off as the animal dashes off through thick bush. It must strike at about ninety degrees: if it strikes at too acute an angle, it will whip about on impact and may break off.

Dr King's first experiments in darting rhino were carried out in the Makindu district of Ukambani, which is thickly populated by a tribe of inveterate hunters and poachers. The rhino, which were very numerous, had to be moved to make room for an agricultural settlement scheme. It was far from easy: through association with man, they had become very crafty: they used to raid crops and gardens at night, and in the hour before dawn retire to dense thickets of wait-a-bit thorn where they could only be followed on foot down narrow tunnels. It was six months before King succeeded in immobilizing his first rhino, but thereafter success came more easily.

When first struck by a dart, a rhino may take practically no notice, but go on quietly browsing. He may charge, and have to be shot. More commonly he sets off at a brisk trot, covering perhaps a couple of miles in about a quarter of an hour before he collapses. The hunters must be close behind him, for he may be unconscious for only an hour, during which he must be secured by strong ropes to a sledge which is winched into a crate on a lorry. They cannot be sure, as they follow, that the drug has taken effect: the dart may have missed the muscle, or failed to inject properly: but they cannot risk a second shot, for an overdose may be fatal. They can, however, if the animal is 'out' for too long, inject him with an antidote, antagonist cypreno-morphine (M285).

King and his colleague, Nick Carter, discovered that it was better to operate from a Land Rover, driving up close to the running animal before taking a shot and then following until he drops. Easiest of all, but of course expensive, is darting from a helicopter.

Darting rhino does not always go as planned, for the rhino is perhaps the most aggressive of the big animals, addicted particularly to charging vehicles. 'The Land Rover', writes Nick Carter, 'was hurtling over the ground. . . . It bucked and roared and the suspension crashed as it hit unseen obstacles in the thick grass. . . . We were travelling at about thirty miles an hour and I was amazed when the cow [rhino] again turned in her own length and came charging back at the Land Rover. Once more Barrie swung the wheel hard to save the radiator from a ton and a half impact, and once more centrifugal force pitched me over to the door. . . . I fell on my left hand as the great animal hurtled past, missing us but jabbing with her sabre-like horn, and somehow I raised the bow with one arm and let fly the dart into her shoulder at point-blank range.' She dropped twenty minutes later.

Another cow charged like a battering-ram. In a flash a ton of inert flesh was transformed into a sort of grey torpedo on legs . . . Barrie swung the wheel hard and accelerated. He was a fraction too late and her horn caught the wheel on my right side with a clang and I saw the metal spread and tear. . . . I leaned over on the turn and shot the dart into her shoulder.'

Darting rhino on foot could be an even more traumatic experience. 'He was charging a fraction to my flank when he saw me, which gave me a chance to press the trigger as I aimed at his neck. At the range of ten yards I heard the dart smack home even as I dropped the bow and leaped for an overhanging branch. Baringero reached down and pulled me up as he thundered underneath, and then there was a series of fading crashes in the distant bush and finally silence while we giggled with relief.'

King has even darted rhino from an elephant. This was in Nepal, where some Indian rhinoceros calves were needed for presentation to zoos and parks in other countries. The problem was to separate each half-grown calf from his large and angry mother. In the past this has always been solved by half a dozen trained elephants knocking the cow rhino about until she capitulates, a cruel and messy business, which both mahouts and Nepalese authorities much disliked. King, from the back of an elephant, put the cows out quite painlessly for long enough to enable the calves, also drugged, to be captured and removed.

It might be thought that, once the drugged animal is crated, the difficulties are over. Far from it. Release in a strange environment is a dreadful experience for any wild animal: he has no 'base', no home, he wanders helplessly around until he starves or is killed. So he must be released gradually – at first into a small enclosure, with his familiar crate available as a refuge: then the enclosure is enlarged; finally, his confidence restored, he is free to come and go as he pleases. But some rhino are far from pleased to go: in a few days' captivity, they seem to find human company congenial, and it is quite difficult to persuade them to take again to the wild.

4

Villainous Saltpetre

Antiquarians dispute on whether gunpowder was first invented by wily orientals, subtle Byzantines or by a semi-legendary monk-alchemist named Bertold Schwartz who is portrayed in a sixteenth-century woodcut peering benevolently, at a distance of some 4 inches, into a devastating explosion in his laboratory. On the whole the dubious credit for this unfortunate invention can most plausibly be attributed to Roger Bacon, Fellow of Merton College, 1214–92. The first primitive cannon, shooting stones, are recorded defending Seville in 1247. So by the battle of Crécy, 100 years later, cannon were already old hat. This book, however, is not concerned with cannon.

The first record of a 'handgone' is on the equipment list of King Edward I's ship *Christophe de la Tour* in 1338. The town of Aachen is on record as having bought four in 1354. In 1355 they figure in the accounts of the Grafschaft Holland and by 1364 there are records of 500 being made in Perugia. Then and for the next 100 years or so the handgun consisted of an iron tube, some 2 feet long, open at one end, fixed at the other to a straight wooden pole, with a touch-hole near the breech end. The intrepid hand-gunner poured down the barrel a measure of powder, pushed down a wad and a ball. Then he poured more powder into the touch-hole, grasped the pole under his arm, directed the piece towards the foe and, commanding himself to his patron saint, applied a live coal or slow-match to the touch-hole. He could not, of course, aim, but on the rare occasions when the ball struck the target at a range of 20 or 30 yards, it would penetrate plate-armour which would turn an arrow. This, no doubt, encouraged soldiers to go on with this unpleasant and dangerous weapon, and try to improve it. Later, they began to rest the stock on the shoulder, which enabled them to take rather better aim.

There is even an oft-reproduced picture of a heavily armoured horseman firing this handgun from his horse, the weight of the barrel taken by a forked rest affixed to the saddle. Those with any experience of horses or firearms will suspect that the artist, was drawing on his imagination rather than on his experience.

It was not easy for the hand-gunner to aim his ponderous tube while one hand was fully occupied in managing the hot coal or glowing match. If he grasped the pole under his armpit and the fore-end in one hand, applying the match with the other, he could hold it tolerably steady, and point it in the right direction, but could not easily judge what elevation to give it. If he rested the pole on his shoulder, holding it with only one hand, he could aim better, but could not hold it steady. One answer to the problem was to have two gunners to each gun, one to aim and the other to load and fire. A better answer was the matchlock.

103

Opposite page
The weapons of 15th-century man: stone, crossbow, bow and handgun

The early hand-gun was fired resting on the shoulder. Here the butt is hollowed to fit the shoulder

In this, the slow-match* was fixed in what was called a 'serpentine', an S-shaped gadget, resembling the modern hammer and trigger combined, which was fixed to the gun by a pin through the centre. As the trigger part of the serpentine was pulled up and back, the hammer moved down and forward, pressing the glowing end of the match into the touch-hole.

An obvious improvement was a spring-actuated serpentine: normally the pressure of the spring kept the serpentine head, with its glowing match, safely away from the touch-hole. But when the trigger was raised, against the pressure of the spring, the serpentine head was lowered until the match ignited the powder in the touch-hole. The next development was that the serpentine should be operated by a spring when pressure on the trigger – no longer a long lever – disengaged it from a gear. The serpentine was generally lowered towards the shooter, not, like the hammer of a flint-lock, away from him.

* A length of cord impregnated with a solution of saltpetre or spirits of wine.

Mercenaries armed with this weapon were employed in the Wars of the Roses; and Henry VII, not a man to waste his money on status symbols, armed with it half the Yeomen of the Guard.

With a 5-foot barrel and a ¾-inch bore, this was quite a formidable weapon. To fire it the barrel was laid on a forked rest stuck in the ground, and the butt, if crooked in the French style, placed 'just before the right pap'; and if straight, in the Spanish style, against the right shoulder. This 'arquebus' is a recognizable firearm. Its ball could pierce almost any armour, and would have some chance of hitting a man at 80 yards. The Spaniards were the acknowledged experts, replacing English bowmen as the most feared infantry in Europe. Armed with the arquebus, they were nearly always victorious in Italy, Mexico, and Peru.

Improvement in the powder had greatly improved the performance of firearms. The charcoal, sulphur, and saltpetre was now mixed when moistened, preferably by human urine, a wine drinker's being considered more efficacious than a beer drinker's, and a wine-drinking bishop's the best of all, particularly if drawn straight from tap.* The end product of this exotic compound, granules composed of the ingredients in the proper proportions, was known as 'corned powder'. For military use, a measured charge of this, with its ball, was contained in a cylindrical paper bag known as a cartridge, about a dozen of which were hung from the shoulder-belt or bandolier. There was a special fine powder for the touch-hole, known as 'priming-powder'.

Powder was carried (if not in a made-up cartridge) in a horn, the nozzle of which contained the exact charge. Sportsmen, who did not carry proper cartridges, needed two horns – one for ordinary and the other for priming-powder, the latter known as the 'touch-box'.

Reloading was a task to be undertaken systematically and not without apprehension. First, the lighted match must be removed from the serpentine and held in the left hand, its glowing end well away from the powder-horn or cartridge. The piece was then 'ordered', butt on ground, barrel also in left hand. With the right hand the powder-flask was tipped up, the mouth blocked by the forefinger and a spring thumb-catch pressed to allow the nozzle to fill. When it was full, the thumb-catch was released and the charge poured carefully down the barrel. Wadding and bullet (or shot) were rammed down in turn. Some priming-powder from the touch-box was poured into the priming-pan, the pan closed by its cover and any loose powder blown away before the match was replaced and screwed into the serpentine. The arquebusier was then, at last, ready for his next shot.

During the fifteenth and sixteenth centuries the authorities of the Holy Roman Empire encouraged the formation of shooting guilds, in order to provide a reserve of marksmen in case of invasion by the Turks. Similar guilds developed in Switzerland. At first these concentrated on practice and competition shooting with the crossbow, but by the mid-fifteenth century they were using firearms: the first guild devoted purely to shooting with firearms seems to have been set up in Lucerne in 1466. Target competition was held on Sundays. Each competitor used his own gun, but the authorities provided powder and ball for their shots at a maximum range of

* I am indebted to Mr Robert Held's *The Age of Firearms*, published by Cassell, 1959, for these recondite details.

Ioan. Stradanus inuent.
Corn. Galle. Sculp.

Ioan. Stradanus inuent. Ioan. Collaert fecit. Ioan. Galle excud.

about 100 metres. (Crossbow matches were shot at about 130 metres.) The winner's prize was strictly utilitarian – a pair of hose, say, or breeches. Singularly enough, the winner was always detailed as butt-marker the following Sunday, to signal the hits; while he who came second was given the unexciting but responsible task of seeing to competitors' slow-matches.

Such competitions soon became extremely popular in Central Europe: people would travel for days to take part in a shoot, and the winners on their return home were fêted as heroes. To a famous meeting at Zürich in 1504, marksmen came from as far as Innsbruck and Frankfurt-am-Main: 460 crossbowmen and 236 arquebusiers competed. Besides the business which brought them, games, horse-racing, jousting and displays by professional swordsmen enlivened the days; dancing and feasting helped pass the nights. Gipsies and strolling players offered their wares, whatever these might be, and no one urged competitors to eschew, if they wished to shoot straight, the pleasures of the flesh. (How different, how very different from the dedicated, ascetic atmosphere of Bisley!) The cost of these meetings was borne by the local municipality, often with the aid of a lottery. Unfortunately in the chaos of the Thirty Years War the shooting guilds declined; and after it the kings of Europe put not their trust in enthusiastic amateurs but in standing armies as large as they could afford.

There is an illustration of a match between marksmen armed with a heavy musket and a light caliver. It was, no doubt, artistic licence to show the targets only 5 yards away. Markers, sheltering behind butts, signal the hits, and the competitors' accuracy is stimulated by musicians and a coach to give advice.

Inventions of considerable technical interest appeared in the early fifteenth century. A leaden ball is seldom of the same consistency throughout: one part is heavier than the other, like a bowl with a bias, which causes it to wobble in flight, impairing both range and accuracy. It was discovered by empirical methods that one could eliminate this wobble by shooting it from a rifled barrel, which caused it to spin rapidly in its flight. The discovery has been attributed to Gaspard Kollner of Vienna, and to Augustus Kotter of Nuremberg: at all events it was an Austrian or south German invention. The effect of rifling was obvious: it greatly improved the gun's performance. But the reason for this was widely disputed. Some held that tiny imps, who delighted in misdirecting a good Christian's bullet, could not keep their seats on a spinning ball: others that the agents of supernatural powers were, on the whole, more comfortable on a spinning ball, but their influence was beneficial, causing it to fly more truly.

To settle this knotty point an experiment, under archiepiscopal supervision, was held at Mainz in 1547. One competitor was armed with silver bullets adequately blessed, which were reliable even against witches and werewolves: the other with ordinary unblessed lead bullets. The range was the phenomenal one of 200 metres. Strange to tell, of twenty leaden bullets nineteen hit the bull, and of silver bullets not one hit even the target. This suggested that rifle-bullets were, indeed, diabolically guided, and for some years they were in disrepute. (We, with the benefits of a secular education, may surmise that the softer leaden bullets fitted more tightly into the rifling. Moreover, the holy crosses deeply engraved on each silver bullet, so far

posite page
te how the men firing these early matchlocks place
right hand against the butt – to absorb recoil. Has
piece in the lower picture gone off by mistake?

Target shooting in Zürich in 1532. Note how the wall surrounding the fairly large target is peppered with misses

from ensuring their straight flight, might have had precisely the opposite effect.)

Apart from spiritual considerations, there were other reasons why the rifle did not, at this period, find general favour. Sportsmen required a dual-purpose weapon, firing ball or shot: but shot, fired from a rifled barrel, would be widely scattered. Lastly, lest there be an escape of gas, the ball must fit the grooves, not the lands of the rifling. This meant that it could not be just dropped or pushed down the barrel in loading, but had to be fairly hammered down against the resistance of the lands.

But no one could deny that the rifle was accurate to a far longer range than the smooth-bore weapon. Matches were shot at Zürich in 1472 at 230 paces, at Eichstadt in 1487 at 245 paces: during the sixteenth century matches at 250–280 paces were not uncommon. The usual target was wooden, round, of a diameter of about 100 centimetres. The butt-marker repaired shot holes with wooden plugs and signalled the hits which, in early days, counted the same anywhere on the target.

It is a sure sign of better firearms that towards the end of the sixteenth century shooting at moving targets, depicting, say, a Turkish horseman, became popular. Snap-shooting competitions were also held, at figure targets which popped out of a trench and down again.

Sixteenth-century Prague had several shooting ranges, as did most towns in the Empire. One of the most elaborate was at Salzburg, made in the early seventeenth century. It was over 250 yards long and 150 wide, with six targets, each having beside it a roofed shelter for the marker, constructed of 3-inch oak planks. The 'bullet-catcher' was a wall 16 feet high.

It must have been obvious to anyone who gave a thought to shooting that it would be easier and much quicker to load the powder and bullet into the breech than down from the muzzle. There had, after all, been breech-loading cannon in the fourteenth century, though they had not been particularly popular with those called upon to fire them. So throughout the sixteenth, seventeenth, and eighteenth centuries, numerous breech-loaders were made. It was easy enough to make one which worked when new: Henry VIII had several, all by foreign gunsmiths. But with the powder of the day, fouling and corrosion soon damaged the close-fitting working parts so that they could not be properly shut, were no longer gas-tight and were thoroughly dangerous.

Similarly many ingenious gunsmiths made repeating firearms based on the principle of the revolver. The earliest was a sixteenth-century repeating arquebus in

Wildfowler load-
ing his gun (1570),
from a drawing by
Stradanus

Opposite page
Duck shooting
(A.D. 1545) from
shore and boat

which a cylinder, its chambers loaded with made-up charges, was revolved by hand
so that each chamber in turn was aligned with the barrel for firing. This, too, was
excellent in theory, but fouling and corrosion affected it in practice. Furthermore,
there must have been a gas leak between cylinder and barrel, and there was always
the risk that an unlucky spark might explode all charges at once, with dire effects on
the shooter.

So the rifle, the breech-loader and the revolver, all invented in the sixteenth
century, for a long time were just interesting technical devices, without much
practical use.

The great drawback of the matchlock was the match, coils of impregnated cord,
glowing and spitting at each end (lest one end be extinguished), wound round the
arquebusier's waist or arm. There was the obvious danger of an accident, if sparks
landed in a powder-barrel or ignited a cartridge hanging from one's belt. The match
was all too easily put out by rain; it gave away the shooter to an enemy by night and
to a wary stag or wild duck by day. It complicated and slowed down the action of
re-loading since, for safety's sake, it must be removed from the serpentine and held
out of harm's way during that lengthy process. It was not really practical for horsemen. Any invention which would do away with the match would be a great step
forward, and it appeared in 1515 at Nuremberg – the wheel-lock.

This made use of the spark-producing properties of pyrites and steel. The
principle of the wheel-lock was to bring into contact a pyrite held in the doghead of

the serpentine with the revolving edge of a serrated steel wheel. The resultant shower of sparks was directed into the flashpan, which had a hinged cover to retain the priming-powder and keep it dry. The wheel was made to revolve by the main-spring, which was compressed by a small chain wound round the axle of the wheel. To cock the piece, the shooter turned the wheel with a key, winding up the chain and so compressing the mainspring, until the wheel engaged in a sear. To fire, he raised the flashpan cover and pulled (or, no doubt, squeezed) the trigger. This released the wheel from the sear, allowing it to revolve rapidly: at the same time the serpentine was also released and, actuated by a secondary spring, lowered to bring the pyrite into contact with the whirring wheel, and – Bang!

The wheel-lock was a great improvement on the matchlock, but it was expensive. It was used mainly for sporting weapons for the rich and for horse-pistols and carbines, which now, for a short time, became the principal arms of cavalry until Gustavus Adolphus, Prince Rupert and Cromwell between them restored the sword to its proper place as the main cavalry weapon.

The matchlock, costing in the first half of the seventeenth century only 15*s* 6*d*, robust and foolproof in its mechanism, remained the principal infantry weapon until nearly the end of the century. Wheel-locks and, later, flint-locks, costing three or four times as much and with mechanisms which needed a skilled gunsmith to repair, were reserved for horse-soldiers; for grenadiers, who needed their hands free for their special weapon; and, most sensibly, for those whose duty it was to escort artillery and powder-wagons.

The matchlock or arquebus took two forms: the light caliver, with a bore of about 0·75 inch and a 4-foot barrel which could be used without a rest and was eminently

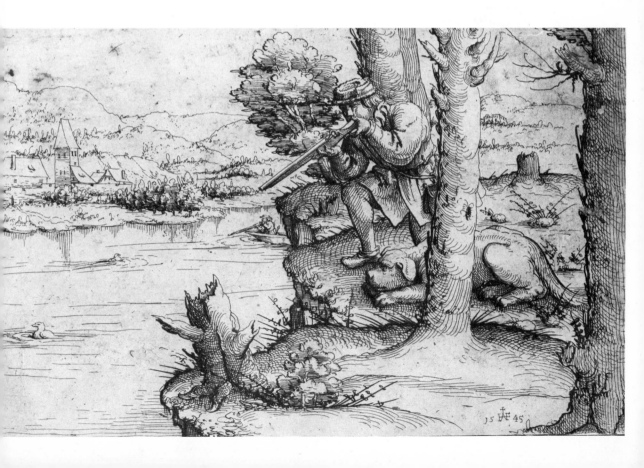

suited to the sportsman, and the heavy musket with a larger bore, a 5-foot barrel, which required a forked rest. For military purposes the musket was generally preferred. It had a longer range and far greater effect against plate-armour up to 200 yards, though a hit at that distance was more the act of God than of man. As for its vicious kick, Sir Roger Williams in his *Brief Discourses on War* (1590) very soon disposed of that frivolous objection. 'For recoiling, there is no hurt if they be straight stocked after the Spanish manner. . . . True it is, were they crooked stocked, after the French manner, to be discharged on the breast, few or none could abide their recoiling by reason of their great charges of powder; but being discharged from the shoulder in the Spanish manner, with the thumb betwixt the stock and the face, there is neither danger nor hurt if the shooter have any discretion.'

Although, by the mid-sixteenth century, cannon had been in use for 300 years and were regarded as more or less acceptable weapons of war, handguns were abhorrent to conservatives, and were condemned for somewhat conflicting reasons, (*a*) that they were too murderous and (*b*) that they were not murderous enough. The chivalrous Montluc, in the reign of Francis I, refused to have anything to do with them. 'I wonder that it could have been the will of Providence that this unlucky instrument have been invented. . . . I have seen horses and valiant men killed with it in such sad numbers, struck to the ground by these abominable bullets which had been discharged by cowardly and base knaves who would never have dared to meet true soldiers face to face and hand to hand. All this is very clearly one of those artifices which the devil employs to induce us human beings to kill one another.'

Shooting deer with arquebus and rest, having approached up wind

Opposite page
Shooting partridges in Spain, mid-17th century

Indeed, the fire, the black, billowing smoke, the sulphur and the stench seemed to confirm the satanic origin of the handgun. Smashing bones, carrying into the body fragments of cloth and leather, it caused horrible wounds which could be cured only by such desperate remedies as: 'Take of oil and wine equal parts, inject them into a living dog, well boil the animal. Its flesh, together with oil, wine and other ingredients, form the application.'

In England firearms were condemned from another standpoint. They were inaccurate and an 'extreme nicety' of aim was required. They became 'hot and dangerous' after seven or eight discharges. 'The fearful spectacle' of a drift of arrows coming towards one was far more alarming than a volley of invisible musket-balls. A bowman was not blinded by the smoke of his own weapon. Arrows jerking about in the wound with every movement galled horses far more than bullets, making them uncontrollable. Above all, a bowman could shoot at least five arrows in the time taken to load and fire a musket once. In short, 'after many hours in great encounters on both sides, and many thousand bullets discharged (often within short distance) very few men are slain or hurt'. The longbow had won the victories of Crécy, Poitiers, and Agincourt: it was the national weapon; and if it wasn't, then it ought to be.

To these arguments, military iconoclasts like Sir Roger Williams retorted that archers 'must discover [expose] themselves to make fair shoots, while the other shots spoil them by reason they discover nothing of themselves unless it be a little through

Duck shooting in winter, 1570

small holes'. In other words, an archer to draw his bow had to stand in the open, while the musketeer could remain under cover and shoot.

In effective range there was not much between the two weapons, but the musket-ball could usually smash through armour and the arrow could not. In accuracy, given equally good marksmen on a still day the bow probably had a slight advantage over the smooth-bore musket, though its accuracy was much more affected by wind. There are records of numerous target contests between the two weapons, and the bow usually won.

As late as 1792, each firing 21 shots at a 4-foot target at 100 yards, the archer scored 15 hits (not very good) and the musketeer only 12. In the same year there was still to be found a lieutenant-colonel of infantry arguing, as had been argued in England and America for 200 years, that the longbow was the better weapon. But the insuperable objection to it was that it took years of practice and the development of special muscles to produce a good archer, while the dullest recruit could learn in a few weeks to shoot a musket. As Sir Roger Williams had put it in Queen Elizabeth's day, 'among 5,000 bowmen you shall not find 1,000 good archers, I mean to shoot strong shoots'.

Anyway, the proof of the pudding was in the eating. English archers in the Low Countries were outshot by Spanish musketeers, and of the 6,000 trained soldiers mustered at Tilbury to repel the Spanish Armada, and inspected there by the Queen, not one was a bowman. But because of their long obsession with the longbow, the English were far behind continental nations in the development of firearms: the best gunsmiths, all the new inventions, were French, German, Italian, or Spanish.

For mounted men the value of firearms was questionable. Sir Roger Williams anticipated the conclusion of Gustavus, Rupert, and Cromwell when he insisted on the superiority of *l'arme blanche*: 'The Almains, during the time they carried lances, carried a far greater reputation than they do now being pistollers. Lances are more sure, for divers pistols fail to go off. . . . Being overcharged, it shakes in a man's hand so that often it touches neither man nor horse; if the charge be too little, it pierceth nothing to speak of. . . . I was often in their company when they ran away, three from one lancer, both in troops great and small . . . always they discharge their pistols eight and five score [feet] off, and so wheel about; at which turns the lancers charge them in the sides, be they well conducted.'

Nevertheless, troopers of horse did practise with their pistols, though how they could have held at arm's length, let alone aimed, such ponderous pieces is one of the minor mysteries of military history.

The English habit of weekly target practice, inculcated by the longbow, did not die, though it was applied more and more to other weapons. In 1537 there was granted to the Overseers of the Guild of St George, forerunners of that most distinguished regiment, the Honourable Artillery Company, a Royal Patent to 'exercise themselves in shooting with the longbow, crossbow and handgun at all manner of marks and butts and at the art of popinjay, and at all other game or games, as at fowl or fowls, as well in the City of London and suburbs as in all other

16th-century matchlock gun with tunnel sight and a
walnut stock inlaid with mother-of-pearl and bone

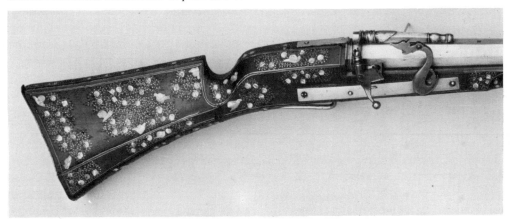

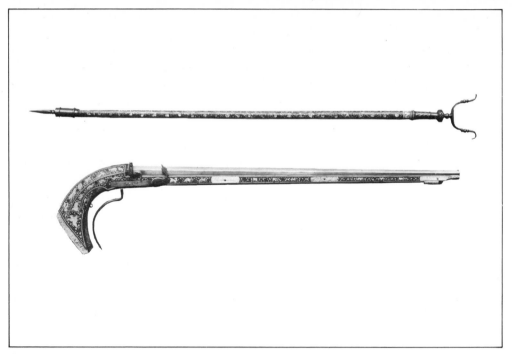

An arquebus and its rest

places whatsoever within the realm of England, Ireland, Calais and the Marches of Wales, and elsewhere within the King's dominions, his forests, chases and parks.'

His forests, chases and parks! Here was privilege indeed, indicating how highly Henry VIII valued marksmanship, even with the deplorable handgun. To give such licence to the Guild of St George was all very well; but every Tom, Dick, and Harry took similar liberties, neglecting at the same time their weekly practices with the longbow, and decimating (so it seemed) the country's wild life. A stream of statutes and exhortations tried to recall them to their duty. The stubborn fellows would not toe the line, but 'daily shoot in crossbows and handguns whereby the King's deer are destroyed and shall be more and more unless remedy be provided. Wherefore be it ordained and enacted by authority of this Parliament that no person shall henceforth shoot in any crossbow or handgun upon pain of forfeiture of the said bow or gun, unless he has lands . . . or other profits to the yearly value of 300 marks (£200).'

Their very repetition, by one Parliament after another, proves how ineffective were these laws. To quote merely one more Act of many, that of 1542: 'Where in the Parliament . . . sundry wholesome and laudable Acts . . . were made and ordained for the avoidance and eschewing of shooting in crossbows and hand guns, since the making of which divers wicked and evil disposed persons . . . have wilfully and shamefully permitted, perpetrated and done divers detestable and shameful murders, robberies, felonies and riots with the crossbows, little short handguns and little hagbutts [arquebuses] to the great peril and continual fear of the King's most

116

loving subjects. . . . And whereas Gentlemen, yeomen and serving men now of late hath laid apart the good and laudable exercise of the longbow, which always heretofore hath been the surety, safeguard and continual defence of the Realm. . . . For reformation whereof be it enacted . . . that no person of whatever state or degree except he hath land . . . to the yearly value of one hundred pounds . . . shall shoot in any crossbow, handgun, hagbutt or demi-hake . . . upon pain to forfeit for every time that he so offend contrary to this Act ten pounds.'

As well fine the tide ten pounds for flooding in, for the King's loving subjects had discovered one inestimable advantage of guns over bows, that they would fire 'hail-shot'. Not merely was a bird or animal far easier to hit with a handful of pellets than with a single missile, but there was no risk of losing a valuable arrow shooting in a forest or at wildfowl on open water. In 1549, only seven years after its stern prohibition of shooting with the gun, Parliament had by implication to accept that guns had come to stay, and content itself with trying to prohibit their latest abuse. 'Whereas . . . there is grown a customable manner of shooting of hail-shot, whereby an infinite sort of fowl is killed and much game thereby destroyed to the benefit of no man; whereby also . . . the shooting of hail-shot utterly destroyeth the certainty of shooting which in wars is most requisite; be it therefore enacted that no person under the degree of Lord in Parliament shall henceforth shoot in any handgun at any fowl or other mark upon any house, church or dovecot, neither shall any person shoot in any place any hail-shot or any more pellets than one at a time.'

The specific prohibition of shooting at marks on houses, churches and dovecots indicates that target shooting was a popular sport, and one hopes that Lords in Parliament continued to enjoy it. As for the ban on hail-shot, it was quite ineffective. The lure of ill-gotten game was far stronger than any Act of Parliament. Bird shooting, difficult with the bow, was fairly easy with gun and hail-shot. It will be recalled

An early adjustable rearsight

The stalking ox

that Falstaff makes a clandestine visit to Mistress Ford while her husband is 'a-birding', and to evade discovery proposes to hide up the chimney. She, however, warns him that this would be inadvisable because 'there they always use to discharge his birding-pieces' – shooting them off in a safe place rather than undertaking the troublesome task of drawing the charges.

The wheel-lock was far better than the matchlock, but was still not entirely satisfactory. The intricate mechanism was very expensive and required the service of a skilled gunsmith. Its action was slow: that is to say, there was an appreciable interval between squeezing the trigger and the discharge, which made it very difficult to hit even a running rabbit, and quite impossible to hit a bird in flight. During this interval, it gave forth a shower of sparks, quite enough to cause a wary mallard to take to the wing. Finally, the pyrites were fragile, apt to disintegrate after a few shots. Something better was needed, and at the end of the sixteenth century, in Holland, it duly appeared: the snaphaunce lock.

The spark to ignite the priming-powder was produced by a concussion between steel and hard flint, instead of friction between steel and fragile pyrites. There were two hammers, facing one another: one, called the 'cock', held in its two jaws a wedge of flint; the other, called the 'battle' or 'steel' presented, when it was lowered into the flashpan, a steel surface for the flint to strike. The cock was actuated by a mainspring, when pressure on the trigger disengaged a gear. To shoot, one lowered the steel so that it was in place over the flashpan, ready for the flint, and squeezed

The ox's horns being used as a rest

the trigger. Simple, effective and comparatively cheap, the lock is believed to have been first used by Dutch poultry-thieves from whom it derived its name – snap-hans, or grab-cock. Confusion is sometimes caused because flint-lock (or firelock) muskets were sometimes incorrectly described in inventories of military equipment as 'strapped snaphaunce' muskets issued to dragoons and grenadiers who could sling them across their shoulders to leave their hands free for other weapons. The true snaphaunce was never a British Army weapon.

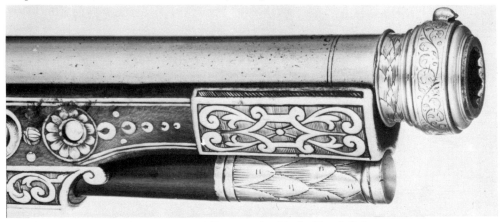

Bead foresight on a superimposed charge German wheel-lock rifle of 1606

Shakespeare was familiar with the snaphaunce. 'Pistol's cock is up' was no doubt an unseemly reference to this rather than to the matchlock or wheel-lock.

From the snaphaunce to the true flint-lock was a very short transition, made first in Spain before the end of the sixteenth century. The hammer known as the 'steel' or 'battle' was reduced to a combined steel and flashpan cover, serving the dual purpose of protecting the priming-powder against rain or being spilt, and producing, when struck by the flint, the necessary spark. Normally it remained closed: as it was struck, it flew open so that the shooter could re-prime with no loss of time. Soon after, the 'half-cock' was devised, by which the cock, or flint-holding hammer was held in a safe position clear of the flashpan, but the piece could not be fired without first drawing the hammer back to full-cock. The downward scrape of the flint against the almost perpendicular steel produced a powerful stream of sparks almost guaranteed to ignite the priming.

This was basically the flint-lock as it remained for over 200 years. Subsequent developments were simply refinements and minor improvements to what everyone must have regarded as the last word in the gunsmith's art.

It was always a slow loader, and the chances of accident were many. Tyros forgot to prime, over-charged, omitted to put the hammer at half-cock and so shot themselves while loading: they even forgot to remove the ramrods from the barrel before firing. So in the army the whole process had to be done 'by numbers', each motion completed on a specific order lest in the excitement of action it be omitted. Here, for instance, is the sequence of order in the British Army for loading and firing a flint-lock musket during the latter part of the seventeenth century:

'Musketeers, have a care for the exercise! – Carry your arms well! – Rest your muskets! Present! – Fire! – Recover your arms! – Half-cock your muskets! – Clean your pans! – Handle your primers! – Prime! – Shut your pans! – Blow off your loose corns! – Cast about to charge! – Handle your charges! – Open them with your

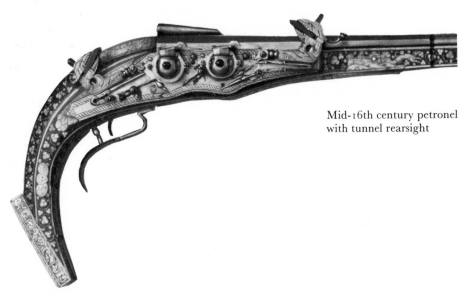

Mid-16th century petronel
with tunnel rearsight

teeth! – Charge with powder! – Draw forth your scourers! – (This done in these motions, the scourer or ramrod then held level, the height of the eye, arm extended.) – Shorten them to an inch! – Charge with bullet! – (The bullet, in the mouth, is spat into the muzzle, the end of the scourer inserted after it.) – Ram down powder and ball! – Withdraw your scourers! – Shorten them to a handful! – Return your scourers! – Poise your muskets! – Shoulder your muskets! – Order your muskets! – Rest!'

Nor was the military musket anything like a precision weapon. In the second Civil War Colonel Lucas, condemned to death by a Roundhead court martial for

Matchlock target gun
of about 1600

commanding the Royalist forces at Colchester, beckoning his firing squad to come nearer, 'I'll warrant you, Sir, we'll hit you,' said one of them. The Colonel retorted, 'I've been closer, friends, and you have missed me!' He had the last word.

On both sides of the Civil War men lucky enough to own 'birding-pieces' used them, loaded with ball, in preference to the regulation musket. At the sieges of the Countess of Derby's Lathom House and of Sherborne Castle Royalist gamekeepers, sniping with their own guns, caused the Roundheads great loss, picking off particularly their officers. Impressed by such examples, General Monck recommended that in the New Model Army six men in every company be armed with 'birding-pieces' and employed as specialist snipers.

A similar sequence had to be followed loading a shotgun, with the additional complication of measuring out the correct amount of shot, and ramming down a wad on top of it to hold it in place. The hazards and complexities of loading were, of course, increased in double-barrelled weapons. It was not uncommon for an accident to occur because a shooter, re-loading one barrel only, had left the other at full-cock. Nevertheless, 'birding' steadily increased in popularity during the seventeenth century, the favourite quarry being duck and geese, probably because they could be easily seen in open water and were often bunched together.

Writing in 1621 Gervase Markham in *Hunger's Prevention or the Whole Art of Fowling* gives far more attention to netting and snaring than to shooting; but his

Approaching

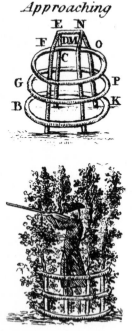

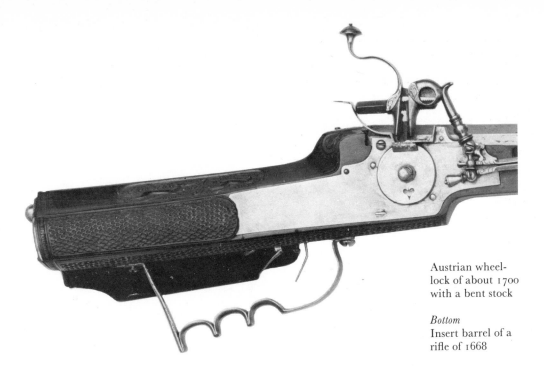

Austrian wheel-
lock of about 1700
with a bent stock

Bottom
Insert barrel of a
rifle of 1668

chapters on shooting are of interest as the first game-shooting treatise in the English language, and containing the first mention of a gun-dog.

'Of the fowling piece you will understand that to be best which is of the longest barrel, as five foot and a half or six foot, and the bore indifferent . . . for these hold the best charges and carry the farthest level, which is a principal thing to be regarded; for fowl are of such a fickell and cunning nature that a man shall hardly get within any indifferent or near station, and to shoot out of level or distance were to shoot against the wind, and scare-crow like, only to affright fowl with the loss of labour. As for the shape or manner of it, tis better it be a firelock or snaphaunce than a cock and tricker, for it is safer and better for carriage, readier for use and keeps the powder drier in all weathers, whereas the very blowing of a coal is many times the loss of the thing aimed at. . . .

'Now for the use of the fowling-piece, it is either for land or water that is passable or may be waded. . . . And herein first the fowler is to observe the finding-out of his game, and which fowl lyeth fittest for his purpose, at no time striving to shoot at a

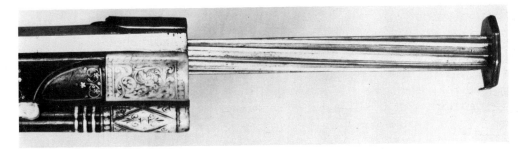

Firing for the King's Prize on 29 August 1719

single fowl if he can by any means compass more within his level. . . . Then shall he seek the convenient shelter he can find, as either hedge, bank, tree or any other shadow, for they are so fearful of the proportion, visage or motion of a man that upon the least suspicion they are gone in a moment. . . . Then shall he make choice of his mark . . . the longest and largest rank or file of fowl as you can find . . . which done, you may instantly and speedily discharge, and then send forth your dog to fetch what you have striken. . . . But by all means you must have your dog in such true obedience that he may not stir from your heels or let so much as his shadow be perceived till you have shot and yourself bid him go.'

In coverts and fields Markham recommended the use of a stalking-horse, 'which is any old jade trained up for that use, which will gently . . . walk up and down' while the sportsman remained concealed behind him, eventually taking a shot under the horse's neck.

Wildfowling became steadily more popular with farmers and small-holders. In 1634 the Ely farmers violently opposed the Duke of Bedford's fen drainage scheme, beating up his employees who seemed to be depriving them both of sport and of a useful supply of winter meat. A Mr Oliver Cromwell, ironically known by Whitehall wits as 'Lord of the Fens', headed an association formed to take legal action against the Duke. Bird-shooting, by the start of the Civil War, was firmly established as an English sport.

The godly soldiers of Cromwell's 'lovely company' were grievously addicted to poaching. During the New Model's campaign in Scotland, the commander-in-chief complained that soldiers 'do straggle at a great distance from their colours with their muskets, and kill and destroy rabbits belonging to warrens and house-pigeons'. He prohibited the practice as 'contrary to the laws of Scotland, dishonourable to the discipline of the army and the cause of frays with the country people'. But soldiers were often given shooting-leave 'to carry a fowling-piece for the killing of fowls for his game, provided he kill no tame pigeons and rabbits'. At the siege of Dunkirk our French allies complained that the redcoats of the New Model neglected to dig proper trenches because they were wholly occupied with rabbit-shooting in the dunes.

It was during the Civil War period that first-class English gunmakers began signing their pieces, indicating their emergence as skilled craftsmen. Amongst the earliest were Harman Barne, Prince Rupert's gunmaker, H. Cripps of London, and William Upton of Oxford. The light flint-lock shotgun, in something like its modern form, was well established by the Restoration; but the lightest, best balanced models were produced on the Continent where Royalist exiles were surprised to see foreign sportsmen actually shooting birds on the wing.

Arquebusiers
shooting at the
popinjay

5

Shooting Flying

Continental gunsmiths were in the mid-seventeenth century far superior to those of England and Scotland. Possession of a French or Italian gun was a status symbol which even so urban a creature as Samuel Pepys did not despise. In 1667 he showed his to 'Truelocke, the famous gunsmith, that is a mighty ingenious man, and he did take my gun to pieces and made me understand the secrets thereof: and upon the whole he did find it a very good piece of work, and truly wrought, but for certain not a thing to be used with much safety; and he do find that this gun was never yet shot off.' Nor was it likely to be, in the hands of Mr Pepys, who was, nevertheless, 'mightily satisfied with it'.

Proof-firing of guns had been compulsory in England since 1637, but during the Civil War and interregnum the law had not been enforced. But with the growing fashion for fowling and the increasing imports of cheap continental guns, which were 'not things to be used with much safety', accidents became more common, and in 1672 the Gunsmiths Company was given adequate powers, which have been used ever since, for the rigorous testing of all native and foreign barrels, using a double charge of powder and a ball.

Lighter guns, faster-acting locks, improved powder had combined to make possible the exhilarating and exacting sport of 'shooting flying' – shooting, that is to say, at birds on the wing. The *Weidmannslied* shows that this was common in Europe in 1560. Less than a hundred years later, the Spanish author of *Arte de Ballestria y Monteria*, writing in 1644, comments on how the number of partridges in Spain had declined since people began shooting them on the wing with the arquebus. According to Nagasawa Shagetzuma's *The Book of Firearms*, written in 1612 on the other side of the world, young Japanese bloods used to shoot flying birds from horseback at full gallop. Exiled Cavaliers were astonished at the skill of the Continental gentry and no wonder when Louis XIV, for example, once killed thirty-two pheasants on the wing with thirty-four shots.

One can date with some precision the tardy introduction of 'shooting flying' to English sportsmen: in the first edition of Nicholas Cox's *The Gentleman's Recreation*, published in 1677, it is not mentioned. But in the second edition, published in 1686, sportsmen are depicted, singularly enough on horseback, shooting at a flying covey of partridges. Although the author recommends a 54-inch barrel, the sportsmen in the picture are clearly not using guns anything like as long. But the slow-burning powder of the day necessitated longer barrels than we use now.

In this book are written the first instructions in English on bird-shooting. 'It is now the mode to shoot flying, as being by experience found the best and surest way,

The text of the 'Hunter's Song' (A.D. 1560) suggests that
shooting flying was not unusual then

for when your game is on the wing it is more exposed to danger; for if but one shot
hits any part of its wings so expanded, it will occasion its fall, although not to kill it,
so that your spaniel will soon be its victor. . . . The gun most proper for this sport
should be about four and a half foot long in the barrel and of a pretty wide bore,
something under a musket. You should have your gun always cocked in readiness,
with your thumb over the cock for fear of its going off contrary to your intention,*
so that when you meet with any game, you must be quick, and having got an aim
to your mind, let fly with all expedition.

'Some are of the opinion that you must shoot something before the fowl, otherwise it will be past before the shot will meet it: but that is a vulgar error, for no game
can fly so quick but that the shot will meet it; for the shot flyeth as wide as about the
compass of a bushel, if rightly ordered in the charging. Yet I am of the opinion, if the
game flyeth as it were over your head, that 'tis best to aim at the head; and if it
flyeth from you, to aim as it were under its belly. And 'tis found best to let the game
fly a little past you before you let fly, for thereby the shot will the better enter the
body.'

Several factors combined to produce, particularly in Britain, a craze for bird-
shooting which, beginning in the seventeenth century, lasted some 200 years. Foremost among these was the disappearance of the forests of medieval England. The
demands of iron-smelting, house- and church-building, and above all of ship-
building† almost destroyed the forests, and no one did any systematic re-planting.

* Very bad advice, particularly when shooting on horseback.
† A single ship of the line required 4,000 mature oak trees.

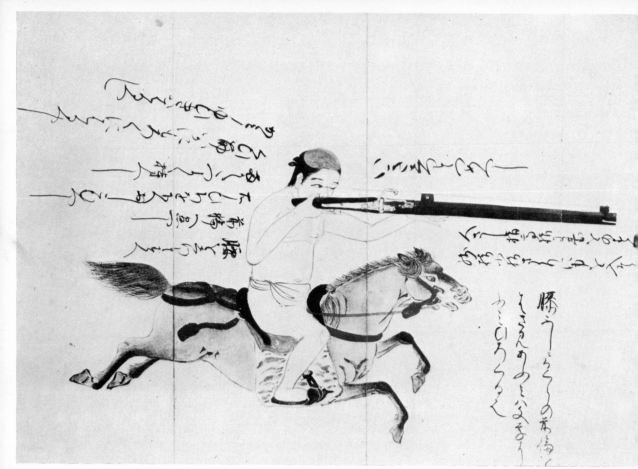

According to the *Book of Firearms* written in 1612 by
Nagasawa Shagetzuma, young Japanese bloods shot
flying birds from horseback while at a gallop

With the forests went the wild deer, red and fallow, the hunting of which had been
the great sport first of the Court and the nobility, then of the richer squirearchy
until about the end of the sixteenth century. By the Restoration wild deer had
disappeared from most of the country and sportsmen had to look elsewhere. At the
same time improvements in arable farming, more acreage under corn and root-
crops, created conditions in which pheasants and partridges flourished; the Game
Laws forbade the killing of game for all, broadly speaking, but owners of land worth
£100 a year; and increasing prosperity encouraged these fortunate 'qualified
persons' to regard shooting more as a sport or perhaps a status-symbol than as a
means of food procurement. Shooting, not hunting with hounds, became the characteristic upper-class sport.

The foxhunter, on whose rude pastime the law imposed no class restrictions,
was widely regarded as vulgar, rustic, addicted to drink, strong language, and
immorality. But the shooter was a different creature altogether. He was doing something which seemed extremely difficult – shooting a flying bird. He derived from
this pursuit steady, healthy exercise which could still be adjusted to his age and

condition. There was a spice of danger, and more than a spice when some gentlemen were out. His sport provided a welcome addition to the larder and brought him into congenial company. There was the fascination of fieldcraft, of planning the defeat of a covey of wary partridges, locating a flight-line of duck, knocking down a snipe in the brief instant before he started his zig-zag, evasive flight. No wonder shooting flying became the rage, and bitter were the reflections of those – general officers, perhaps, admirals, bankers, wealthy merchants, bishops – who were not, by owner-ship of land, 'qualified persons'.

Fashion and competition between gunsmiths brought many refinements to expensive guns – gold vent-plugs to prevent erosion from the firing of the priming-powder, silver foresights to quicken the aim. Gunsmiths who had decorated wheel-lock pieces with gold and silver plates engraved with scenes drawn from the hunting field, from mythology and from the artist's exotic and erotic imagination (some seventeenth-century firearms would hardly have been permitted within the chaste premises of Messrs Holland and Holland), transferred their talents to flint-lock rifles and fowling-pieces: it was not until the end of the eighteenth century that balance, clean lines and efficiency, rather than decoration, became the hallmarks of the best London gunmakers. Improved gunpowder made it unnecessary to keep a special powder for priming. Roughening the inside of the breech retained the shot for a fraction of a second while the powder was fully ignited, thus increasing muzzle

Shooting flying began with the bow and arrow.
Here a Persian party are shooting duck from a boat

velocity and enabling the barrel to be shortened. Choke and half-choke barrels increased the gun's killing power by concentrating the shot. Accurately machined locks and well-tempered springs made locks smoother and faster working, thus cutting down that time-lag between trigger-pressure and discharge which constituted the greatest difficulty in shooting at a running hare or a bird on the wing. Whereas in the sixteenth century magic was widely believed to govern marksmanship, during the Age of Reason the governing factor was science and the skill of the gunsmith.

There were numerous books on shooting, of which the best known is *Pteryplegia, or the Art of Shooting Flying*, written in 1727, which combines advice to the beginner with a description of a day's sport.

The day begins with the sportsmen's preparations.

> Our sport almost at hand we charge the gun,
> Whilst every well-bred dog lies quietly down.
> Charge not before. If over-night the piece
> Stands loaded, in the morn the prime will hiss:
> Nor prime too full, else you will surely blame
> The hanging fire and lose the pointed aim.
> Should I of this the obvious reason tell:
> The caking powder does the flame repel.
> Yet cleanse the touch-hole first: a partridge wing
> Most to the field for that wise purpose bring.
> In charging, next, good workmen never fail
> To ram the powder well, but not the ball.
>
> See a cock-pheasant sprung! He mounts – he's down!
> Trust to your dogs! Quick, quick – Recharge your gun
> Before the air gets in and damps the room!
> A chamber hot will to the powder give
> A benefit, and will the same receive.
> The open touch-hole, too, if haste you make
> Its little fatal train will freelier take.
>
> There sprung a single partridge – ha! She's gone!
> Oh! Sir, you'd time enough, you shot too soon;
> Scarce twenty yards in open sight! for shame!
> Y'had shattered her to pieces with right aim!
> Full forty yards permit the bird to go
> The spreading gun will surer mischief sow;
>
> When a bird comes *directly to your face*.
> Contain your fire awhile and let her pass,
> Unless some trees behind you change the case.
> If so, a little space above her head
> Advance the muzzle, and you strike her dead.
> Ever let shot pursue when there is room;
> Marks hard before thus easy will become.

A high seat was
needed for
shooting wolves
even in the 16th
century

But when the bird *flies from you in a line*,
With little care I can pronounce her thine;
Observe the rule before, and neatly raise
Your piece till there's no *open under-space*
Betwixt the object and the *silver sight*;
Then send away, and timely stop the flight.

The unlucky *cross mark*, or the *traverse shoot*,
By some thought easy (yet admits dispute,
As the most common practice is to fire
Before the bird) will nicest time require.
For, too *much* space allowed, the shot will fly
All innocent, and pass too nimbly by;
Too *little* space, the partridge, swift as wind,
Will dart athwart, and bilk her death behind. . . .

But see, the stiffened earth by frost is bound,
The flocking larks bestrew and peck the ground.
Now let the sportsman so dispose his charge
As may dispense the circling shot at large;
The shot and powder well proportioned be,
Neither exceeding in the quantity
Destruction thus shall a wide compass take,
And many little bleeding victims make.
And now proceed, not by approval, but storm:
Run briskly, fire amid the rising swarm,
And you will treble slaughter thus perform.

131

This is perhaps
the earliest
picture of a
handgun being
fired (from a
MS. of 1473)

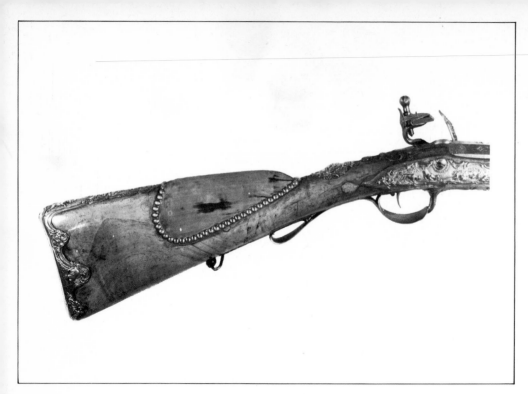

The modern sportsman will deprecate 'browning' a flock of larks, and note that
the poet seems to have no conception of the technique of swinging through a crossing
bird. We prefer nowadays to take in front a bird flying directly overhead, rather
than let it pass and shoot it in the tail. Yet the technique of shooting flying had
advanced since the author of *The Gentleman's Recreation* advised against 'shooting
before the fowl'. The comparatively slow-acting flint-lock and the slow-firing
powder of that day, the fact that there was an appreciable delay – and by no means
always the same delay – between trigger-pressure and discharge made it far harder
than it is now to bring down a flying bird. Unless it is going straight away from him,
the shooter had to swing through it, and to hold the correct lead for some time after
squeezing the trigger. This is still the secret of a crossing or overhead shot, but was
even more so in the days of slow-firing flint-locks.

The French were the acknowledged experts on shooting flying. 'It is as rare',
wrote an English author in 1727, 'for a professed marksman of that race to miss a
bird as for one of ours to kill. . . . They are trained up to it so very young that they
are no more surprised or alarmed by a pheasant than a rattle-mouse.' This being so,
it is well to quote Magné de Marolles, an early French writer on the subject, whose
advice was briefer and better than that of the author of *Pteryplegia*.

'The real way not to miss crossing game, on the wing or running, is not only to
swing forward, but even more, to avoid involuntarily stopping your swing at the
moment of pulling the trigger, as do most unskilled shots; because then the hand
stops swinging to fire and in that instant, however brief, the bird, which does not
stop, passes the line of aim and is missed behind. . . . It is essential to accustom the
hand to follow the game without stopping.'

134

The slowness of the flint-lock made it necessary for sportsmen to use larger shot than they do now, so as to kill at long range a bird going away. 'Prinny's crony, Colonel George Hanger,* generally used Number 3's, which would penetrate forty-eight sheets of writing paper at forty yards. 'Upon my word,' he wrote, 'I should not imagine I should be in any degree of danger of receiving material injury were I to allow any person to fire at my hinder parts at four-score yards with Number 6, provided I had a good pair of buckskin breeches.'

But the younger sportsmen like Peter Hawker were more interested in quick shots at driven game than in long shots at birds going away, so they preferred 6's or even 7's.

Clearly the author of *Pteryplegia* never contemplated using a double-barrelled gun, for the barrels of his day were so long and heavy that a double would be too clumsy to shoot flying. But improvements in boring had by the end of the eighteenth century made barrels so short and light that doubles were in general use. Neverthe-less, beautiful and deadly as the late flint-lock guns were, they had their disadvantages. It was very difficult to make a weatherproof flashpan: either raindrops seeped in, or a high wind blew away the powder. The flint, even of best quality, had to be changed fairly often and perfectly adjusted. It produced a flash, just before the dis-charge of the gun, which gave ample warning to a wary bird.

These drawbacks, particularly the last, stimulated the inventive genius of the Reverend Alexander Forsythe, of Belhevie, Aberdeenshire, a keen wildfowler and amateur gunsmith. He observed that the flash of a flint-lock an appreciable time before discharge gave warning to flighting geese, which had time to change course. He recalled that chlorate of potassium and fulminate of mercury fired faster than gunpowder, giving a spark which might ignite the charge; and he tried them as his priming-powder in an ordinary flint-lock. These fired fast indeed but with not enough force to ignite the charge. Experimenting, he found that when set off by percussion they fired equally fast but with a much stronger spark. In his own work-shop he made a percussion-lock for his trusty flint-lock – and, behold, it worked, beyond all his expectations.

Full of patriotic ardour, the reverend gentleman hastened in 1806 to London, eager to place his invention in the hands of the Government, which was in its familiar state of not quite knowing what to do next in the war against Napoleon. He arranged a *locum tenens*, paid out of public funds, at Belhevie and started manu-facture in a workshop in the Tower. That is to say, he tried to start manufacture, but was frustrated by vexatious delays imposed by red-tape and lethargy. In 1807 the Whig Government, known without much conviction as 'the Ministry of all the Talents', fell, and a Tory Government took office. Searching for economies, their attention was drawn to the activities of Mr Forsythe, himself an arrant Whig, who was ordered forthwith to remove himself and his 'rubbish' from Crown premises. This he did and, turning from patriotism and piety to profit, set up shop in Piccadilly in partnership with James Purdey.

The new device was, of course, fiercely criticized by *laudatores temporis acti*. 'An

---

* It was George Hanger who replied to an impertinent question, 'Sir, I do not know whether I am a gentleman, but I do know I am a *dead shot*.'

English Gentleman', writing appropriately enough to the Editor of *The Gentleman's Magazine*, set little value on a lock which infallibly fired in wind and rain, because 'gentlemen do not go sporting in that weather. If, moreover, the new system was applied to the military, war would shortly become so frightful as to exceed all bounds of imagination, and future wars would threaten, within a few years, to destroy not only armies but civilization itself. It is to be hoped, therefore, that many men of conscience and with a reflective turn will militate most vehemently for the suppression of this new invention.'

The military authorities, noted then as always for their power of reflection, decided that the best thing to do with the Forsythe percussion-lock was to ignore it: perhaps it would then go away. But it did not. It became, instead, the rage among sportsmen, many of whom bought Forsythe guns while others brought in their old guns for conversion.

When the Forsythe lock is in the priming position, a pinch of the detonating medium drops into the detonating chamber. The lock is turned through a half-revolution and is then ready for action. When the hammer falls it strikes a firing-

Preceding page
The earliest form of handgun was just a tube attached to a pole; the next stage was to have the pole resting on the shoulder as here. Note that the 'marksmen' in the embrasures have tunnel sights though they do not appear to be using them

Perhaps the first form of mechanical flying target, precursor of the clay pigeon

Shooting pigeon from a trap

pin which detonates the priming mixture with a crisp, clean spark which passes through the touch-hole to the powder-charge.

Some die-hards maintained that the Forsythe gun lacked killing-power. It was, in fact, not the Forsythe gun which had this defect, but some converted flint-locks, those which had a very slight choke and a roughening of the barrel at the breech end designed to hold back the wad until the charge was fully exploded. With such guns, the percussion-lock system produced such a violent recoil that the charge had to be reduced, to the detriment of the gun's killing-power: but the guns made by Forsythe and Purdey did not have this defect. Forsythe even invented a magazine-lock, holding enough of the detonating medium for twenty shots, in which exactly enough was measured out for each charge; but this was not a success as there was some risk of an accidental explosion of the whole quantity at once.

After various experiments, there developed a muzzle-loading percussion-lock gun in which the detonating medium was a small tube of thin copper filled with fulminate of mercury. This was held in position by a spring clip, with one end resting on a small 'anvil' to receive the blow of the hammer, while the other end fitted into a vent through which the spark passed to the powder-charge in the chamber.

The explosion so produced – crisp, hard, instantaneous – altered the style of shooting. 'The present quick way of shooting,' wrote the author of a manual written in 1837, 'greatly surpassed the old style, when with the use of a flint-lock and with the cock to it having a large sweep, it was thought necessary to aim some way in advance of the object, and never to pull till it had been followed to a respectable

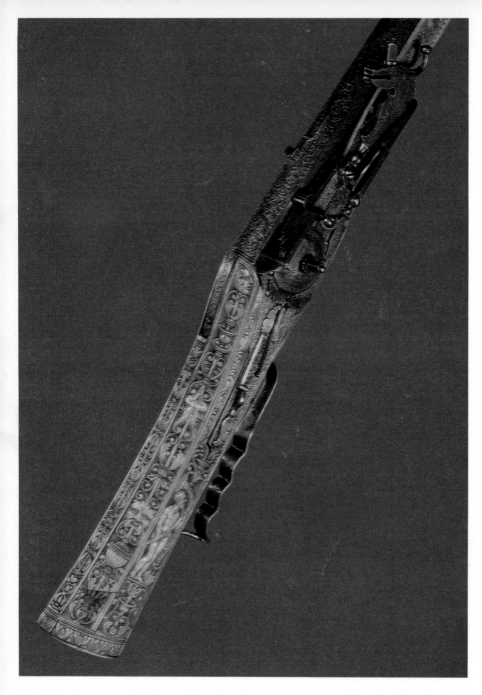

The high grooved rear sight of a German matchlock rifle of 1598

Opposite page Backsight and part of the barrel of a gun of 1624. The motto on the barrel is 'It strikes before the flash is seen'

distance. The dexterity, with which it is now done, is such, that a rabbit can scarcely stir from his seat before he gets knocked over.'

For most of the eighteenth century the orthodox form of shooting was walking-up over open country. But as the number of sportsmen multiplied while game and acres disappointingly failed to do so, covert shooting became more popular because it gave more shots. The flint-lock had been a bit slow for quick snap-shots at pheasants and woodcock swinging away between trees and bushes, but the per-

140

cussion-lock was not. By the time of Waterloo the pheasant had largely replaced the partridge as the common game-bird, and was often hand-reared.

To make pheasants fly (they prefer to scuttle away through the undergrowth) the battue was developed, a method of concentrating game and shots, of providing instant sport. 'It signifies a party of sportsmen beating a covert by walking in line, at equal distances apart, with a number of beaters and game-gatherers following, generally one between two sportsmen. . . . Whenever a shot is fired by either of the party, the whole of the beaters and sportsmen halt in lines abreast, whilst the discharged gun is re-loaded. . . . It is usual to place nets about three or four feet high round the further end, sides and boundaries of the covert. . . . On reaching the net, after attempting to get through, the pheasants run back in the direction of the guns and are then compelled to fly. The best shooting always takes place at the end of the covert; where, being driven into close quarters, the birds are at last obliged to take to their wings. Without nets few shots only could be had; but immense slaughter may be had by preventing the pheasants running out of the covert.'

Battues got a bad name as unsporting and murderous, though many birds must have escaped during the lengthy process of reloading muzzle-loaders. Moreover 'one of the most heinous objections alleged against it is that it engenders jealousies and

At first people seem to have gone out shooting on horseback and one wonders how they managed to make their horse stand while they took their shot. Perhaps they did not and that is why the shooter of pheasant, partridge, etc. was soon back on his own two feet

a bad spirit. Now it is certainly true that it may excite a little jealousy in the breasts of some, when they find their neighbours knocking down every thing right and left, and they themselves are doing little more than beat the air. It may occasion a less exhilarating sensation in these, when the return is brought in and talked over amidst the liberal potations of the night ... but then the elevation of the spirits, that is excited around the table by a good day's sport, serves to banish such selfish mortification.'

Undeniably, the battue must have provided a good many pretty easy shots.

Something more difficult, more sporting, was required. It was found in driving birds over guns, which differs from the battue in that birds, often put up some distance off, come high and fast: indeed, lines of trees, coverts and whole plantations were designed so as to make them come higher and faster, giving ever more difficult shots.

The controversy between advocates of walking-up and driving started before Waterloo and still rumbles on in the correspondence columns of the sporting Press. The former claim that walking-up is more sporting because it requires on the part of the guns physical fitness and fieldcraft. With driving, they say, only the head-keeper, who plans the shoot, needs any fieldcraft, and only the beaters get any exercise. Walking-up is not so destructive of game, and it is certainly cheaper than driving. To this it is retorted that driving requires more skill from the guns, since game flying overhead, high and fast, is far harder to hit than the bird which flaps up 20 yards away and flies slowly off in a straight line. Driving, say its advocates, is more humane than walking-up, since more birds are clean killed by a shot in the head or breast, and fewer fly off to a lingering death with pellets in the guts. Moreover, it is better for the stock, since old birds, who lead the covey, are generally shot in a drive, while young birds, at the tail of the covey, are shot walking-up.

What cannot be denied is that driven birds are more difficult to shoot, particularly if the drive is planned to make them so. Many field sports are governed by unwritten rules designed to make it difficult to kill, and in bird-shooting this strange foible of civilized man is carried to what some would call ludicrous extremes. It is with driven birds that it becomes absolutely necessary to swing through the bird, from tail to head and 'let fly', with the gun still swinging, when one has given the correct forward allowance. In the words of *The Dead Shot*, published in 1861, 'To avoid missing a cross-flying or running object, you must not only aim before it, but take care that you do not involuntarily stop the motion of your arms and gun, as they follow the bird, at the moment of pressing the trigger. Want of attention to this simple fact is too often the reason why the shot passes below and behind the object. Accustom yourself to keep the gun to the shoulder after you have pulled the trigger, and you will . . . gain a capital point towards becoming a dead shot.'

Skill in shooting flying was developed by 'trap-shooting' at live pigeons released by pulling a long string, from a trap set some 20 yards away; or, more cheaply, by shooting at sparrows similarly released, round whose necks was fitted a paper ruff to make them fly more or less straight, like a pheasant or partridge. Trap-shooting was a very fashionable occupation, and large sums were wagered on it. Humanitarians, particularly foxhunters, condemned it as cruel.

But in shooting muzzle-loaders, flint- or percussion-locks, the risk was not all borne by the game: the chances of mishap were manifold. A spark from, say, a cigar or a pipe could cause an explosion while the gun was being loaded or primed. A gun was customarily carried on a shoot with the hammers at half-cock, which should be safe but was not entirely so. It was not uncommon for a shooter, loading one barrel, to be shot by an accidental discharge of the other. A clod of mud in a barrel, a double charge of powder or shot could burst the barrel with dire results. Charles James Fox, who lived for his annual bout of puffing, blowing, banging-off-in-all-directions partridge shooting, was badly wounded in this way. It was partly to reduce

Man loading his
musket – from a
MS. in the British
Museum

Opposite page
A Moghul hunting
party setting out
armed with flint-
locks. Detail from
a miniature in the
British Museum

the danger from a burst barrel that the shooter supported his gun with his left hand
not well forward, as we do now, but as close as possible to the trigger-guard.

Nor were safety-rules universally observed, even by the highest in the land. The
Prince of Wales, 'Prinny', shooting with Lord Claremont, had a misfortune which
was described by *The Times* in hilarious detail. 'Lord Claremont, having eaten too
hearty a breakfast, retired in a resting posture behind a furze-bush. Two of the
Prince's dogs scented the noble peer and came to a point. His Royal Highness let fly
at the furze-bush, wounding his lordship in the defenceless portion of his body. The
Prince's gun hung fire, or the snipe would have received the full charge. Twenty-
seven and a half grains of Number Three shot were extracted from Lord Claremont's
bum.'

The Duke of Wellington was a notoriously dangerous gun. It was charitable
indeed to describe him as 'unlucky at Wherstead: he peppered Lord Glanville's
face with nine shots'. On another occasion he terrified Lady Shelley's little girl by
his carelessness with a gun.

Two ways of holding the gun recommended by
the author of *The Crack Shot*

'What's this, Fanny?' exclaimed her ladyship. 'Fear in the presence of the
Lord of Waterloo?' She added the sage advice that Fanny stand close behind the
Duke, where she might be comparatively safe.

Having added to his bag a dog and a beater, the 'Lord of Waterloo' peppered an
old woman at a cottage window. She made an awful fuss.

'I'm wounded, milady!'

'My good woman,' Lady Shelley rebuked her, 'this ought to be the proudest
moment of your life. You have had the distinction of being shot by the great Duke of
Wellington.'

But it cost the Duke a guinea before she could feel any real pride in her misfortune.

It is not, therefore, surprising that beginners set out on a day's sport with some
nervousness and were advised by an expert, 'The first object is to get the better of
trepidation or apprehension at the moment of discharge. . . . If you feel inclined to
flinch, take a sandwich and a glass of brandy; after which stand as still as possible
for at least five minutes, and then proceed.' Professional assistance, however, was
generally at hand. 'Do not forget', wrote the author of *Directions for a Gamekeeper*, 'the
sandwich-case and a flask of brandy for when their nerves are a little affected. Assist
them in re-loading, during which time let them stand as still as possible till they get
quite cool and collected. The trembling being quite off, proceed very deliberately.'

The shooting school

Firing a musket resting on the right
shoulder, from an oriental MS. in the
British Museum

Swinging on to a clay

Sportsmen had a prodigious quantity of paraphernalia. The well-equipped shooter carried, as well as his gun:

(a) A ramrod fitted with a worm for drawing out charges.
(b) Spare flints.
(c) Leather patches to be wrapped round flint heads so that they were properly secured in the hammer and not damaged or loosened by jar.
(d) Screwdrivers for adjusting the lock.
(e) A pricker for clearing the touch-hole.
(f) Oil and tow for cleaning the barrels.
(g) Brushes for cleaning the flash-pan and lock.
(h) Circular wads of felt or pasteboard.
(i) Either a shot-belt, made with separate pouches for measured charges of powder and shot, or
(j) A soft leather shot-pouch and
(k) A copper (fireproof) powder flask. Expensive models had an adjustable nozzle to measure out 2, $2\frac{1}{4}$ or $2\frac{1}{2}$ drachms of powder. Some shooters, impatient of gadgets, preferred to measure their powder charge in a clay pipe-bowl which held about 1 drachm.

The clay shatters

The gamekeeper must carry, besides spares of everything which his charges might have forgotten, *aqua laudanum* for insect- or dog-bites.

The percussion-lock breech-loader was the sportsmen's gun for half a century, but in the Great Exhibition of 1851 the French gunmaker, Lafauchaux produced the first efficient and safe breech-loader. Gas-leakage and powder-fouling at the breech, which in early breech-loaders had caused the mechanism to jam and corrode, was prevented by enclosing powder, shot, and wad all in a single cartridge with a copper base which, when it was fired, expanded and sealed the chamber. The percussion-cap was at first in the form of a small projection from the rim of the cartridge, but this was rather dangerous and soon the centre-fire cartridge was produced.

Early breech-loaders received somewhat grudging acceptance. They were certainly heavier and were supposed to be less hard-hitting than muzzle-loaders: they were expensive, noisy, liable to burst, and troublesome to keep clean and dry.

The Hunt by
A. C. Bieldemaker

Chinese wildfowler
with a bag of cranes

Opposite page
Duck shooting from
capanelle in the
Venetian lagoons

'I use a breech-loader', confessed a sporting writer in 1861, 'for tame game and early in the season; but for all purposes of wild game and real sport, long shots and security at the breech, I give infinite preference to muzzle-loaders.'

But the time it took to load a muzzle-loader and the amount of paraphernalia it required gave the breech-loader a decisive advantage. In 1872 the first ejector gun was made, and in 1877 the first hammerless ejector, which is still virtually unchanged, the sportsmen's gun today.

Another development of the 1870s was the choke-bore, a slight contraction of the muzzle which concentrates the shot so that more pellets hit the bird if the aim is true. (With a full 12-bore load of 304 Number 6 pellets, fired at a 30-inch circle 40 yards away, 70 per cent will hit the target from a full-choke barrel, but only 40 per cent from a true cylinder barrel.) The choke does not increase the muzzle velocity or penetration of the gun, but the concentration of shot increases the effective range, making birds harder to hit, but easier to kill if they are hit. Most modern guns have the right barrel a true or 'improved' cylinder (i.e. a very slight choke) and the left barrel a full- or half-choke.

Since Victorian times there has been a tendency to shorten barrels from 28 or even 30 inches, to as little as 25 or even 24 inches. This lightens the gun by about an ounce for every inch cut, and therefore makes it more handy for a quick shot. It has surprisingly little effect on the range and killing power.

The breech-loader made battues altogether too easy, and promoted the newer sport of shooting driven game. Fortunes were spent on planning estates, planting coverts, hedgerows and belts of trees, for the sole purpose of making birds fly over the guns high and fast. This was the fashionable sport for those who could afford it from about 1870 until 1914. It did not escape criticism. Here is the somewhat hostile account, by a lady tenant farmer, of a drive on the Prince of Wales's sporting estate of Sandringham in the seventies:

'A complete silence having been secured for miles round, the day was ushered in by a procession of boys with blue and pink flags, like a Sunday School treat, a band of game-keepers in green and gold, with the head man on horseback, an army of beaters in smocks and hats bound with Royal red, a caravan for the reception of the game, and a tailing off of loafers to see the fun, for H.R.H. is very good-natured in allowing people to look on at his amusements, provided they do not interfere with

S. Howitt: *Grouse shooting*, 1796

Stand of the musket shooters at the great Shooting
Tournament held at Zürich in 1504

them, and, if it could be conveniently managed, would perhaps have no objection
to everybody's life being "skittles and beer" like his own.

'At about 11 o'clock the Royal party arrive in a string of waggonettes and range
themselves in a long line under the fences or behind the shelters put up for that
purpose, each sportsman having loaders in attendance with an extra gun or guns to
hand backwards and forwards, to load and reload. The boys and beaters are

157

Shooting on stilts
in the Landes

Opposite page
Shooting pike in
the water calls for
its own expertise

stationed in a semicircle some distance off, and it is their place to beat up the birds and drive them to the fences, the waving flags frightening them from flying back. On they come in ever increasing numbers, until they burst in a cloud over the fence where the guns are concealed. This is the exciting moment, a terrific fusilade ensues, birds dropping down in all directions, wheeling about in confusion between the flags and the guns, the survivors gathering themselves together and escaping into the fields beyond. The shooters then retire to another line of fencing, making themselves comfortable with campstools and cigars until the birds are driven up as before, and so on through the day, only leaving off for luncheon in a tent brought down from Sandringham, or in very cold weather it is carried into the nearest house.

'It requires good, steady marksmanship for this style of shooting (for involving neither danger nor fatigue it can hardly be called "sport"), and the birds have a chance of escape; indeed, after a few engagements, the old ones become quite strategical and know the flags are their friends and fly back through them, or veer round to the right or left out of range. This is altogether superior to the pheasant battue, when the birds are brought up in hen-coops and turned out tame into the woods to be shot down in thousands. Any fine autumn evening at Sandringham you may see them perched on the park wall and not greatly disconcerted at your approach.

'The hares are despatched upon a still lower scale of slaughter, and they might as well have fired into a flock of sheep in a fold, an amusement which I am thankful to say did not suggest itself to them, or I tremble to think of what the uncompensated consequence might have been.'

In contrast here is the lady farmer's description, perhaps somewhat idealized, of an old-fashioned, more leisurely conducted and (in her view) more sporting day.

'Next to setting off with a "southerly wind and a cloudy sky", I know of nothing more invigorating than an old-fashioned "shuttin' day", in Norfolk; the crisp air

R. Pollard: *Pigeon shooting*, 1812

Opposite page
Frankland: *Shooting Signals*

Shooting Signals.

Have you marked any Birds?	Birds are marked.	No.

Bring the Powder and Shot.	Dog wanted.	Luncheon.

The straight-arm hold

with a spice of salt in it, the gossamer hanging over garden and hedgerows, a slight mist now, but the sun promising to come out presently and light up the gorgeous autumn colouring and the deep blue of the distant strip of sea. The Squire and his friends appear in promiscuous-looking garments, well booted and gaitered, for walking all day up and down turnips is as drenching as a pond; the gamekeeper, master of the situation, in the old brown velveteen of strictly professional cut, and the pockets bulging out into the shape and make that none but a keeper could contrive to wear them into; the retrievers wild with excitement, and everyone off at last.

'At the sound of the guns, friendly carts and gigs appear from no one knows where – the butcher, baker, and candlestick-maker on their rounds; and the cheerful little parish doctor suddenly remembers that the nearest road to his patients lies in that direction, is always going every minute, can't even stop to take a glass of sherry, but staying on and on to see the sport; and at noon time the rustics will saunter up, the antediluvians on parish day following at a creeping pace, and lean over the gates and hover near the luncheon cart. The parson, if he is of a good, sociable sort, will be with the shooting party; and though it may all seem very slow work by comparison with the thousands that fall before the driving battues, yet every one is satisfied and no one the worse for it, and if our duty to our neighbours is any consideration, that ought to count for something.'

The double-barrelled hammerless ejector is the modern sportsman's weapon.

162

The single-barrelled gun weighs the odds too heavily against him, while multi-shot pump- and automatic guns are generally considered to be implements of the pot-hunter. Most men use 12-bore; boys, women, the old and the infirm often use 16-bores which are lighter, but have less killing power. Guns smaller than the 16-bore are not really much use.

Cartridges are graded by the size of their pellets. The smaller the shot, the more pellets in a cartridge and the greater the chance of a hit; the larger the shot, the greater the penetration at long range. Most shooters use 8's for snipe, 5's for duck, 6's for partridges, grouse, and pheasants, but on this subject there is much controversy.

Broadly speaking there are three forms of game-shooting with the shotgun – walking-up, driving, and flighting.

In walking-up, the gun or guns, with beaters and dogs, walk in line across country, putting up game-birds, hares, and rabbits, shooting them as they fly or run away. It is the simplest way to shoot, and so long as you walk slowly, keep as quiet as possible, investigate every scrap of cover, and keep a proper line, you should have sport. The shots are fairly easy – except when snipe-shooting – as they are generally at pheasants and partridges as they rise and fly straight away before they get up full speed; but hard exercise and a good deal of fieldcraft is required from the guns.

In driving, the guns remain stationary, more or less concealed, and beaters

Bent-arm hold
(from the left shoulder)

Williamson:
*Peacock shooting
in India*

drive the birds over them high and fast, giving shots as difficult as possible. For the guns it involves little exertion, no fieldcraft, but excellent marksmanship.

The third and by far the most difficult form of game-shooting is flighting. The shooter by observation and experience estimates the line taken, generally by pigeon and wildfowl, on their way to feed, and conceals himself on this line to ambush them as they fly over. Fieldcraft of a high order is required to estimate the *exact* line of flight (for it is no good being 50 yards out) and camouflaging oneself from birds that are very observant and wary. The camouflaging is of vital importance: in the words of the Prophet Isaiah, 'All our righteousnesses are as filthy rags, and we all do fade as a leaf.' Except for the gent who pots birds as they are just settling, the shots are difficult, just as difficult as at driven pheasants, for the birds are generally flying high and fast, and often swinging round as well.

Shooting technique has hardly changed in the past century. The proper way to shoot a flying bird or running hare is to swing through it and fire while still swinging. This means, with a crossing target, or one flying straight overhead, starting the swing with your bead behind your bird, swinging so that the bead passes the bird, and firing, *without checking the swing*, when you have the correct lead. With a bird rising and going away, the swing starts below the bird and the shot is fired when the gun is pointing slightly above it. The correct lead depends on the range, the quickness of the shooter's reactions, the speed and angle at which the target is moving. It can only be learned by personal experience: most birds, especially large birds which look as though they are flying slowly, are missed behind, through not giving enough lead: it is not uncommon to hit the second bird in a covey when you have aimed at the one in front. The commonest and worst faults are to hold the aim and to check the swing at the moment of squeezing the trigger.

The quicker you raise the gun to the shoulder, swing and shoot, the better. The whole movement should with practice become smooth, flowing, and almost instinctive. Many indifferent shots find that they hit the bird which appears suddenly, giving the chance of only a quick shot; but miss the duck or pheasant seen approaching from a long way off, giving ample time to aim.

Footwork is all-important. Assuming you shoot from the right shoulder, your feet should be about 12 or 15 inches apart, left foot forward, at a comfortable, natural angle, and so placed that you are facing your right-front but can easily swing in either direction. You should, if possible, stand on level ground, with no clods, tufts or stones to hamper free movement.

Whether the shot is at ground game or at a high bird, most of the weight should be on the left foot, and the left leg should be nearly straight. It is a capital error, in taking a high bird coming overhead, to lean back and put the weight on the right foot.

Eighteenth-century sportsmen generally took an overhead bird while it was

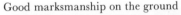

Good marksmanship on the ground

167

Reloading during
a shoot

An early form of clay pigeon, a glass ball filled with feathers. When shattered the glass broke and the feathers flew

Opposite page
Going out shooting in France

going away, on the grounds that the feathers then offered less resistance to the pellets. We, on the other hand, prefer to shoot an oncoming bird, as it is more likely to be killed stone-dead by a shot in the head or breast and less likely to fly off wounded by a pellet in the tail or guts.

Driven birds should be taken as far forward as possible; for the bird taken well ahead is within the lethal zone of the spread of the shot three or four times as long as that taken overhead and is therefore more likely to be hit. A good shot will drop two birds of a covey before they cross the line.

No sensible person will go out shooting before he has learned to shoot in a shooting school, and many an expert fires off hundreds of rounds before the start of each season to get his eye in. Nowadays, for humanitarian and economic reasons, trap-shooting has been replaced by shooting at the 'clay-pigeon' or 'clay-bird', a saucer-like disc, made of pitch and pulverized limestone, discharged from a spring-actuated launcher to simulate a flying bird. Its flight is not quite the same as a game-bird's: it cannot, for instance, be set to swerve or jink; and from the moment it leaves the launcher

The Emperor
Awragreb
shooting nilgais.
Note the length of
the barrel and the
way he is using an
attendant's
shoulder as a rest

The ejector

it goes slower and slower until, losing its impetus, it falls to the ground – whereas a live bird may be accelerating, slowing down, or maintaining a steady pace. But it is the obvious target on which to learn, and many first-class shots, to find their form, fire hundreds of rounds at clay-birds before the start of each season.

There are shooting schools in many big cities in Europe and North America, and clay-bird clubs all over the world. Clay-bird or 'Skeet-shooting' has become a sport in its own right, competed for at the Olympic Games and practised by thousands of marksmen who seldom or never shoot at a living bird.

The basic form of clay-bird competition is known as Trap-shooting or Down-the-Line. Five competitors take their stance at numbered stands, firing in turn five shots from each stand. The clay is thrown so as to reproduce a bird getting up 16 yards ahead and going away. Thrown usually from the same trap, all the clays rise at the same angle: but their direction is varied, and of course their angle from the shooter varies as he changes his stand.

In most Down-the-Line competitions he is allowed to stand with the gun at his shoulder, safety-catch off. He calls 'Pull!' and immediately the clay is thrown. Knowing exactly where and when the clay will appear, and roughly in what direction it will go, he aims rather than swings through the bird. For a hit (or 'Kill') with the first barrel he scores two points, with the second barrel one point.

Regarded as practice for game-shooting, Down-the-Line is the most artificial and least useful form of clay-bird shooting. But it should not be so regarded. It is a sport in its own right, with its own set of rules and to a great extent its own weapons, for most experts prefer to aim along a single barrel rather than between two barrels,

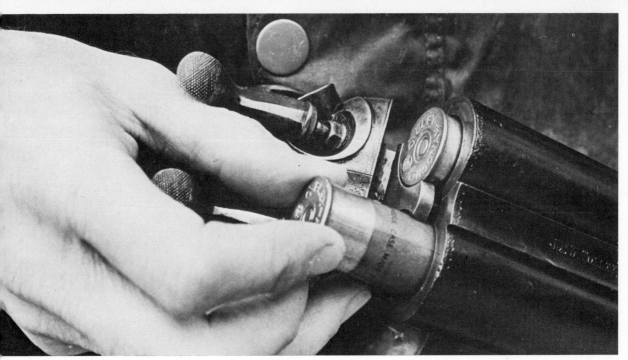
The non-ejector (removing, in this case, unfired
cartridges)

and use under-and-over, or automatic guns rather than conventional doubles.

The standard of accuracy is something far beyond the game-shooter's emulation. A hundred kills in a row is a not uncommon feat. A shooter classified as Class AA is one who gets 95 per cent kills, and even a Class C shot gets 85 per cent.

A refinement of ordinary Down-the-Line shooting, known as the Olympic Trench, is used in international competitions under the rules of the International Shooting Union. In this, too, the shooter changes his stand to give variety to his shots. Further variety is given by the fact that the clays are thrown from fifteen traps, with extra strong springs, in five batches of three, and set so as to throw at different elevations as well as in different directions. This, of course, makes the shooting much more difficult, but the rule is 'Kills to count', which means that a kill counts the same whether it is by the first or second shot: many experts invariably fire two shots in very quick succession, not waiting to see if the first kills before firing the second. Scores are lower than in Down-the-Line, and for a long time 199 hits out of 200 was an unofficial world record.

The clay-bird competition which most resembles game-shooting is known as Skeet. Clays are thrown from a 'high house' and a 'low house', and the guns change their stands so as to get crossing, diagonal and overhead shots, from each side, from behind and from in front, high and low. In most competitions one must remain in the 'gun down' position until the clay is thrown, and there may be a varying delay after one calls 'Pull!' The greater resemblance to game-shooting is emphasized by the fact that most Skeet-shooters use ordinary sporting guns with side-by-side barrels.

Cover, or the lack of it, determines the wildfowler's stance

Opposite page
Dispatching a wounded duck

177

Shooting wood-
cock in Czecho-
slovakia

Opposite page
Shooting pigeon
from a hide

Finally, there are 'sporting clays', thrown from varying positions as the gun
walks through typical shooting country, at varying angles and heights so as to
reproduce so far as possible the conditions of game-shooting. These are most useful
for teaching beginners and for bringing experienced shots up to form at the beginning of a season. They are used for these purposes in shooting schools.

Apart from the rules of Down-the-Line which make things easier for the shooter,
there are basic differences between clay-bird and game-shooting. A single pellet is
enough to 'kill' a clay, but it is probably not enough to kill a pheasant. But it does

178

not in the least matter if a clay is shot to pieces, for no one wants to eat it; so the clay-bird shooter likes to take his shot at as close a range as possible, using a gun with a wide spread, which puts a premium on speed. A clay-bird cannot be thrown so as to swerve or jink. Above all a clay starts off at a high speed, slows down and begins to drop; while a game-bird is generally gaining both speed and height as one shoots. Nevertheless, clay-bird shooting is quite obviously first-class practice for the sporting shot; and, even more, a fascinating sport in its own right.

Two unsporting variants of the shotgun deserve mention. The first is the sawn-off shotgun, with barrels shortened to some 18 inches. Since it can be easily concealed under a coat or down a trouser-leg, it has always been a weapon favoured by poachers, bank-robbers, and miscellaneous criminals, as well as (in the Wild West) by bar-tenders and stage-coach guards who could use it effectively in a confined space. The short barrels allow the shot to spread so that one can hardly miss a close shot. Loaded with buckshot, it is a terrible weapon at 10 yards, but not so good at 20.

Somewhat similar is the blunderbuss, a single-barrel gun with a very large bore and a very heavy barrel, firing a handful of slugs or musket balls. The customary flaring muzzle has no effect whatsoever on the spread of the shot, which would be exactly the same if the barrel were sawn off where the true cylinder ends. The blunderbuss had many of the advantages of the sawn-off shotgun, and was much used by assassins, highwaymen, and coach-guards. Furthermore the heavy barrel, often made of brass so as to withstand corrosion by sea-water, took a big charge of powder and shot. This was useful in a naval battle, particularly for shooting at boarders and at the rigging and grappling ropes of an enemy ship, so blunderbusses were part of a warship's armoury until well into the nineteenth century.

We may conclude this section on the sporting gun with some miscellaneous notes on shooting, its etiquette, and peripheral subjects, all culled from *The Dead Shot* (1861).

A young shot on the moor

Opposite page
Open pheasant country produces high fast birds

'The sportsman should never take the field without a knife, a drinking horn and a shilling for largesse.'

'Always allow game to cool thoroughly before packing it; you may have the mortification of receiving an acknowledgement from your friends at a distance, of a hamper of game, which arrived "*un peu trop haut*".'

'In shooting with a young sportsman, or a stranger, always allow him to precede you in getting over the fences: it may be that you save your life, or a limb, by the precaution.'

'Always correct and point out errors which you perceive in young sportsmen; and rebuke anyone, whether old or young in whom you detect carelessness in handling the gun.'

The wildfowler's country

Hare shooting in the s

Village clay pigeon shoot – pull!

Opposite page
Wildfowler and mud flats

'However generously disposed you may be towards your friends and neighbours, if you have a valuable dog, never lend it: and the same may be said of a
favourite gun. If your friend or neighbour thinks you unkind in refusing to lend
either, show him this page in *The Dead Shot*.'

'Many a retriever puppy is spoilt by children, who, innocently enough, delight
in throwing sticks and stones for the dog to fetch; first spitting on them, in order (as
they say) "that the dog may find it by the smell; and not bring a wrong one". The
little innocents, however, unless they happen to have uncommon foetid breath,
should know, that the spittle is of no great assistance to the dog in retrieving their
missiles.'

187

Shooting clays from the high tower at the annual
British Open Gamekeepers' Championship

Opposite page
A double in the air – the Partridge Tower

189

Taking a second
gun from a loader,
enabling four shots
to be fired at each
covey

The try gun which ensures that your gun is made to
fit, so that you can give of your best

'If the young sportsman who is troubled with "nervous anxiety" were to say to
himself before firing, "Steady, Ed'ard Cuttle! Steady!" and act up to it, ten to one
he would soon find himself considerably improved.'

'The young sportsman must always shun spirits; the old one sometimes requires
a stimulus of the kind to help him over the hedges, and to lift his legs out of the heavy
soil fallows.'

'Any person who has been drinking freely should not touch a gun until sober; and
a sportsman should not, under any circumstances or persuasion, be induced to walk
out, or even to remain in the company with another who is in the least degree the
worse for liquor, and yet has a loaded gun in his hands. The best plan is to take the
gun from him unawares, and fire it off.'

6

Musket and Rifle

It will be recalled that seventeenth-century marksmen and gunsmiths were generally defeated by the problem of ramming down the barrel, against the resistance of the lands, a ball which must exactly fit the grooves of the rifling if it was to be gas-tight. In theory the problem could be solved by loading the ball at the breech end, and various methods were invented for doing so, notably a screw-plug breech which, having been loaded, could be screwed into place; and a screw-barrel, which could be unscrewed for loading and then screwed back again. But these were almost as slow to load as the muzzle-loader; the screw-thread was soon fouled and choked by carbon deposits from firing, the action became loose through corrosion and finally dangerous to the shooter.

Well-to-do continental sportsmen, hunting heavy and dangerous game such as the wild boar, needed something with a longer range, more accuracy and more striking power than a smooth-bore musket, but preferred muzzle-loading rifles, with all their drawbacks, to unreliable breech-loaders. The loader's job was no sinecure but, given ample time, a stout iron ramrod and a heavy mallet, he could force down the ball from muzzle to breech and hand to his impatient employer a ponderous weapon which would throw a ball of some 0·85 or 0·80 inch calibre with reasonable accuracy to about 200 yards. In a carefully observed and recorded test held in 1776, a marksman with a heavy German rifle at a distance of 150 yards shot a ball six times out of eight within the circumference of the crown of a hat; at 400 yards he shot within half a yard of the mark.

But the heavy ball flew in a high trajectory, so the rifleman had to be a good judge of distance. Smooth-bore muskets needed, for aiming, no more than a plain bead foresight, though some had backsights too. But for rifles something more elaborate was needed, backsights adjustable for different ranges. The usual form was a V-sight, with one, two, or three leaves. Tube-sights, similar in use to aperture-sights, were sometimes fitted. An effective telescopic sight is mentioned in a book published in Nuremberg in 1702. Royal marksmen naturally required something special, so Louis XIII had made a rifle with a silver backsight in the form of a nude female reclining in an inviting posture, her raised knees forming the shoulders of the sight.

Such rifles, fitted with the best wheel- or flint-locks, and some with hair-triggers too, were very expensive. But for a Bavarian or Tyrolean sportsman who wanted to stop a charging boar or bowl over, so that he could not escape, a chamois or ibex on the other side of a deep ravine, they were worth the money. They had a shattering recoil and were very heavy, so they were not everybody's weapon.

Of their accuracy there could be no doubt, and this led to more elaborate

Opposite page
Homeward bound

Drinking-cup
of 1646 depicting
a Swiss rifleman

targets. Picture targets came into fashion, landscape scenes painted by local artists. A very satisfying target was at the castle of Lysice in Moravia. The 'bullet-stopper', 200 paces from the firing point, was gaily painted to resemble a castle wall with a gate in the centre. In front of this were two round targets, each with a bull's-eye in the centre. If the marksman hit the bull, the castle gate opened to reveal a pretty girl with a bouquet: if he missed, the devil appeared and put out his tongue. This was still in use in 1928

The rifle's principal defect was slow-loading, especially when powder fouling had clogged the grooves. A Spanish marksman, Alonso Martinez de Espinar, writing in 1644, both diagnosed the trouble and hit upon an ingenious way of overcoming it.

'There must be a rule in knowing how to load them, for the greater power of these arquebuses over smooth bores consists in this, that the fire has greater resistance in the former kind of barrel, because it forces itself into the twists of the rifling, and because there is an obstruction in the passage through which it has to find its way it multiplies its force. And for this reason it should be observed that its force is increased by ramming down the charge. And it is necessary to have felt wads, cut with a punch, which must be exactly fitted to the mouth of the barrel. They must be pitched with Greek pitch (colophony), wax and tallow. All this should be dissolved and the wads thrown into it, and after they have absorbed the pitch they must be put to cool, and then they remain very hard and greasy; these are very important indeed for rifled arquebuses, because with them the balls go in more easily, for they have to fit very closely to the barrel, having to be driven to the bottom by blows of the ramrod. And as they enter in this manner it is impossible to get them in for two shots running from the fouling which the powder leaves, and there is no other remedy but to wash the barrel. And that this may not be necessary, and that you may be able to fire as many as a dozen balls, these wads are applied, which drive down the fouling left by the powder, and leave the barrel clean and slimy with pitch. And in the same way, the ball entering with so much pressure, helps to stop the windage of it, and in this consists the greater or less range that it has, according as the fire uses more of its force.'

But soon riflemen hit upon an even better idea, to use a ball which fitted the lands of the rifling, but to wrap it in a patch of greased leather or cloth which fitted tightly into the grooves. There was thus no escape of gas and the ball took the spin. This could be loaded fairly quickly, usually without the aid of a mallet, but not so quickly as the ball of a smooth-bore musket.

As a weapon of war the latter was still on balance the better weapon. A typical pattern was the Tower musket, used by the British infantry from the days of William III until well into the 1840s, and still used by hunters in many parts of the world. It was known affectionately to its users as Brown Bess, and to its enemies, with respect rather than affection, as *la Besse brune* or *die braune Liesl*. It had a simple flint-lock, modified from time to time – the details are not germane to this book – to make it more hard-wearing and reliable in action. Ten pounds in weight and sturdy in construction, it was built to stand the knockabout of active service, the slam-bang of arms drill, the various shocks of fighting with bayonet and butt. Its bore was of

Aperture rear sight of a flint-lock rifle of 1675

0·75 inch; but the ball only about 0·71 inch in diameter. This detracted from the weapon's accuracy, but made for quick loading since the ball could generally (except when the barrel was badly fouled by firing) be dropped down the barrel: the ramrod was needed only for seating it firmly on top of the charge, which could often be done simply by tapping the butt on the ground. Indeed, a tap of the butt could eliminate the separate operation of priming, by forcing a few grains of the charge into the touch-hole. But the practice was officially discouraged, for it produced too many mis-fires, even when the touch-hole was enlarged. The ball of the Brown Bess weighed about an ounce, that of the French musket (in Marlborough's wars) about two-thirds of an ounce which, as the veteran Captain Parker observed, makes 'a considerable difference in the execution'.

196

Multiple aperture rear sight of a rifle of 1680

To load, the soldier tore off with his teeth the end of the paper cartridge and poured a pinch into the priming pan, the remainder down the barrel. He next dropped down the crunched-up paper of the cartridge, to use as a wad, followed by the ball which might or might not have to be rammed home. All this could be done by an average trained soldier ten times in three and a half minutes, a good deal faster than the French or German soldier could load his musket with a more tightly fitting ball, especially when the barrel was foul from repeated firing, and far faster than a rifle could be loaded.

The fact that the ball was smaller than the diameter of the barrel meant that the Tower musket was not very accurate. It had too much 'windage'; that is to say, the ball, so to speak, bounced from side to side in its passage down the barrel. Exhaustive

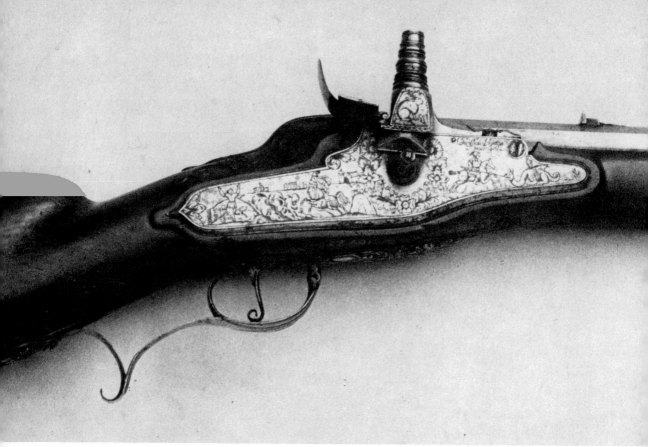

A German wheel-lock carbine of about 1700 with a
chimney on the lock to protect the marksman's eye from
sparks and smoke

official tests carried out under the best possible conditions, the range being known
to an inch, proved that at 200 yards one had to aim $5\frac{1}{2}$ feet above the target; fired
from a rest at a target 11 feet 6 inches × 6 feet, ten shots at 250 yards all missed, and
at 150 yards only half the shots hit. A larger, more tightly fitting ball, gave greater
accuracy, but slowed down the rate of fire. A good shot would think twice before
backing himself to hit a man-sized target at 80 yards. But in battle his target was not
a man: it was a line or column of hundreds of men, shoulder to shoulder, generally
much closer than 80 yards and obscured by dense clouds of acrid powder-smoke.
The infantry fight was won not by long-range marksmanship, but by repeated,
murderous volleys, delivered at close range with shattering effect and followed up by
a bayonet charge. The British Army of the eighteenth century had its faults, notably a
sluggish and over-conservative command, a corps of officers who prided themselves
on being amateurs and scorned the study of their trade, and a cavalry which suffered
from an excess of courage and dash, but a deficiency in horsemanship, swordsmanship, and control. But the annihilating volley-firing of the British infantry, like that
of the English bowmen, was the best in Europe.

For this sort of work the rifle was of little use. But for skirmishing, for reconnais-

sance, for sniping it was found that a weapon accurate at a longer range than the
musket, even though slower in loading, had certain advantages. So German
potentates during the wars of the Polish Succession, the Austrian Succession and
the Seven Years War, raised a specialist corps of riflemen known as Jägers. These
were in theory hunters, foresters, and gamekeepers, expert shots with the rifle,
trained in light infantry tactics. But their use was peripheral: in the pitched battle
they could not compete with the ordinary infantry of the line.

There was, however, one theatre of war in which the terrain – mountain and
dense forest, walls, fences, and timber stockades – gave few openings for conventional infantry tactics and great advantages to the riflemen. For in these circumstances individual marksmanship was all-important, volley-firing ineffective at
elusive, invisible targets, and the bayonet a mere irrelevance when the enemy
melted into the trees before a charge. Moreover in America the rifle, first brought by
German and Swiss armourers, had undergone some very important changes.

Along the frontiers of the Thirteen Colonies a firearm was not a luxury for the
rich sportsman, but a matter of life and death. An accurate, long-range rifle was
better for hunting and Indian-fighting than a musket. But the German rifle was not
quite what was wanted. The frontier trapper did not need to knock down a charging
boar or a man in plate-armour: his quarry was the deer, turkey, or squirrel, his

Two German flint-lock rifles of about 1700. The top one
has a blued and gilt rear sight, the bottom one a blued
rear sight, both with notched bar and folding leaf

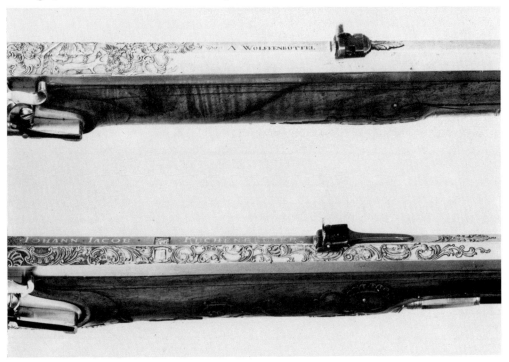

Rear sights –
of a rifle of about
1680

of a flint-lock
sporting rifle of
1710

of a Canadian
plains rifle of 1865

of a Purdey rifle
of 1865

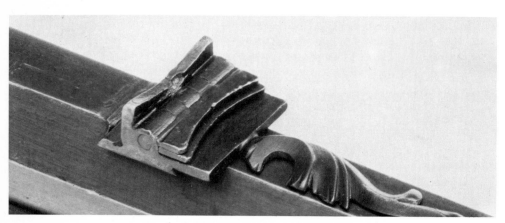

enemy naked. Far from the nearest store or trading-post, travelling on foot in the wilderness perhaps for months on end, he had no use for delicate, complicated locks, for a rifle weighing up to 20 lb which required vast quantities of powder, and bullets weighing fifteen to the pound.

So there was developed, originally in Pennsylvania, what is usually known as the Kentucky rifle. This had a simple (some would say crude) flint-lock which stood up to hard wear and could easily be repaired. The bore was usually less than 0·5 inch, and the bullets weighed about fifty to the pound, with powder-charges proportionately small. With such charge and ball, the rifle could be less than half the weight of its European counterpart, and the barrel longer – say 42 to 48 inches – which made for a flat trajectory and long-range accuracy. The flat trajectory facilitated quick snap-shooting at unknown ranges and did away with the need for an adjustable backsight: a simple, fixed V-sight was good for any range up to 150 yards, beyond which the rifleman could simply aim a little higher. He could be reasonably sure of hitting a deer, an Indian or a redcoat at 300 yards and might well do so at 400 yards. The rifle was not designed to carry a bayonet, nor was it sturdy enough for use as a club, but what did that matter?

Not many used eighteenth-century Kentucky rifle bullets have been found. Two, found in the graves of Indians in Tennessee who had obviously been killed by them, oddly enough bore clear-cut marks of the rifling, indicating that they had not been wrapped in a greased patch. It seems likely that the American frontiersman used a greased patch only when he had ample time to load: if he was in a hurry, he loaded the ball 'naked', accepting a loss in accuracy due to a leakage of gas along the grooves. In the early nineteenth century consideration was given to issuing British riflemen with balls of two different sizes, one to be used with a patch, one for short-range work without a patch. But this arrangement was found to be too complicated for active service.

The Kentucky rifle was not in all circumstances a better weapon than the

An early adjustable rear sight

Top: Muzzle and foresight of a flint-lock breech-loading rifle in the form of an open-mouthed monster

Middle: Silver bead foresight of a German flint-lock of about 1780

Bottom: Profile foresight of a flint-lock of about 1730

German rifle or the musket, but it was better in the circumstances which generally prevailed in the War of American Independence. These facts escaped the comprehension of the British military authorities: nor, to be just, were they grasped more readily by Congress which ordered for the Continental Army large numbers of ordinary muskets. However, a year after Bunker's Hill Congress did belatedly order the raising of ten companies of expert riflemen from Pennsylvania, Maryland, and Virginia. These, and their successors, had an effect totally disproportionate to their modest numbers.

Colonel Hanger relates an incident which illustrates the American rifle's deadly accuracy.

'Colonel, now General, Tarleton and myself, were standing a few yards out of a wood, observing the situation of a part of the enemy which we intended to attack. There was a rivulet in the enemy's front, and a mill on it, to which we stood directly with our horses' heads fronting, observing their motions. It was an absolutely plain field between us and the mill; not so much as a single bush on it. Our orderly-bugler stood behind us about three yards, but with his horse's side to our horses' tails. A rifleman passed over the mill-dam, evidently observing two officers, and laid himself down on his belly; for in such positions, they always lie, to take a good shot at a long distance. He took a deliberate and cool shot at my friend, at me, and the bugle-horn man. Now observe how well this fellow shot. It was in the month of August, and not a breath of wind was stirring. Colonel Tarleton's horse and mine, I am certain, were not anything like two feet apart; for we were in close consultation, how we should attack with our troops, which laid 300 yards behind in the wood, and could not be

Various types of sight used down the centuries

perceived by the enemy. A rifle-ball passed between him and me; looking directly to the mill I evidently observed the flash of the powder. I directly said to my friend, "I think we had better move, or we shall have two or three of these gentlemen, shortly, amusing themselves at our expense." The words were hardly out of my mouth when the bugle-horn man behind us, and directly central, jumped off his horse and said, "Sir, my horse is shot." The horse staggered, fell down, and died. He was shot directly behind the fore-leg, near to the heart – at least, where the great blood vessels lie, which lead to the heart. Now, speaking of this rifleman's shooting, nothing could be better; but, from the climate, he had much in his favour. First, at that time of the year, there was not one breath of wind; secondly, the atmosphere is so much clearer than ours, that he can take a more perfect aim. I have passed', he adds, 'several times over this ground, and ever observed it with the greatest attention; and I can positively assert that the distance he fired from, at us, was full four hundred yards.'

The British Government could have raised an even more effective corps: they had the men, highlanders and German Jägers, perfectly suited to light infantry tactics. They had the money. They even had the rifle, the Ferguson rifle, a weapon far in advance of its time.

Matchlock used by Arabs

This was something of a compromise between the German and the Kentucky rifle, having a smaller bore (0·68 inch) than the former, a shorter barrel (34 inches) than the latter, and carrying a bayonet. Its special distinction is that it was the first effective breech-loading rifle. To load it a plug attached to the trigger-guard was unscrewed, leaving an opening on top of the barrel, behind the chamber. Into this was loaded first the ball, then the powder. The explosion forced the ball into the eight-groove rifling; and because the screw plug was behind the chamber (not, as in previous breech-loaders, in front of it) the single breech-loading mechanism did not foul up and corrode but remained gas-tight for many years. It had a leaf backsight adjustable for ranges up to 300 yards.

Ferguson's rifle was very accurate and, by the standards of the day, very fast firing. In a demonstration at Woolwich on a day of heavy rain and high wind, 'Captain Ferguson performed the following four things, none of which have ever been accomplished with any other small arm. 1. He fired during 4 or 5 minutes at a

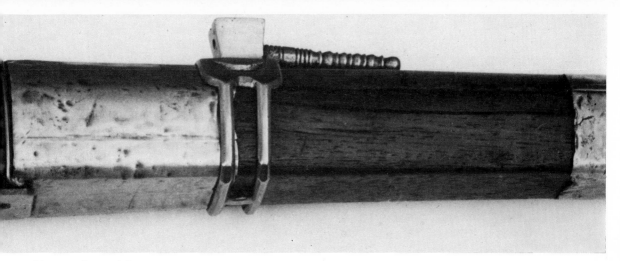

and its tunnel rear sight

target, at 200 yards distance at a rate of 4 shots a minute. 2. He fired six shots in one minute. 3. He fired four times per minute advancing at the same time at the rate of 4 miles in the hour. 4. He poured a bottle of water into the pan and barrel of the piece when loaded so as to wet every grain of the powder and in less than half a minute fired with her as well as ever without extracting the ball. He also hit the bulls-eye at 100 yards. . . . He only missed the target three times in the course of the experiments.'

Unfortunately, we are not told the size of the target or the bull's-eye, but clearly the spectators were most impressed. Later, demonstrating his rifle before the Royal Family, Ferguson told George III that he could fire seven shots a minute, but 'would not undertake in that time to knock down above five of His Majesty's enemies'.

A company of riflemen, armed with these rifles and commanded by Ferguson himself, performed very well against American riflemen. It is related that George Washington owed his life to Ferguson failing to recognize him when seeing him within easy range at the Battle of Germanstown. It is surprising that only 100 Ferguson rifles were issued to the British Army. The reason seems to have been that it did not take the standard cartridge; that it required more skill and training than the musket; and that there was a weakness in the stock which was cut away to take the plug-housing. Some of the few surviving specimens are fractured at this point. Ferguson died in action, a disappointed man, and most of the rifles used on the British side were those belonging to Carolinan and Virginian loyalists.

It is sometimes claimed that the Kentucky rifle won the war for the Americans. It is more true to say that it was lost by the single-minded ineptitude of Lord George Germaine, George III's Secretary at War. But the war certainly proved the military value of the rifle.

It is a commonplace of military history that nations, even the British, learn more from their defeats than from their victories. The painful experiences of the War of American Independence suggested that the weapons and tactics of Marlborough were not the last word in military science. The war against the French revolution and the turmoil on the Continent produced a prolifera of volunteer middle-class regiments with the minds and money to experiment, and an influx of foreign volunteers

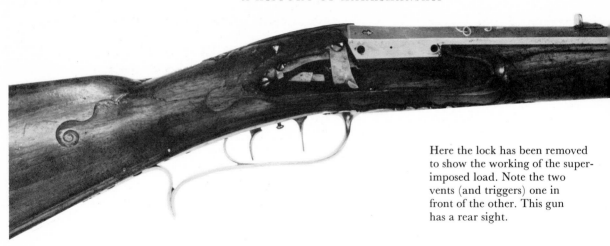

Here the lock has been removed
to show the working of the superimposed load. Note the two
vents (and triggers) one in
front of the other. This gun
has a rear sight.

and refugees, many of whom knew all about the heavy, short-barrelled rifles of German and Austrian Jäger. For some years the idea of specialist units of riflemen was discussed exhaustively and bounced briskly from one department to another. In 1800, however, it was actually translated into action: an experimental rifle corps was formed, trained in light infantry tactics and armed with a rifle developed by a Whitechapel gunmaker, Ezekiel Baker.

This had a bore of 0·615 inch, with seven grooves which made a quarter-turn in the 30-inch barrel. There was a conflict between the demands of accuracy and serviceability, the point at issue being the 'spirality' of the rifling, i.e. the number of turns the rifling made in the barrel. Accuracy was attained by a relatively sharp spirality, giving the ball a rapid spin which it retained over a long range; but such a barrel was peculiarly liable to fouling after a few shots, and the patch could, if the spirality was too sharp, fail in its function. The Baker rifle was not noted for accuracy: the ball was inclined to cease spinning and stray off course after about 200 yards; it was, in fact, sighted for 100 yards, with a folding 200-yard leaf; but its inventor insisted that sharper spirality would make it a weapon less suitable for military use. For the rest, it was a tough, robust weapon, suited to carry the rifle regiment's sword bayonets and for any other military purpose. Being comparatively slow to load, it never replaced Brown Bess as the standard infantry weapon, but in the hands of specialist riflemen it was of great value, outshooting the smooth-bore muskets of the French *voltigeurs*. The only other weapon of roughly similar performance was the Tula rifle of the Russian Army. Anyhow, it remained in service for thirty-five years.

From Ezekiel Baker's own book, *Remarks on Rifle Guns*, we know a good deal about its performance. Official tests were held in 1800 and 1803, in the presence of His Majesty and at the command of the Board of Ordnance. The results were exactly recorded. Set in mortar so that it was quite immovable, the rifle was made to fire twelve shots at a round target of 9-foot diameter at 300 yards. Eleven of the shots made a 4-foot 10-inch group, centred round the middle of the target. Firing from the shoulder, without a rest, at a 7-foot-diameter target at 100 yards, Baker himself scored fifteen hits out of eighteen rounds. These fifteen shots made a group of about

3 feet 6 inches. At a man-sized figure target at 100 yards he scored thirty-two hits out of thirty-four shots.

Having studied such official records of the Baker rifle, one treats with some incredulity a story which nevertheless seems to be authentic. It concerns the 2nd Battalion, Rifle Brigade, whose commanding officer in 1805 was Lieutenant-Colonel Wade, an excellent rifle-shot. He and two private soldiers named Smeaton and Spurry used to hold targets for each other up to 150 and even 200 yards. When the Earl of Chatham, inspecting the battalion, remarked on the danger of this practice, Wade protested that there was no danger, and, bidding a rifleman hold a target for him, aimed and hit it. Lord Chatham was horrified, but Wade nonchalantly informed him, 'Oh, we all do it.' He then held a target for the rifleman's fire. The story reflects high credit not only on the Rifle Brigade's marksmanship, but on the relations between officers and men: it cannot have been a regiment where discipline was maintained by the lash.

There are no really authentic contemporary records of the Kentucky rifle, and modern experiments with eighteenth-century weapons may be misleading because black powder and lead balls are now of a more uniform quality than could be made two centuries ago. With these qualifications, one can say with some confidence that the Kentucky rifle was a good deal more accurate than the Baker rifle. Fired in 1922 from a rest, at 100 yards, an ancient seven-groove rifle known as 'Old Killdeer' put five bullets into a 2·10 inch group and made equally accurate shooting at silver dollars and half-dollars.

There are, of course, many accounts less meticulously recorded of the Kentucky rifle's performance. At the annual fairs of Green River, Popso Agie, and Pierre's Hole mountainmen, trappers and Indians used to meet to sell beaver skins, buy powder and shot, race horses, drink moonshine whisky, and traffic for young squaws. Shooting contests, with heavy side bets, were a popular feature of these gatherings. There was no difficulty in preparing targets: a slash with a hatchet sliced a square of bark from a tree so that bullet holes would show, a piece of paper was nailed to the middle of it – and there was a target. Sometimes a slit was cut in a tree and filled with gunpowder or powdered charcoal, which gave most satisfactory results if struck by a bullet. More exotic contests were to blow out a candle (quite easy: a ball passing within a couple of inches of the flame will do the trick) or drive in a nail with a bullet. Each competitor fired one shot only, with a rest, at 80 or 100

Like Johnny Walker these old rifles are still going strong. Here is a veteran being fired at Bisley in 1971

Left rear sight
on a gun of
about 1780 by
Durs Egg

yards, or standing without a rest at 40. To drive in a nail at that range the best shot
needed luck, but it was good, clean fun, with a bit of a gamble as well. An exacting
test of friendship and trust, as well as marksmanship, was 'shooting the tin cup': each
competitor took turns in shooting at a cup balanced on his opponent's hand or held
between his knees. The range varied, depending on whether or not the contestants
had been lunching; where 'whisky flowed in streams', 'twenty to thirty fathoms' was
quite enough. But by the 1840s on the Great Plains, where the terrain favoured long-
range shooting, riflemen were paying five dollars to compete at 300 yards.

It is lamentable to record that even the innocent diversion of marksmanship was
not free from sharp practice, especially when exhibited on the stage. A certain
Bartholomew Bosco used to 'catch' bullets, fired at him, in mid-air. The rifle was
duly loaded with powder and ball in the presence of the audience or even by one of
them. But the flash-hole led not to the rifle's ostensible barrel with its lethal bullet,
but to another barrel underneath, disguised as a ramrod holder, which was loaded
with a small charge of powder and a special 'bullet' made of mercury in a gelatine
case which disintegrated a few inches from the muzzle. Balls used for trick shooting
were often made of wax, painted to look like lead and filled with small shot: Eley
made special trick-shooting cartridges with a ball, a very small powder charge, and
a dozen wads to fill the consequently empty space: if the ball missed the target,

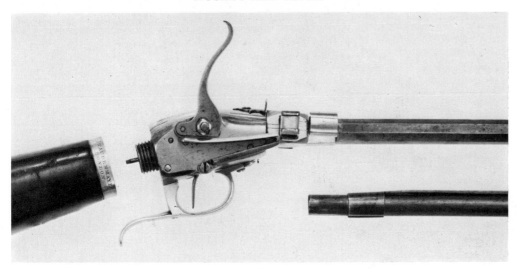

The air reservoir (left) and the other
parts of the magazine air rifle

commonly a glass ball, one of the wads was sure to hit and break it. In some exhibitions the impact of the bullet on the back-stop operated a mechanism which cut a string and made the target fall, or an unseen assistant snuffed out the candle with a blow-pipe. Where the target was held in the hand of a beautiful female assistant walking across the stage, a pause in the music, or other signal given by the orchestra, warned her to stop so that the target was for a moment stationary. To such sad subterfuges were professional marksmen reduced, particularly (it must be said) in the New World.

But even the Island Race was not entirely innocent of sharp practice. There is on record a shooting match held in 1811 between riflemen of the Duke of Cumberland's Sharpshooters and the Nottingham Robin Hood Club. 'The Notts took 2 hours and 40 minutes to fire their shots, in order to draw the Cumberland into the night, but the Cumberland fired theirs in 43 minutes, beginning at a quarter past five', and deservedly won.

Although the Chinese may have invented gunpowder, firearms reached the Far East unquestionably from Europe, and oriental invention in this field always lagged behind that of Europe.* Matchlocks, for instance, were used in Asian and North African wars well into the late nineteenth century. But the long-barrelled Afghan jezail and similar weapons used by Moorish tribes in the 1840s, rested on a rock and fired from behind cover by mountaineers, easily outshot the muskets used by European troops in the first Afghan War and the early French colonial wars. The French, indeed, developed a special long-range rifle to deal with them. Like the Kentucky rifle, they did not carry a bayonet and were not sufficiently robust for hand-to-hand combat, but for that they were not needed: the tribesmen had plenty of swords and long knives.

* The common oriental word for a gun, *bundook*, may be a corruption of the Turkish 'Veneduq', the 'product of Venice'.

Flint-lock breech-loading rifle by Durs Egg with a silver holed plate mounted vertically in a sprung housing giving both an open and an aperture sight with vertical adjustment

Opposite page
Pennsylvania flint-lock rifle of about 1800 with a scooped rear sight

The expansion of Europe to America, Asia, and Africa brought European sportsmen into contact with far larger and more dangerous animals than even the wild boar: but their weapons up to the mid-nineteenth century were still the muzzle-loading rifle or smooth-bore, improved only by percussion caps instead of flint-locks. These had a terrific knock-down power against medium-sized, soft-skinned game like lions and tigers, but lacked the penetration and bone-smashing capacity necessary to kill, or even to halt, larger animals such as buffalo, bison, and elephant. To kill one of these huge creatures not one but several bullets might be required, and a sportsman on foot would need an armoury of rifles, with half a dozen loaders, if he was to have any hope of stopping a determined charge.

British sportsmen in India adopted the Indian custom of shooting from the back of an elephant, from a howdah which held the necessary spare rifles and loader. In the great plains of North America and in the new hunting grounds of South Africa they hunted on horseback, often with dogs to help.

It was exciting and pretty dangerous to gallop across rough country in the midst of a thundering herd of American buffalo (or, to be more pedantic, bison), firing into a huge bull's shoulder at a range so close that the powder singed his hide. No doubt many hunters did so, but not many wrote an account of it. Here is George Catlin's description of a buffalo hunt near the Yellowstone River in 1837:

'We all crossed the river, and galloped away a couple of miles or so, when we mounted the bluff; and to be sure, there was in full view of us a fine herd of some four or five hundred buffaloes, perfectly at rest, and in their own estimation (probably)

A scooped rear sight in chiselled steel on a breech-
loading flint-lock rifle

perfectly secure. Some were grazing, and others were lying down and sleeping; we advanced within a mile or so of them in full view, and came to a halt. Monsieur Chardon "tossed the feather" (a custom always observed, to try the course of the wind), and we commenced "stripping" as it is termed (i.e. every man strips himself and his horse of every extraneous and unnecessary appendage of dress, etc. that might be an incumbrance in running): hats are laid off, and coats – and bullet pouches; sleeves are rolled up, a handkerchief tied tightly round the head, and another round the waist – cartridges are prepared and placed in the waist-coat pocket, or a half dozen bullets "throwed into the mouth", etc. etc., all of which takes up some ten or fifteen minutes, and is not, in appearance or in effect, unlike a council of war. Our leader lays the whole plan of the chase, and preliminaries all fixed, guns charged and ramrods in our hands, we mount and start for the onset. The horses are all trained for this business, and seem to enter into it with as much enthusiasm, and with as restless a spirit as the riders themselves. While "stripping" and mounting, they exhibit the most restless impatience; and when "approaching" – (which is, all of us abreast, upon a slow walk, and in a straight line towards the herd, until they discover us and run), they all seem to have caught entirely the spirit of the chase, for the laziest amongst them prances with an elasticity in his step – champing his bit – his ears erect – his eyes strained out of his head, and fixed upon the game before him, whilst he trembles under the saddle of his rider. In this way we carefully and silently marched, until within some forty or fifty rods; when the herd discovering us, wheeled and laid their course in a mass. At this instant we started! (and all *must* start, for no one could check the fury of those steeds at that moment of excitement), and away all sailed, and over the prairie flew, in a cloud of dust which was raised by their trampling hoofs. M'Kenzie was foremost in the throng, and soon dashed off amidst the dust and was out of sight – he was after the fattest and the fastest. I had discovered a huge bull whose shoulders towered above the whole band, and I picked my way through the crowd to get alongside of him. I went not for "meat", but for a *trophy*; I wanted his head and horns. I dashed along through the thundering mass, as they swept away over the plain, scarcely able to tell whether I was on a buffalo's back or my horse – hit, and hooked, and jostled about, till at length I found myself alongside of my game, when I gave him a shot, as I passed him. I saw guns flash in several directions about me, but I heard them not. Amidst the trampling throng, Monsieur Chardon had wounded a stately bull, and at this moment was passing him again with his piece levelled for another shot; they were both at full speed when the bull instantly turned and receiving the horse upon his horns, and the ground received poor Chardon, who made a frog's leap of some twenty feet or more over the bull's back, and almost under my horse's heels. I wheeled my horse as soon as possible and rode back, where lay poor Chardon, gasping to start his breath again; and within a few paces of him his huge victim, with his heels high in the air, and the horse lying across him.'

But the buffalo was comparatively easy to kill. Sioux and Comanches, after all, did the job with bows and lances. The African lion and elephant was a very different proposition. One of the first European elephant-hunters was Rowaleyn Gordon Cumming, a Scottish sportsman if that term can be properly applied to a man possessed of an extraordinary callousness and blood lust.

He set out from Port Elizabeth on a year's hunting trip equipped with three English double-barrelled rifles by Purdey, William Moore, and Dickson of Edinburgh, 'the latter a two-grooved, the most perfect and useful I ever had the pleasure of using'; one heavy, single-barrelled 12-bore German rifle; an enormous Boer rifle of 6-bore (0·924 inch); and 'three stout double-barrelled guns for rough work when

The rear sight of the Baker rifle of 1800

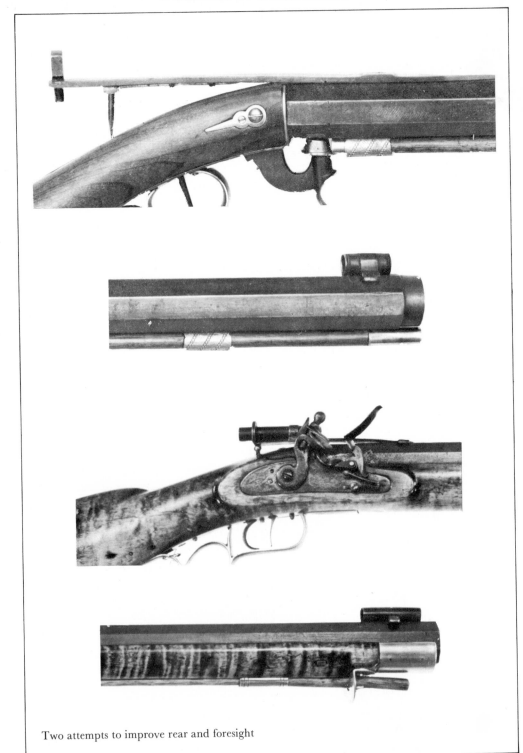

Two attempts to improve rear and foresight

hard riding and swift loading is required'. He does not mention the bore of his English rifles, but they seem to have been not less than 12-bore, or 0·747 inch. Even his 6-bore was not the largest elephant rifle in use: some redoubtable hunters braved the recoil of 4-bore, 1·052 inches, rifles. With his two-grooved Dickson rifle he thought he did well to bring down a blesbok with a single shot in the shoulder at 250 yards. In a shooting match, he was confident of hitting a board 6 inches by 4 at 100 yards.

His ancillary equipment included 'several lead-ladles of different sizes, a whole host of bullet-moulds, loading-rods, shot-belts, powder-flasks; 3 cwt of lead, 50 lb of pewter to be used for hardening the balls to be used in destroying the larger game, 10,000 prepared leaden bullets, 100 lb of fine sporting gunpowder, 300 lb of coarse gunpowder, 50,000 best percussion caps, 2,000 gun-flints, greased patches and cloth to be converted into the same.'

He usually hunted on horseback. 'When hunting elephants, my after-rider carried ammunition and a spare rifle; and my own personal appointments consisted of a wide-awake hat, secured under my chin by "rheimpys", or strips of dressed skin, a coarse linenby shirt, sometimes a kilt, and sometimes a pair of buckskin knee-breeches, and a pair of "veldtschoens", or home-made shoes. I entirely discarded coat, waistcoat, and neck-cloth, and I always hunted with my arms bare. My heels were armed with a pair of powerful persuaders, and from my left wrist depended by a double rheimpy an equally persuasive sea-cow jambok.

'Around my waist I wore two leathern belts or girdles. The smaller of these discharged the duty of suspenders, and from it on my left side depended a plaited rheimpy, eight inches in length, forming a loop in which dangled my powerful loading-rod, formed of a solid piece of horn of the rhinoceros. The larger girdle was my shooting-belt: this was a broad leather belt, on which were fastened four separate compartments made of otter-skin, with flaps to button over of the same material. The first of these held my percussion-caps, the second a large powder-flask, the third and fourth, which had divisions in them, contained balls and patches, two sharp clasp-knives, a compass, flint and steel. In this belt I also carried a loading mallet, formed from the horn of the rhinoceros; this and the powder-flask were each secured to the belt by long rheimpys, to prevent my losing them. Last, but not least, in my right hand I generally carried my double-barrelled two-grooved rifle.'

On one occasion, while moving away from a dry-weather bush-fire, he found himself looking down from a hill at the backs of a herd of bull-elephants. 'There they stood quietly browsing on the side of a hill, while the fire in its might was raging to windward within two hundred yards of them.

'I directed Johannus to choose an elephant, and promised to reward him should he prove successful. Galloping furiously down the hill, I started the elephants with an unearthly yell, and instantly selected the finest in the herd. Placing myself alongside, I fired both barrels behind his shoulder, when he instantly turned upon me, and in his impetuous career charged head foremost into a large bushy tree which he sent flying before him high in the air with tremendous force, coming down at the same moment violently on his knees. He then met the raging fire, when, altering his course, he wheeled to the right-about. As I galloped after him I perceived another noble elephant meeting us in an opposite direction, and presently the gallant Johannus hove in sight, following his quarry at a respectful distance. Both elephants held on together, so I shouted to Johannus, "I will give your elephant a shot in the shoulder, and you must try to finish him." Spurring my horse, I rose close alongside, and gave the fresh elephant two balls immediately behind the shoulder, when he parted from mine, Johannus following; but before many minutes had elapsed that mighty Nimrod reappeared, having fired one shot and lost his prey.

'In the mean time I was loading and firing as fast as could be, sometimes at the head, and sometimes behind the shoulder, until my elephant's fore-quarters were a mass of gore, notwithstanding which he continued to hold stoutly on, leaving the grass and branches of the forest scarlet in his wake.

'On one occasion he endeavoured to escape by charging desperately amid the thickest of the flames; but this did not avail, and I was soon once more alongside. I blazed away at this elephant, until I began to think that he was proof against my weapons. Having fired thirty-five rounds with my two-grooved rifle, I opened fire upon him with the Dutch six-pounder; and when forty bullets had perforated his hide, he began for the first time to evince signs of a dilapidated constitutition. He took up a position in a grove; and as the dogs kept barking round him, he backed stern foremost among the trees, which yielded before his gigantic strength. Poor old fellow! he had long braved my deadly shafts, but I plainly saw that it was now all over with him; so I resolved to expend no further ammunition, but hold him in view until he died. . . .

Standing position
using a sling, 1800

Opposite page
Kneeling position, 1800

'A few days later . . . I came full in view of the tallest and largest bull elephant I had ever seen. He stood broadside to me, at upwards of one hundred yards, and his attention at the moment was occupied with the dogs, which, unaware of his proximity, were rushing past him, while the old fellow seemed to gaze at their unwonted appearance with surprise.

'Halting my horse, I fired at his shoulder, and secured him with a single shot. The ball caught him high upon the shoulder-blade, rendering him instantly dead lame. Finding himself incapacitated, the old fellow seemed determined to take it easy, and, limping slowly to a neighbouring tree, he remained stationary, eyeing his pursuers with a resigned and philosophic air.

'I resolve to devote a short time to the contemplation of this noble elephant before I should lay him low; accordingly, having off-saddled the horses beneath a shady tree which was to be my quarters for the night and ensuing day, I quickly kindled a fire and put on the kettle, and in a very few minutes my coffee was prepared. There I sat in my forest home, coolly sipping my coffee, with one of the finest elephants in Africa awaiting my pleasure beside a neighbouring tree.

'Having admired the elephant for a considerable time, I resolved to make experiments for vulnerable points, and, approaching very near, I fired several bullets at different parts of his enormous skull. These did not seem to affect him in the slightest; he only acknowledged the shots by a "salaam-like" movement of his trunk, with the point of which he gently touched the wound with a striking and peculiar action. Surprised and shocked to find that I was only tormenting and

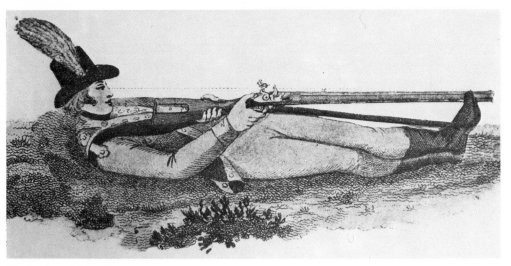

The back position, 1800

prolonging the suffering of the noble beast, which bore his trials with such dignified composure, I resolved to finish the proceedings with all possible despatch; accordingly I opened fire upon him from the left side, aiming behind the shoulder; but even there it was long before my bullets seemed to take effect. I first fired six shots with the two-grooved, which must have eventually proved mortal, but as yet he evinced no visible distress; after which I fired three shots at the same part with the Dutch six-pounder. Large tears now trickled from his eyes, which he slowly shut and opened; his colossal frame quivered convulsively, and falling on his side he expired. The tusks of this elephant were beautifully arched, and were the heaviest I had yet met with, averaging 90 lb weight apiece.'

This elephant was fortunate; another needed fifty-seven balls to finish him off. It is not a very edifying story, and Gordon Cumming, intrepid hunter though he was,

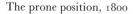

The prone position, 1800

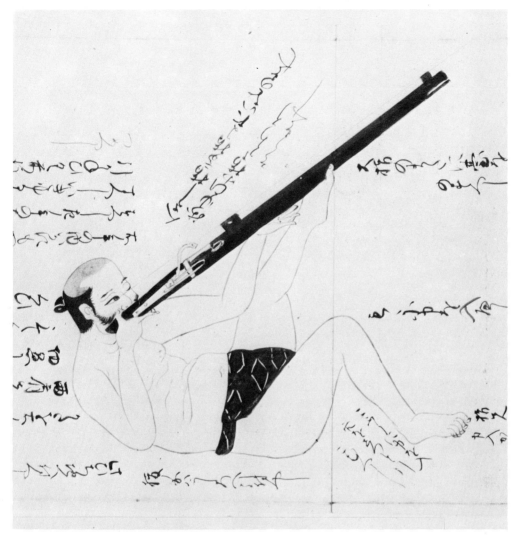

The back position illustrated in Nagasawa Shagetzuma's
The Book of Firearms, written in 1616

cannot have been a very nice man. No animal has suffered, and still suffers, more from man than the African elephant.

When a rifle was foul, it was difficult, even with the rhino-horn loading-rod and mallet, to ram down a ball while galloping across country. For this reason, he eventually decided that for hunting on horseback, when the shots were taken at very close range, a smooth-bore was 'the proper tool for a mounted man when quick loading is necessary.

'I remember having a discussion with the commanding officer of a regiment of heavy dragoons on this subject, and he and I agreed that nothing can surpass a double-barrelled smooth bore for practical utility. When a two-grooved has been

219

Joseph Lang's Shooting Gallery in Pall Mall, 1837

Opposite page
A muzzle-loader at Bisley, 1970

once or twice discharged, the bullet required considerable power to drive it home;
and to a mounted man this is extremely inconvenient. I consider that no regiment
in the service was more effectually armed than my own old corps, the Cape Mounted
Rifles, who were furnished with short double-barrelled smooth-bore pieces, carrying
a ball of twelve to the pound, and having stout percussion-locks. Give me a weapon
of this description to war against the larger game of Africa. To accelerate loading,
the hunter ought to have his balls stitched up in their patches, and well greased before
taking the field. This was my invariable custom: I found it a great convenience, and
after a little practice I could load and fire in the saddle, although riding in rough
ground at a swinging gallop.'

The middle of the nineteenth century produced some important developments in
rifles, which, however, can only be dealt with briefly because their technical details
are germane to a book on firearms rather than to one on marksmanship.

Wrapping a rifle ball in a greased patch was reasonably effective, but time-
consuming and clumsy. Could not a ball be devised which would be easily rammed
down the barrel, and yet fit into the grooves of the rifling? Experiments were made
with various types of belted balls, but they brought no great improvement in
accuracy or ease of loading. Obviously a pointed bullet, if it spun properly, would
have a higher velocity than a spherical ball: but the old difficulty cropped up again:
it could not spin properly unless it fitted the grooves, and if it fitted the grooves, it

Bisley, 1970

could not be rammed down the barrel. (The greased patch was really no solution: it was all right for a spherical ball, which need not spin very fast: but a pointed bullet must spin fast and true on its own axis, or it will turn over in the air.) A French officer, Captain Minie, hit upon the solution in 1848: a pointed bullet (technically known as cylindro-ogival) with a hollow base. It could be pushed easily down the barrel, fitting the lands of the rifling, but the explosion of the charge into the cavity in the base made the base expand so that it fitted the grooves. The Minie ball was soon adopted, in one form or another, for all rifled firearms, and is still invariably used today.

During the 1830s all European armies adopted the muzzle-loading rifle as the principal infantry arm, the British Army's choice falling first on the Brunswick rifle firing a belted ball. Then, after much experiment and examination of foreign rifles, the British military authorities settled on an adaptation of the French Minie rifle, firing the Minie bullet but reduced to a bore of 0.577 inch with three grooves making half a turn in the 39-inch barrel. With this rifle, known as the Enfield, it entered the Crimean War. It was a good rifle, sighted for line regiments up to 200 yards and for rifle regiments up to no less than 800 yards.

During the same decade fixed cartridges first appeared, though not yet for military purposes: the bullet, charge, priming-powder, and detonator were all combined in a single case, loaded into the breech in one motion. The detonator was first in the form of a projection from the rim of a 'pin-fire' cartridge; then placed

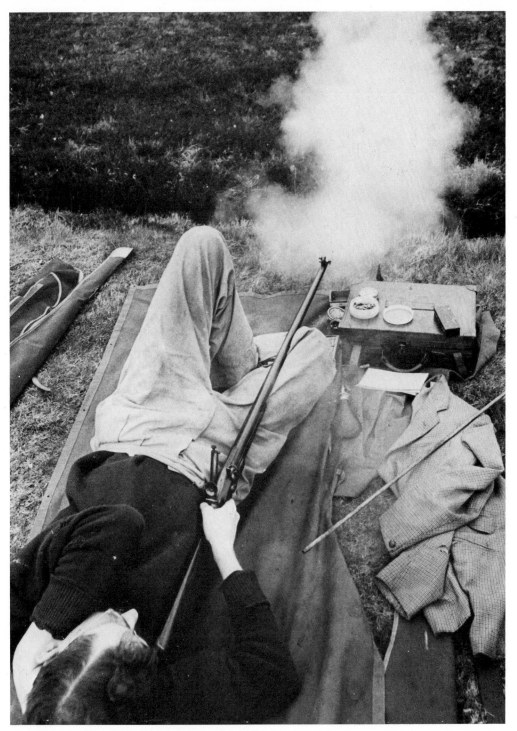

The prone position, Bisley, 1970, and the cloud of
smoke from the black powder used by the competitor

Loading, Bisley, 1970

Aiming, Bisley, 1970

under the rim of a 'rim-fire' cartridge; finally set in the centre of a 'centre-fire' cartridge as it is today. The essential point was that the cartridge was made of brass: as the charge exploded, this expanded, completely filling the chamber, forming a gas-tight seal so there could be no blow-back. This at last made possible a safe and gas-tight breech-loader. Innumerable patterns of breech-loading rifles were made, single-shot and repeating.

Perhaps the most efficient single-shot action was the 'falling block', exemplified by the Martini. A lever behind the trigger-guard raises and lowers a block which incorporates the firing-pin. When the lever is lowered, the block drops and exposes the chamber, into which a cartridge is inserted. Raising the lever and block closes the chamber and the rifle is cocked and ready for firing. Extractors draw the empty case back from the chamber as the lever is lowered and the block drops again.

Many people have wondered why it was not possible to apply to the rifle the simple repeating-mechanism of a revolver. The reason is that it is almost impossible to align exactly the chamber and the barrel. In a smooth-bore weapon, firing spherical bullets, this does not much matter: but a rifled barrel must be slightly smaller in diameter than the chamber, so unless they are exactly aligned, one side of the bullet is scraped, which of course spoils it for consistent, accurate shooting. Moreover, the small gap between chamber and barrel results in a leakage of gas, a loss of power. In a short-range weapon like a revolver, this does not greatly matter: but in a rifle it does, so would-be inventors of repeating rifles had to seek a solution elsewhere.

The earliest efficient repeating rifle was the Winchester, 'the gun that won the West'. Cartridges were held, nose to tail, in a tubular magazine below the barrel. The operation of a loading lever fed the new cartridge into the chamber and cocked the firing-mechanism.

Finally, towards the end of the century, there appeared the bolt-action magazine rifle, of which the prototype was the Mauser. This, for the modern reader, needs no explanation.

7

Pistols and Revolvers

As has already been related, the invention of the wheel-lock made the pistol a practicable proposition: one could not very well have a matchlock pistol, if only because it could not be safely holstered with the match alight.

Some of the early wheel-lock pistols, of the late sixteenth and seventeenth centuries, were not merely beautiful weapons, chased and gilded and engraved, but accurate and hard-hitting. This is particularly so of pistols with rifled barrels. These seem to have been more successful than rifled muskets, perhaps because, being shorter in the barrel, they were not so difficult to load. 'Screw-barrelled pistols', of which the rifled barrel could be unscrewed from the butt so that the ball and charge could be loaded into the breech, were not uncommon. Presumably they, like all forms of early breech-loading guns, deteriorated, becoming loose and dangerous with powder-firing and corrosion: but neither in war nor sport would a pistol be fired nearly as often as a musket. It seems to have been with a screw-barrelled, rifled wheel-lock pistol that Prince Rupert hit the weather-vane on top of St Mary's church tower at Stafford: when his uncle, Charles I, suggested that it was a fluke, he drew the other pistol and sent the vane spinning a second time.

Wheel-locks were always expensive; but the flint-lock pistol was a cheap and common weapon, carried by every cavalry trooper and many others. The 'horse-pistol' was a somewhat clumsy weapon with a barrel about a foot long, but other pistols were shorter in the barrel and beautifully balanced, and pocket-pistols had barrels of only 4 or 5 inches.

Gentlemen commonly practised up to 50 yards with smooth-bore pistols, and occasionally up to 100 yards with rifled pistols. Sometimes a detachable shoulder-butt was supplied with a pistol, making it a short-barrelled carbine. There is no reason why a rifled flint-lock should not have been as accurate as any modern pistol. The claim that an expert could, at 15 yards, hit a bottle-cork ten times out of ten is probably no exaggeration.

During the eighteenth century the pistol gradually replaced the sword as the duellist's favourite weapon, especially in England, Ireland, and America where the standard of swordsmanship was generally low. The procedure and rules of duelling, at first pretty loose and imprecise, became increasingly rigid: a duellist who ignored them was far more likely to suffer the penalties of the law than one who fought fair. The injured or insulted party sent a friend, his second, to demand an apology, failing which a challenge would be issued. The party challenged had choice of weapons. The time, place, range, number of shots, and such details were not settled by the principals, but were 'submitted to the calm deliberation of their seconds'. The latter were no longer, as in earlier, more bloody days, expected to fight themselves: their job was to see fair play, to arrange for the attendance of a surgeon and to load the pistols. The last duty was particularly important, for the duellists themselves were generally in a very nervous state, and sometimes quite ignorant of firearms: when, for instance, Warren Hastings and Philip Francis fought at Calcutta, neither had ever fired a pistol before. A carelessly loaded pistol, a badly adjusted flint, failure to ensure that the weapon was properly primed – any of these could produce a misfire, cause a gentleman to be shot down while unarmed and helpless, or subject the principals to intolerable nervous strain while the charges were drawn and the weapon re-loaded. One writer on the subject had known a pistol snapped a dozen times before it went off, though the flint was often chipped; this was putting a man in serious apprehension of his life eleven times oftener than he expected.

Occasionally seconds took it upon themselves to ensure that no blood was shed: William Hickey tells of a duel in which the seconds, believing that the cause of the quarrel was too trivial, by mutual agreement loaded both weapons with powder only, no ball.

It was not 'done' to take a deliberate aim: a gentleman should fire as soon as his pistol 'came up'. This made the balance of the pistol and the angle of barrel and butt of vital importance. A weapon too heavy in the barrel, or with the barrel and butt set at too acute an angle, fired low: the opposite flaws caused it to fire high. A good duelling pistol, like a good shotgun, was made to measure, so that it came up easily, the barrel horizontal. Since in a duel between two good shots the first to fire lived and the other died, gunmakers like Joe Manton perfected fast firing locks and hair-triggers. In Britain and the United States rifled pistols were, however, considered unfair. Only a cad would use a pistol rifled at the breech end but smooth near the muzzle, so that the rifling could not be seen.

At one time it was not considered fair to take the prudent precaution of practising with one's own pistol before a duel. Samuel Martin, before fighting Mr Wilkes, the 'patriot' and demagogue, put in hours of practice, 'even on Sundays', and was thereafter known by such derisive names as 'the Celebrated Targeteer'. This convention

Wheel-lock pistol with an etched barrel and stock and
butt inlaid with engraved ivory. It was made for
Emperor Charles V by Peter Bech of Munich about 1540

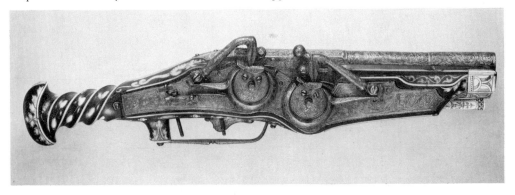

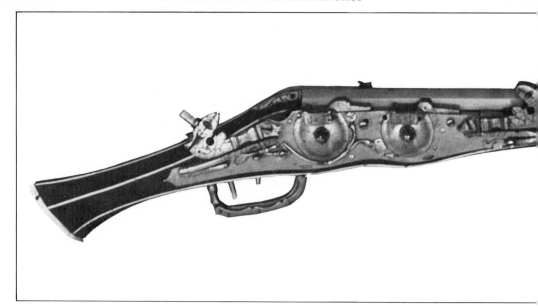

A Saxon wheel-lock pistol of 1561

seems, however, to have died out: nineteenth-century manuals of duelling enjoin frequent practice, always with the same weapons, to 'ascertain the exact throw of the ball'.

A gentleman about to fight a duel 'should not allow the idea of becoming a target to make him uneasy': he might do worse than pass the evening before playing cards, or splitting with a couple of friends a bottle of good port. If he finds difficulty in sleeping, a good light book – one of Sir Walter Scott's, for instance – may do the trick. Having been called by his servant with a cup of coffee and a biscuit, he should calmly dress, wash, and shave, taking particular care to bathe his eyes with cold water. He must leave the house without disturbing his wife and children who must, of course, be kept in ignorance of the affair, lest their natural apprehensions cause them to inform the authorities. On the way to the duelling ground, should he feel the slightest qualms, a small glass of brandy and soda may be efficacious in calming his nerves.

On arrival, he should pace calmly up and down, coolly puffing his cigar, while the seconds measure the ground and load the pistols. He should not address his adversary, but should watch closely to see if the latter showed any nervous tremulation, being careful himself to remain 'as firm and stiff as a statue'. When the preliminaries are concluded, he takes his stance.*

A duellist generally stood sideways on to his opponent, so as to present a narrow target. Some, however, argued that if one was hit standing sideways on, the ball was

---

* Sometimes, instead of taking their stances and awaiting the signal, they stood back to back and on the signal, walked apart an agreed number of paces, turned and fired.

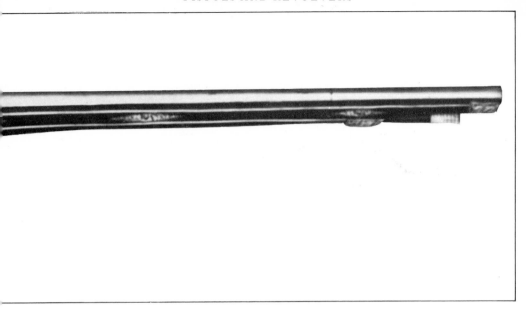

bound to do serious damage: but if one faced the fire, it might pass through the body without touching anything vital. Charles Fox faced his opponent fair and square, characteristically explaining that he was as broad one way as 'tother.

The duellist should single out some particular point on his adversary, a gilt button for instance, and concentrating all his attention on that, 'think of nothing but placing his ball on the proper spot'. When the signal or word is given, he should immediately raise his pistol and pull the trigger carefully, moving 'only the fore-finger and that with just sufficient force to discharge the pistol'. If the first shots miss, the parties go on firing until one is hit or until they have fired the number of shots, generally two each, agreed by the seconds.

If the duellist is hit, he must 'not be alarmed or confused, but quietly submit the part to the examination of a surgeon . . . and, if he dies, go off with as good a grace as possible'. Statistically a duellist had a 20 per cent chance of being killed.

The usual method of firing was with the pistol almost at arm's length, the elbow almost straight. Some, however, fired in an awkward, cramped position, the arm bent and the elbow down so as to give some protection to the body. An expert known as Fighting Fitzgerald used to 'reduce his height five or six inches'. His plan was to bend his head over his arm till the upper portion of him resembled a bow. His right hand and arm was held in front of his head in such a manner that the ball would have to pass all up his arm before it touched a vulnerable point.

As an example of how a duel should not be fought one cannot do better than relate the encounter of Mr Wilkes with Samuel Martin.

The cause of their quarrel was an anonymous description of Martin, in Wilkes's scandalous rag, *The North Briton*, as 'the most treacherous, base, selfish, mean, abject

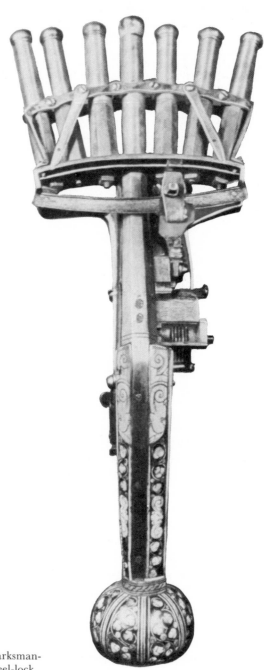

The antithesis of marksmanship: a German wheel-lock
pistol adapted to fire seven
barrels

and low-lived fellow that ever wriggled himself into a Secretaryship'. Martin nursed his wounded honour for eight months, practising with his pistols, until Wilkes was in disrepute over some observations in *The North Briton* on his Majesty himself, and an obscene poem entitled *An Essay on Woman*. In the debate which led to the Patriot's expulsion from the House, Martin in a voice shaking with passion and looking Wilkes straight in the face, twice repeated 'A man capable of writing in that manner without putting his name to it, and thereby stabbing another man in the dark, is a cowardly, malignant and scandalous scoundrel.'

Next morning Wilkes wrote (he could hardly help writing) to Samuel Martin.

Sir,
    You complained yesterday, before five hundred gentlemen, that you had been *stabbed in the dark*; but I have reason to believe that you was not so *in the dark* as you affected to be. To cut off every pretence of ignorance as to the author, I whisper in your ear, that every passage of *The North Briton* in which you have been named or even alluded to was written by

Your humble servant,
John Wilkes

Martin, who must have expected such a letter, took great pains over his reply, his draft showing many corrections.

'As I said in the House of Commons yesterday, that the writer of *The North Briton* who had stabbed me in the dark, was a cowardly as well as a malignant and infamous scoundrel; and your letter of this morning's date, acknowledges that every passage of *The North Briton*, in which I have been named or even alluded to, was written by yourself; I must take the liberty to repeat, that you are a malignant and infamous scoundrel and that I desire to give you an opportunity of showing me whether the epithet of *cowardly* was rightly applied or not. I desire that you may meet me in Hyde Park immediately, with a brace of pistols each to determine our differ-ence. I shall go to the Ring in Hyde Park, with my pistols concealed; and I will wait in expectation of you one hour. As I shall call in at your house to deliver this letter, I propose to go from thence directly to the Ring in Hyde Park; from where we may proceed, if it be necessary, to any more private place. And I mention I shall wait one hour, in order to give you the full time to meet me.'

Two points about Martin's letter are of interest. First he arrogated to himself the choice of weapons although that choice should have been made by Wilkes as the party challenged. He gave Wilkes no time to find a second or a surgeon.

One can only wonder at Wilkes's extraordinary rashness in going to meet Martin in such circumstances. However, with his loaded pistols concealed, he set off for Hyde Park, arriving a few minutes late.

'I beg your pardon, Mr Martin,' he said, 'for keeping you so long. I was out when you called, engaged with my lawyer.'

'Very well,' replied Martin. 'See, those people are too near us. We had better retire to a more private place.'

As they walked across the turf, Wilkes asked, 'What, are we come without seconds or previous regulations?'

Flint-lock pocket
pistol, front

'I have come,' said Martin, 'to risk my life and am under no apprehension of unfairness.'

'But it is usual on these occasions to settle some preliminary rules. Indeed, it is an absolute necessity.'

'We shall walk from each half a dozen paces then turn round and fire.'

Wilkes asked, 'Shall either of us receive the other's fire, or shall we both fire immediately?'

'We shall fire together if we can, or in what way each thinks fit.'

Thus, through Wilkes's unusual gullibility, the challenger had chosen not merely the weapons, but the time of the duel, the range and the conditions.

'Shall there,' asked Wilkes, 'be any begging of life in case of emergency?'

'Let that be left to chance and occasion when it happens.'

While they were talking, a man and a woman passed close by. Wilkes took Martin's arm and they walked on as though engaged in friendly and earnest conversation.

Reaching a rail which divided the park at a low, watery place, Wilkes said, 'This is the spot.' Martin agreed. It was the only right of choice that Wilkes exercised. They stooped under the rails and Wilkes proposed that they each use one of the other's pistols. Martin assented.

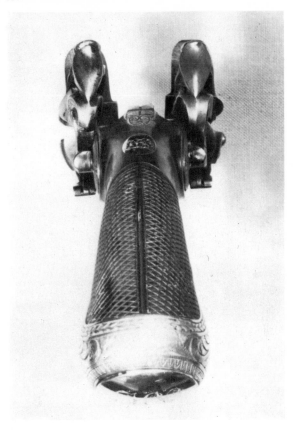

The same pistol
seen from behind

Wilkes laid both his pistols on the grass. 'Make your choice, sir.'

Martin chose one of his opponent's weapons, and laid down one of his own. But Wilkes said, 'If you please, Mr Martin, I shall have the one you have kept in your hand.' Martin gave it to him. They then parted from one another each six paces.

When Martin turned round to fire he saw Wilkes stooping, as though examining the priming of one of the pistols.

'Stay a little!' said Wilkes, 'I am not ready.'

'I will stay until you are ready.'

Wilkes then standing upright, they presented at each other.

'Now, sir!' said Martin, and fired.

They fired, Martin wrote, nearly together, and both missed.

Wilkes then ran forward several paces, presumably intending, as a bad shot, to close the range. Martin retreated a step or two with his pistol pointed; then, when Wilkes presented his second pistol, Martin fired. Wilkes 'snapping his pistol in his hand at the same moment'.

Wilkes threw down his pistol.

Martin asked, 'Did it miss fire?'

'No, dammit, I am wounded.' Unbuttoning his *surtout* frock and waistcoat, Wilkes showed on his shirt a large stain of blood about the middle of his belly.

233

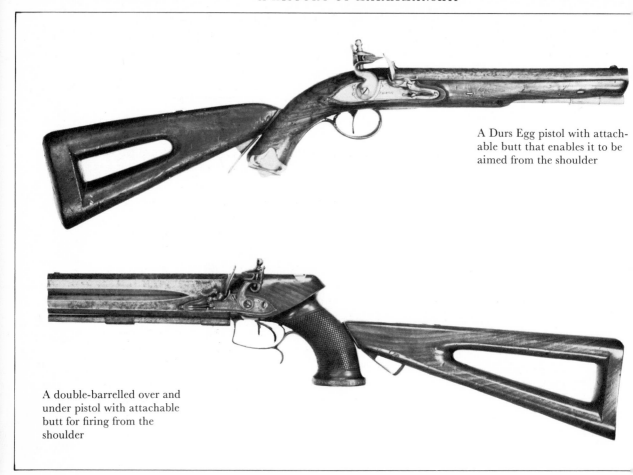

A Durs Egg pistol with attachable butt that enables it to be aimed from the shoulder

A double-barrelled over and under pistol with attachable butt for firing from the shoulder

Said Martin, 'I have killed you, I am afraid.'

Wilkes buttoned up his clothes, and ducking under the rail, walked off towards Grosvenor Gate. Martin, pocketing the pistols, followed. At the top of the slope he saw someone helping Wilkes along. Martin ran up and offered help. 'No, no!' exclaimed Wilkes. 'Take care of yourself. I will say nothing of you.' Thereupon they parted.

Concluding his story of the duel with a postscript, written with a different pen, so possibly some time later, Martin wrote, 'on examining the pistol on his return, Mr Martin found it loaded, but the pan clean and without powder. Mr Martin thinks that when he saw Mr Wilkes stooping down, he was employed in opening the pan of Mr Martin's pistol to see whether it was primed, and supposes that by some accident Mr Wilkes did then spill the powder: Mr Martin having loaded both the pistols and primed them with his own hands before he left the house. The flints too were new and had been put in the cocks of Mr Martin's pistols but two or three days before this happened.'

Their contemporaries were convinced that the duel was unfair because:

(a) Martin did not challenge in a sudden rage, but practised for eight months beforehand, 'even on Sundays'. What seems to us a prudent precaution shocked eighteenth-century gentlemen.

(b) Martin, by the form of his challenge, chose the weapon though that choice should have been Wilkes's. Wilkes was a better swordsman than pistol shot.

(c) Martin's challenge gave Wilkes no time to arrange for a surgeon, and find a second to see fair play, load the pistols, give the signal to fire, and so on.

(d) Martin chose the range, presumably that at which he had long been practising. At 12 yards a good shot will probably hit his mark; a bad shot will probably miss.

(e) Martin himself in the first exchange gave the signal 'Now, sir!' to fire. He would, therefore, be almost certain to get his shot off first. In the second exchange he does not seem even to have given a signal but, already on the aim, fired as soon as Wilkes presented.

(f) Martin, a West Indian, could not have been ignorant of duelling etiquette.

There are many unexplained and now inexplicable points of detail in the story of this duel. One is left, however, with the certainty that Martin did not fight fair; and with the impression that, had he been charged with attempted murder, he might have fared badly under cross-examination. But of course Martin, Secretary to the Treasury and Treasurer to the King's Mother, was never cross-examined on shooting the author of *The North Briton* and the *Essay on Women*.

As one might expect, democratic Americans dedicated themselves with peculiar zeal to the aristocratic custom of the duel. One of the most famous duels was that fought in 1806 between Andrew Jackson ('Old Hickory') and Charles Dickenson. Both were dead shots: Dickenson could, at eight yards, put four successive bullets into a circle the size of a silver dollar; and on his way to the duelling ground he severed, with one shot, a dangling string outside an inn, requesting the landlord, 'If General Jackson comes along this road, be kind enough to show him that.'

At the signal, Dickenson fired first. He hit his antagonist, but Jackson did not fall. Slowly Old Hickory raised his pistol, took careful aim and fired – but the hammer stuck at half-cock. He recocked it, and taking his time over it, while Dickenson stood like a rock, took another deliberate aim, and shot Dickenson dead. Only then was it noticed that Jackson's shoes were full of blood from a dangerous wound in his chest. It appears that he wore a very loose-fitting coat, so that Dickenson was deceived as to the exact position of his heart – a trick which some purists condemned as savouring of sharp practice.

Duels were sometimes fought on horseback, the parties firing as they galloped past one another at a distance of 8 or 9 yards, marked by posts, their pistols charged either with ball or with swan-shot. After two passages in this manner, if neither was hit, they fought it out with swords. In 1665 in France Madame de la Pré-Abbé and Mademoiselle de la Motte fought such a duel.

Slowly opinion gained ground that shooting somebody or standing up to be shot was an unnecessarily emphatic way of settling a quarrel. The practice died out first in Britain and northern Europe, but in the United States it was still common in the mid-nineteenth century, and in France until the twentieth: indeed, it is still not quite extinct. Italians were great duellists: in the decade 1879–89 2,759 duels were fought in Italy, but 93 per cent were fought with the sword, and less than 2 per cent of the combatants died – about one-tenth of the proportion of fatalities in pistol duels.

Until duelling was condemned not only by the law but, far more important, by upper-class opinion, refusing a challenge could be difficult and embarrassing. One who refused in style was the American Judge Breckinridge. Challenged by a British officer in 1798, he replied:

> Sir,
>
> I have two objections to this duel matter. The one is lest I should hurt you; the other, lest you should hurt me. I do not see any good it would do me to put a bullet through any part of your body. I could make no use of you when dead for any culinary purpose, as I could a rabbit or a turkey . . . for though your flesh might be delicate and tender, yet it wants that firmness and consistency which takes and retains salt. At any rate, it would not be fit for long sea voyages. You might make a good barbecue, it is true, being in the nature of a racoon or an opposum, but people are not in the habit of barbecuing anything human now. As to your hide, it is not worth taking off, being little better than that of a two year old colt. As to myself, I do not much like to stand in the way of anything that is harmful. I am under the apprehension you might hit me. That being the case, I think it most advisable to stay at a distance. If you want to try your pistols, take some object – a tree or a barn-door – about my dimensions, and if you hit that, send me word. I shall then acknowledge that if I had been in the same place you would have killed me in a duel.
>
> I have the honour to be,
Sir,
Your humble and obedient servant.

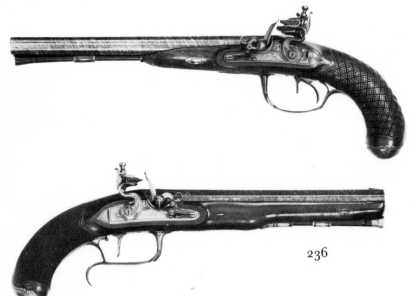

Flint-lock duelling pistols

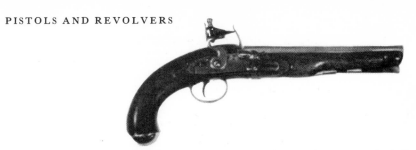

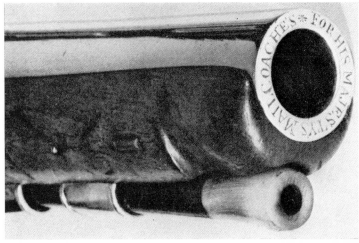

A flint-lock pistol with a brass barrel made for the Royal Mail guards in 1835

Bottom
Detail of its muzzle

An acquaintance of mine in more recent years evaded a challenge with in-genuity and even panache. *Plenus Bacchi*, he was in a Belgium night-club when he observed at the next table a living model of Hercule Poirot himself – bald, musta-chioed, with a head shaped like a pear. On his own table was half of an over-ripe melon. It was the work of a moment to pick up the half-melon and crown 'Poirot' with it. A challenge resulted. As the party challenged, my friend had the right to choose his weapon. 'The weapon I choose,' he replied with a dignity which was hardly disturbed by his companions' hilarity, 'is the pick-axe.' No more was heard of the matter.

Of equal ingenuity was a duellist who insisted on stripping off all his clothes, lest a pistol wound be complicated by fragments of cloth. His opponent withdrew in disgust, refusing to make himself ridiculous by shooting at a man *in puris naturalibus*.

Duelling attained its full absurdity in the early twentieth century when duelling pistols were deliberately made to be almost innocuous. The barrels were so badly bored that even fired from a vice they generally missed a man-sized target at 20 paces. The trigger-pull was so hard that a herculean effort was required to discharge the weapon, or so light that it generally exploded prematurely if the duellist was (as was not infrequently the case) agitated. Some 'duelling pistols' could not be fired at all, because the touch-hole did not connect with the chamber. Duels, however, were still staged with all the solemnity of fights to the death.

An ingenious Frenchman made pistols which fired bullets of wax up to some 20 metres. Protected by fencing masks and padded clothing, their hands safeguarded

Prince Dolgorouki
and Baron de
Heeck duelling at
Thionville in 1873

by a small shield attached to the butt, members of a pistol club could blaze away at one another without the slightest danger. Similar 'small impact' cartridges are made today in Germany and the United States. At 6 to 8 metres they are as accurate as ordinary pistol ammunition. They do not seem to be used for make-believe duels, but they could be safely used at any distance over 30 metres.

The duel, regulated by every kind of custom and tradition, was, so to speak, at one end of the pistol shooting scale: at the other was the concealed or disguised pistol of which, during the seventeenth and eighteenth centuries, many different and ingenious varieties were manufactured. There were pistols made to resemble daggers or riding whips, pistols so small that they could be carried in the cuff of a coat, dual-purpose pistols and swords. One cannot readily see the utility of knife-and-fork pistols, unless one proposes to assassinate someone across the dinner-table, but plenty were manufactured. Perhaps the most singular device was a pistol fitted into a Highlander's sporran, cocked, which fired as soon as an unauthorized hand groped within. Highlanders must have worn a sporran thus armed with some apprehension, lest they suffer grievous personal injury.

For some three hundred years all effective pistols were single- or double-barrelled, single- or two-shot weapons. The principle of the revolver was an old one: revolvers, or repeating muskets made on the revolver principle, were invented as early as 1500, but the bright idea could not be translated into an effective weapon. It proved difficult to line up accurately the revolving chamber with the barrel, and impossible to prevent fouling and corrosion which would jam the mechanism. There was always a danger that the explosion in one cylinder would set off a chain-reaction through all the others. Pepper-box revolvers, quite common in the late eighteenth and early nineteenth century, were safer, but extremely heavy and clumsy, having five or six complete, revolving barrels. It was not until Samuel Colt took out his first patent in 1835 that the revolver proper became a practicable proposition.

The first Colt 'cap-and-ball' revolver was, of course, a percussion-cap weapon, much less liable to accidental multiple explosion than revolvers with loose priming-powder in the touch-hole of each barrel or chamber. The caps were deeply recessed, as another safety precaution. Otherwise it contained no startling innovations. The unique virtue of the early Colt revolvers lay in the accurate fit of the working parts, and in the fact that these excellent practical weapons, an early essay in mass-production, were cheap, rugged, long-ranged, and interchangeable in their components so that broken parts could be easily replaced from any frontier store.

There were three subsequent cap-and-ball models – the Dragoon of 1848, the Navy of 1851 and the Army of 1861, all used in vast numbers in the Civil War. The last of these, converted to shoot centre-fire cartridges, re-appeared in 1871 as the famous 'Peacemaker'. This and the ·44 Frontier immortalized in Glorious Technicolor, were the favourite weapons of cowboy, sheriff, and bad man. They all had the same characteristics. With long barrels ($7\frac{1}{2}$ inches), heavy bullets (200–250 grains) and powder charges (38–40 grains), they had fair long-range accuracy and great stopping power.

They were all 'single-action' revolvers: that is to say, they had, like older pistols, to be cocked before firing. Adams and Webley produced the first double-action revolvers, which did not have to be cocked: pulling the trigger drew the hammer back until it was released from a sear, when it struck forward. The Adams and the

In 1868, Marie P . . . and Aimée R . . ., both of whom were so-called 'horizontals', fought a duel (two shots at twenty paces) over the heart (and purse) of a rich young man of Bordeaux. Marie P . . . was hit in the thigh at the first exchange. The victor shortly afterwards retired and married

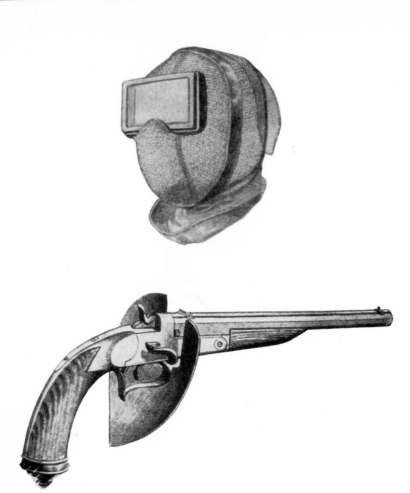

Pistol and its hand
shield used when
shooting with Dr
Devillier's bullets

Mask and protec-
tive clothing used
when shooting
with Dr Devillier's
wax bullets

Opposite page
Poacher target
used in Germany
up to 1950

Right
Gangster target
used in U.S.A.

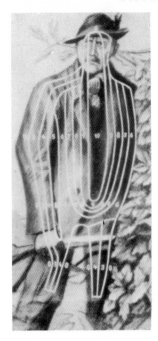 

Webley were perhaps better revolvers than the Colt, being faster shooting; but they did not have the Colt's long-range accuracy, they were more expensive and the parts were not readily interchangeable.

Nowadays one can practise at very little cost with ·22 ammunition. In the pistol ranges in the cellars of the C.B.I. in Washington are, or were, tubs full of ammunition, and agents are encouraged to come and help themselves whenever they have a few spare moments for practice. But ·45 ammunition is very expensive, and it is very doubtful if Jesse James, Wild Bill Hickok or Wyatt Earp could afford the hundreds – nay, thousands – of rounds required to make a dead shot.

In 1884 the celebrated American marksman, Ira Paine, gave a carefully recorded exhibition of pistol shooting with the Colt ·45, using both $7\frac{1}{2}$- and $5\frac{1}{2}$-inch barrels. His best performances, in 6-shot practices, were

At 12 yards	2-inch group	5 shots in 2-inch bull
At 25 yards	5-inch group	3 shots in 4-inch bull
At 50 yards	7-inch group	(no record of number of bulls)

Contemporary trials of the ·45 Webley produced comparable results. It seems unlikely that any western gunman could have done better, but by the standards of modern competition shooting these are mediocre performances.

No doubt some law-enforcers and law-breakers were very deadly pistoleros, but the emphasis was on speed, not on accuracy. Having in his gun five* shots instead of

* It was customary to carry a six-shooter with an empty chamber under the hammer, lest a knock on the hammer cause an accidental discharge.

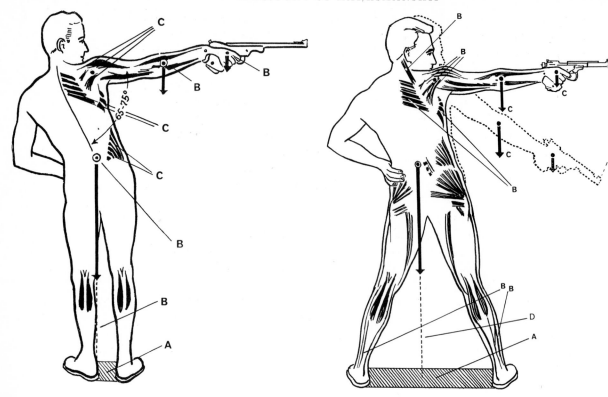

the duellist's one, the western gunman could afford a miss or two. Speed was all important, the quick draw, getting your shot off before the other fellow, then four more quick shots, one of which would probably hit.

Wyatt Earp, professional gambler and gunman, marshal of Dodge City and of Tombstone, was an exception: he took his time, firing a single well-aimed shot while his antagonist was spraying the countryside with lead. To this he owed his long life and prosperity but there is no evidence that he was by modern standards a very good shot.

Holsters were originally just like army or police holsters with a buttoned flap, attached to the belt waist-high. But to facilitate a quick draw, the westerner took to wearing an open holster, with no strap or flap to undo, low down on the right hip (assuming he was right-handed) or on the left hip if he preferred a 'cross-draw'. If he wore two guns, he did not usually use both hands to shoot: he drew both guns, fired five shots with his right hand, dropped or holstered the first gun, transferred the second from left to right hand and went on firing. It does not seem that he shot from the hip, except perhaps at very close range: contemporary drawings generally show gunmen shooting with arm extended.

The automatic pistol appeared in the late nineteenth century. There are innumerable makes and patterns, but all operate on the same principle. There is a long, spring-operated magazine, generally in the butt of the pistol. When the round in the chamber is fired, the recoil drives back a sliding jacket which in its backward movement ejects the empty case and cocks the action; as, driven by a spring, it returns to its forward position, it pushes the next round from the top of the magazine into the chamber, ready for firing.

In the wake of the two world wars, with violence condemned throughout the civilized world, it might reasonably be supposed that pistols and revolvers, like gentlemen's small swords, would fall into disuse. On the contrary: more and more people – police, security guards, ordinary citizens living in dangerous places – find it necessary to carry them. A few words on the handgun as a weapon of defence are not out of place. The author can speak with modest authority, having carried a gun constantly, and lived among people carrying guns, for several years, and having used it more than once.

The first question is, should the ordinary peaceful citizen ever be armed? The answer is, only when the police cannot, for various reasons, protect him against murder or armed robbery. These occasions are rare in western Europe, but not uncommon outside it. It can, of course, be argued that a pistol carried by someone who cannot use it properly is not merely a useless encumbrance, but a temptation to the evil-doer. True. But the answer is, if one has to carry a gun, learn to use it. During the Mau Mau rebellion in Kenya most Europeans and Asians, and many thousands of loyal Africans, carried guns, though very few ever used them. I am quite sure that, if they had not been armed, if it had not been known that they were armed, hundreds would have been chopped to death with pangas.

Stance, muscles and
body weight employed
in pistol shooting

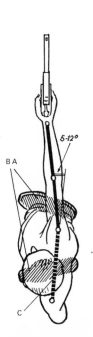

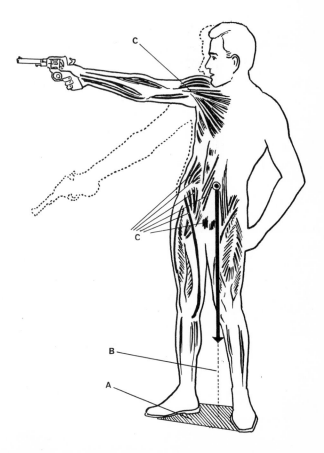

A Russian
crackshot

Opposite page
Little
marksmanship
here

While the rebellion was brewing, I had occasion to carry, late at night, some Top Secret papers from my boss's office to my own house. As I was setting out, he asked, 'Have you got a gun?'

'Of course not.'

'Good heavens! You're not carrying those papers around unarmed!'

I realized he was right. Robbery in the dark streets of Nairobi was not as common as, say, in Washington; but it did happen, and the consequences of losing these papers would be very serious.

'Here, take this.' He handed me a large, heavy ·45 Webley revolver, which I stuck awkwardly in my trouser pocket.

As I walked to my car and drove home, I realized that it was not only uncomfortable there, but pretty useless, for I could never, if attacked, have time to draw it. I decided that, with the shape of things to come, I had better discover the best type of gun for my purpose and the best way to carry it.

The choice lies between a revolver and an automatic pistol. The automatic holds eight or more rounds against the revolver's five (or six if one has all the chambers loaded). It is a trifle quicker in action, being self-cocking. One can much more rapidly slide a fresh magazine into the butt of an automatic than reload, one by one, the chambers of a revolver. Some people find the automatic easier to shoot straight. (On this, opinion varies: personally I shoot better with a Lüger than with any service pistol or revolver.) On the other hand the revolver, having a much simpler mechanism, never jams or gets clogged up with sand: one can just leave a revolver in a holster and it will always work, but an automatic needs frequent cleaning and oiling. To my mind, however, one single factor makes the revolver the better weapon. An automatic cannot safely be carried in the holster at full cock: the safety-catch is not sufficient insurance against accident. It has, therefore, to be drawn and cocked before it can be fired. Most automatics need two hands to cock: even those with an external hammer are, compared to a revolver, difficult to cock in a hurry. A modern revolver can, however, be carried perfectly safely with the hammer down: on drawing, one can either cock with the thumb or, more probably, 'pull through', firing double action. So, with due regard to safety, one can get off the first shot much quicker with a revolver than with an automatic.

In my opinion the bore should not be less than 0·32 inch or 9 mm. A light bullet may not stop your man unless you are a very good shot. A ·38 is better, and a ·38 magnum, which has an extra-heavy charge, best of all: it will send a man spinning even if it hits only his arm or leg. A ·45 is, to my mind, too large and heavy, especially if you want to carry it concealed. My own revolver, which I found satisfactory in every way, was a Colt ·38 Special (or magnum). Magnum revolvers pack a terrific wallop and were originally designed, I believe, for police use in the United States for shooting at gangsters' cars, because an ordinary revolver would not crack a car's water-jacket.

How should you carry it? Not, if you are a lady, in a handbag: this is the very worst place. You cannot draw it in a hurry, your handbag may be snatched or you

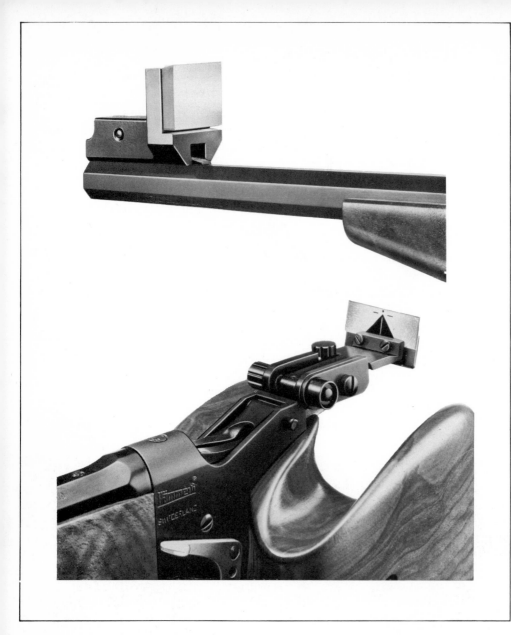

Fore and rear part
of the Reuss sight
(see page 249)

Opposite page
The target seen
over ordinary
pistol sights and
over the Reuss
sight

have not got it when you need it. Not in a pocket either: it spoils your suit, you cannot get a hand to it in a hurry; and when you try to pull it out, the hammer catches in the lining.

(To this, incidentally, a kinsman of mine owed his life. During one of the bad times in Ireland, while he was riding down the road, a man ran towards him tugging at a revolver in a pocket. The revolver caught in the lining, and Trench was able to fight the fellow off with his heavy hunting-crop. What infuriated him was that during the fracas a farmer strolled past: 'One of my own tenants, mind, and all the damn fellow said was, "Och, why can't you leave the poor gentleman alone?"' Although on this occasion caught unarmed, 'Townie' Trench was himself a dead shot, addicted to potting at trees and bushes as he drove around. Asked if he was not afraid of being ambushed, he replied simply, 'Not a bit. They know that if they hit me, they'll get a far worse landlord; and if they miss me, God help 'em!')

A holster attached to the belt is better, if you do not mind it being seen: it should, if you are right-handed, be on the left side, butt to the front, conveniently placed for a 'cross draw'.

A holster slung low on the hip was the favourite place for the westerner's gun. Certainly it facilitates a very quick draw, but it has certain disadvantages in modern life. It is no use in a car, or sitting in a chair: indeed in either position it may, if the holster is an open one, fall out. I find it very inconvenient on a horse, since the gun always seems to work round between one's thigh and the saddle. Perhaps this did not happen with the westerner since he rode with a long stirrup leather and a straight, almost vertical leg.

By far the best place for the revolver is in a shoulder holster carried under the left armpit. The weight is taken by a broad strap over the left shoulder. The holster is held steady and in place by an elastic band and narrow strap across the back and round the right shoulder. Provided you are not bathing, the gun is invisible – often an important point – and does not spoil the appearance of a coat. Since the left arm prevents the revolver from slipping out accidentally, the holster can safely be open, which is absolutely necessary for a quick draw, with or without a spring clip to hold the gun in place. Walking, riding, driving a car, sitting in an armchair or at a table – the gun can always be drawn in an instant. Only in a bath or in bed

Free pistol

need it ever be taken off, so you do not need to put it beside you when you are eating or writing at a desk, and are not made to look foolish when, after a convivial dinner, your host's servant enters the drawing-room bearing on a silver tray a selection of pistols and revolvers carelessly left on the dining table.

I do not now own a revolver, and I hope I shall never again be obliged to carry one around with me. It is such a responsibility and a *bore*. But if I am, it will be a ·38 Special or magnum revolver in a shoulder holster.

A revolver, if required at all, will probably be needed very quickly, at short range, against an enemy on the same level as yourself. For quick action – coming out of a house, say, to investigate something suspicious in the garden, or entering a dark hut where someone may be waiting behind the door – it should be held in front of the navel, the barrel horizontal and pointing straight to the front. Your body is in what Grant Taylor, the greatest expert of World War II (who shot the gangster, Dillinger), called the 'battle crouch'; this presents a smaller target to the enemy than an upright stance, and helps to hold the revolver butt firmly into the pit of the stomach. You 'aim' simply by facing your man, shoot (double-action) and hit him in the midriff. Holding the gun horizontal and pointing by turning the body is a trick very quickly learned. It gives you, up to about 10 yards, all the accuracy you need. At longer ranges it is better to adopt the ordinary straight-arm, target shooting position, use the sights, cock the hammer and fire single-action. At very long ranges, hold the revolver in both hands.

Normally one raises the gun to shoot. But on horseback when your gun is drawn you must carry it with the muzzle pointing to the sky, lest you inadvertently shoot your horse. If your horse is moving faster than a trot, you cannot really aim, but (so to speak) you chop down at the target and shoot. It is not difficult thus to hit a man-sized target at 15 yards.

248

Target shooting (except for competitions reserved for full-bore military pistols) is a very different matter. Here nothing counts but accuracy. A quick draw is unnecessary, because there is no one shooting back. A flat trajectory is irrelevant, because the exact range is known and sights are adjusted accordingly. Striking energy and penetration are of no account, for all that needs to be struck is a target, and all that must be penetrated is a piece of paper. So the competition pistol is a specialized weapon, not much use for any other purpose. The recipe for accuracy today as in the days of the duel is a heavy bullet and a light charge, giving the least possible recoil; so the target pistol fires a ·22 rim-fire cartridge. The butt is nothing like an ordinary pistol butt: it resembles a mould fitted round the hand, and may even be built to fit an individual owner, so designed that his grip for every shot is exactly the same because he *can* grip it only in one way. It has a hair-trigger, with a pressure so light that it would be highly dangerous in any other context; the action is smoother, quicker than in ordinary pistols, and less disturbing to the aim. To help in aiming, the foresight and backsight are as far apart as possible – the latter protruding from the rear of the pistol so that it is directly over the shooter's wrist.* The line of sight is as close as possible to the barrel. For its bore, it is a very heavy weapon, generally weighing from 1·0 to 1·3 kg (over 2 lb), with a centre of gravity over the middle finger. The butt is set at such an angle to the barrel that the recoil pushes

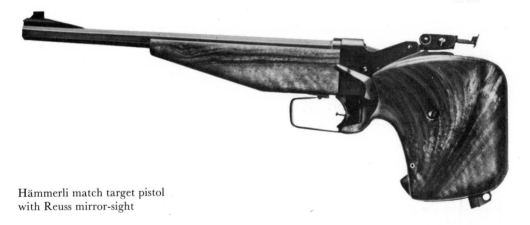

Hämmerli match target pistol
with Reuss mirror-sight

the weapon straight back, without tilting up the muzzle. The accuracy of such a pistol is, in the words of a German writer, 'absolute', any error is that of the marksman. A free pistol costs in England anything up to £157, and a standard pistol up to £122.

In international competitions there are two standard targets – an ordinary ten-ring round bull's-eye for slow fire competitions and a figure or silhouette target for rapid fire. The usual international competition ranges are 25 to 50 metres. (In Britain, 20 and 50 yards.)

* These remarks apply particularly to the 'free pistol'. In the 'standard pistol' the trigger pressure must not be less than 1,000 gr., the barrel length not more than 153 millimetres (6 inches), and the sights not more than 22 centimetres apart.

Pistol with attachable
butt and telescopic sight

It is not my purpose to pad this book with statistics, but particulars of one competition may be given to indicate the standard of accuracy now achieved with a modern ·22 free pistol by a first-class shot. The British Open Championship consists of 60 shots slow fire at 50 metres. The 1969 winner, J. P. Cooke, scored 555 out of 600 (93·5 per cent) at a standard ISU target with a bull's-eye of 2 inches diameter. At shorter ranges the scores are, of course, higher: for 20 shots at 20 yards, 188 (94 per cent) is a very good score, but nothing miraculous. In timed shoots, with four-, six- and eight-second exposures of a target at 50 metres, it is commonplace for several competitors in the Olympic Games to score 'possibles'.

I do not think any pistol shots of bygone days could achieve these scores, or anything like them. The modern marksman has the enormous advantage of perfectly designed and balanced weapons, and of unlimited practice with cheap ·22 ammunition.

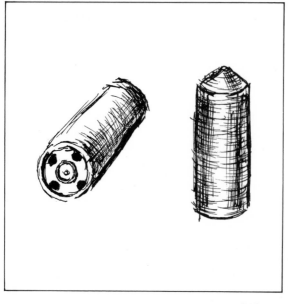

The jet-propelled pistol
bullet, a new and most formidable
projectile as it does not stop until
its fuel is exhausted

250

8

Modern Rifle Shooting

During the second half of the nineteenth century a succession of technical inventions enhanced immeasurably the deadlines of the rifle. The cylindro-ovoidal bullet improved its accuracy and doubled its effective military range. Various forms of breech-loader increased the rate of fire to about five rounds a minute, and repeating rifles brought this up to ten, fifteen, or twenty rounds a minute. The soft lead bullet was unsatisfactory, since it stripped in the rifling if the muzzle velocity was increased: but in 1883 Major Rubin, of the Swiss Army, produced the small calibre,* nickel- or copper-coated bullet which, because it did not strip like soft lead, could be fired at hitherto unimagined velocities – 1,800 or 2,000 feet per second. High velocity gives a flat trajectory, making it far easier to hit a man or an animal than with a low velocity, high trajectory weapon for which the range must be accurately judged. Finally, smokeless powder made it possible for a rifleman to fire many rounds in quick succession without either obscuring his target or giving away his position.

This is not a military history. It is enough baldly to state that the American Civil War, the Franco-Prussian War and the Boer War seemed to prove that the battle-field of the future would be dominated by, in succession, the breech-loading, repeating, and high-velocity rifle. (In the event, the reign of the rifle proved to be comparatively short: from 1915 onwards more lethal weapons were developed. But they are no concern of a history of marksmanship.)

As the effective range increased, range-judging became of capital importance and remained so throughout the wars of the nineteenth and early twentieth century. If, for instance, the Martini-Henry rifleman, aiming at the middle of a 6-foot Zulu standing 450 yards away, over-estimated the range and set his sights at 500 yards, his bullet would pass harmlessly overhead. The ·303 had a flatter trajectory, but the ranges at which it was commonly used in the Boer War were much longer, so range-judging was just as important: at 700 yards there was no more than 100 yards margin of error. It was not, of course, possible for every rifleman to carry a portable range-finder. Graticules on field-glasses and telescopes helped estimate range: a 6-foot man who filled the distance between two graticules would be *x* distance away. The same principle could be applied to various tubes or funnels – threads stretched across them, a fixed distance from the eye, subtended an angle corresponding to a man a certain distance away. But none of these were better, and most were less practical, than various rule-of-thumb methods of range-judging taught to recruits. For instance: 'At 600 yards the head is a dot, the body tapered; at 300 yards the face is blurred; at

---

* His original model was of 7·5 millimetres or 0·295 inch.

Inn sign in Alsace Lorraine

200 yards all parts of the body are distinctly seen.' The size of a man in relation to the foresight, or to the bore of the rifle, the bolt having been removed, was also a useful aid to judging distance, provided he was obliging enough to stand upright in full view.

Recruits were taught that distances were apt to be over-estimated when the enemy was lying or kneeling, or when he could not be seen clearly against the background; across valleys or over broken ground; along avenues, ravines, or long, straight roads; in shade, mist, or rising heat-waves. They were apt to be under-estimated when the sun was behind the marksman or when, owing to the clean atmosphere or the background, the target could be clearly seen; over level ground, snow, water, or (oddly enough) over a deep chasm; up or down hill. Practice and training in these weapons gave good results, but in the wars of the mid-twentieth century range-judging became less important: the trajectory of the rifle bullet was flat enough to hit a man up to 400 or 500 yards, and beyond that range (owing to the large number of light machine-guns) rifles were seldom used.

Jahangir taking aim

The Boer was a very fine marksman, and the best instructor the British Army ever had. Time and again British attacks over open ground withered before accurate, medium-range Mauser fire, skimming the surface of the veld from concealed trenches at the bottom of kopjes. In close fighting Boer snap-shooting was equally deadly: hundreds of British tommies were shot through the head as they peered over a parapet or round a rock. Up to 2,000 yards and more, Boer harassing fire proved painfully effective. In contrast, British musketry, based on disciplined volley-firing at charging hordes of Zulus or Fuzzy-Wuzzies, proved singularly useless.

The British Army learned its lesson. Even the cavalry were taught to regard the rifle, not the sword, as the principal weapon. Civilian marksmen and what might be

The beginnings of the modern rifle: its barrel and bullets

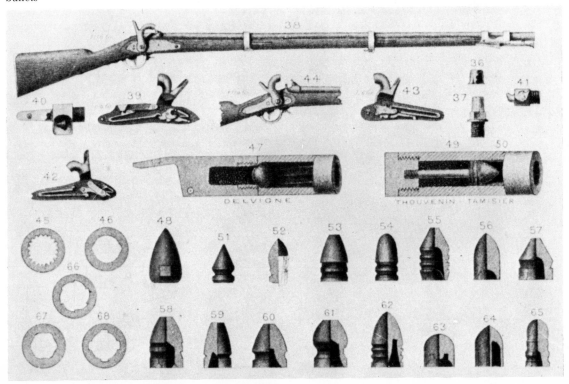

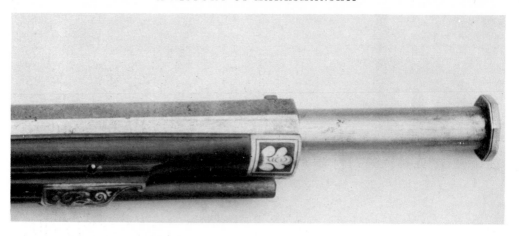

called the 'Bisley lobby' to some extent learned the wrong lesson. For instance T. F. Fremantle, a great authority on target shooting, wrote in 1901 that future battles would be fought at very long ranges, and that riflemen should be trained accordingly. The British military authorities, however, laid far more stress on rapid firing at short and medium ranges, up to 500 yards, a battle-winning tactic now for the first time made possible by the magazine rifle and smokeless powder. The opening months of the Great War showed that Fremantle was wrong; training in the 'mad minute', fifteen or twenty aimed shots in sixty seconds, alone saved the British Expeditionary Force and perhaps France itself from defeat before Christmas.

In trench warfare artillery, mortars, machine-guns, and grenades were far more useful than ordinary rifles in the hands of ordinary riflemen. But the specialized form of marksmanship known as 'sniping' was developed to an extraordinary degree during the next three and a half years, especially by certain German units who were acknowledged masters of the art.

Several novel features distinguished sniping in the Great War from other forms

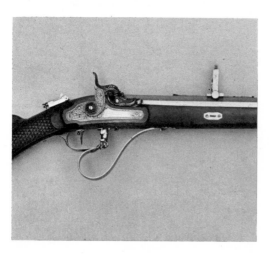

Top
Wheel-lock gun with rifled barrels fitting into each other. When the inner barrel, for small game is removed, the larger outer barrel could be used for big game. It has a twin-leaf sight and was made in 1653 in Salzburg by Cornelius Klatt

Sights of an Italian percussion gun of the 19th century

A double leaf sight. An unofficial modification to a
Martini-Henry of 1899 now in the School of Infantry
Museum

of marksmanship. The range was unknown, and no sighting-shots were allowed.
The target was very small – half a man's head, perhaps, the lens of a telescope, or the
water-jacket of a machine-gun which, if punctured, put the gun out of action as
effectively as a direct hit from a shell. The target was generally a fleeting one, and the
sniper had only a couple of seconds for his shot. Also, of course, the target was apt
to shoot back. This made sniping an extremely dangerous job, but also a fascinating
one: there was never any shortage of volunteers for sniping.

In the British Army circles there was a certain prejudice against sniping. In the
days of the long bow, of Brown Bess and of the ·303 Short Magazine Lee Enfield,
British battle tactics aimed at producing a beaten zone through which no enemy
could pass. A beaten zone depended on rapidity of fire rather than accuracy: indeed
too much accuracy would defeat its own purpose, since it would produce not a zone
at all, but hundreds of arrows or bullets wastefully striking the same spot. The crossbowman, the Kentucky rifleman and the sniper represent another military tradition,
another battlefield tactic – not the arrow hail, the volley or the beaten zone, but a
single shaft or bullet, loaded at leisure and discharged with great accuracy.

But in the early months of trench warfare German snipers had to be taken
seriously. They shot hundreds of British and French soldiers and, especially, officers,
and in some sectors gave their side a superiority which was very marked.

The German Army, especially the Saxon divisions, included many Jägers,

An early leaf sight

Opposite
Note the long coiled match used by this
Tartar huntsman depicted in a scroll
painting in the British Museum

professional foresters, keepers and no doubt poachers from the Kaiser's own shooting preserves in the Rominten and Hubertusstock districts, and other great game preserves. Such men were trained by a lifetime's experience in stalking, camouflage, and quick snap-shots at fleeting targets glimpsed momentarily through the undergrowth. The British Army, too, had its expert marksmen: the Lovat Scouts was full of them, and others were to be found in Canadian and Australian units. But the professional expertise of forest Jägers was more relevant than the art of the highland deer-stalker to front-line sniping.

Moreover, from the very beginning the Germans realized the value of telescopic sights. This is a very old invention, first suggested in *Magisterium nature et artis opus physical mathematicum*, written by the Jesuit Father Francesco Lana in 1684. In 1702 it is described more exactly in *Oculus artificialis teledioptricus sive telescopium* by Johannus Zahn. It does not seem then to have been put to much practical use: presumably the rifle of that date was not accurate enough to justify such a precise sight. But in the American Civil War a few Southern sharpshooters used Whitworth rifles, fitted with telescopic sights, imported from Britain; and American hunters were interested in the device. In 1880 August Fiedler, Chief Game Warden of Prince Reuss IV of Riesengebirge, developed a telescopic sight, adjustable laterally and vertically, which gave his royal master the reputation of a miraculous shot. He made similar sights for the Duke of Pless, Prince Solms-Baruth, and a few other fortunate sportsmen; but he never patented or commercialized his invention, and none of his sights

The acme of marksmanship is shooting at a target
which can shoot back; thus the sniper must be the
marksman *par excellence*. Here is one positioned
(Hawkins's position) under a camouflaging robe eight
yards from the camera

seem to have survived. Another amateur telescopic-sight maker, of the same period, was a wealthy dilettante of Charlottenburg, Eugen von Turnov.

In 1887 Lieutenant von Bülow Marconay, then a student at the Staff College, submitted to the Prussian military authorities his own telescopic sight. A special commission reported on it as 'a good invention, unsuitable for field work but good for fortress work'. Bülow was commended for his zeal, awarded a medal in 1890 and told to do what he liked with his device. During the 1890s various German sportsmen and game wardens built their own sights with telescopes supplied by Voigt-länder, and by the beginning of the twentieth century telescopic sights were being produced commercially in large numbers.

The telescopic sight has certain drawbacks. It is a delicate instrument, easily upset by a sharp knock and misted over in damp weather. It upsets the balance of a rifle, making it rather top-heavy, so that it cannot easily be used, like a shotgun, for an instinctive shot at a running animal. It requires frequent checking and adjustment by a skilled artificer. It should never be fitted to a rifle used for hand-to-hand fighting, and is rather wasted on the ordinary soldier. Its purpose is not so much to facilitate long-distance aiming, as to define clearly, in a bad light, in camouflage or in thick bush, a small and obscure target. It is, therefore, the ideal sight for a sniper, whose chief need is to define his target and who never has to fight hand-to-hand or to swing his rifle like a shotgun.

It is, therefore, not surprising that in 1914, largely through the initiative of the Duke of Ratisbon, the German Army had about 20,000 of these sights, together with the sporting rifles to which they were fitted, Jägers experienced in their use, and artificers skilled at adjusting and serving them.

The Saxon Jäger was not merely a very fine short- and medium-range snap-shot: he was an expert at camouflage, an art of which his officers (long before their British and French enemies) appreciated the value. In 1914 and early 1915 the typical British trench was neatly built of sandbags identical in size, shape, and colour, levelled off on top, laid as symmetrically as bricks or concrete blocks, provided with loopholes as obvious as gaps in a row of teeth. No one could peer over or through this without being seen and probably shot. The typical German trench was a jumble of multi-coloured sandbags, corrugated iron sheets, coils of rusty wire, timber, stones and miscellaneous rubbish, in which snipers and observers were far more easily hidden. Moreover, the sniper, as often as not, was not in the trench at all but behind it, or in no-man's-land, lying in a shallow trough scooped in a field of turnips, or among a tangle of brambles, or even behind a corpse – camouflaged, seeing all, but himself invisible, motionless and deadly. As he fired perhaps only half a dozen shots a day, and these produced no smoke but only, in the early morning, a very slight, misty shimmer of the cold air, he was extraordinarily hard to detect.

An advertisement in a Viennese newspaper for a Reichert telescopic sight attached to the Mannlicher rifle claims that with it Rittmeister von Fark shot 63 Russians *in one day*, and Private Herrenreiter, from an arboreal hide, shot 121 Frenchmen. One cannot escape the suspicion that the Rittmeister and the private were remembering 'with advantages what feats they did', but there certainly was in 1915 a plague of head wounds in the French, Russian, and British armies, and almost a collapse of morale in certain sectors where it was tantamount to suicide to peer for a moment over the parapet or through a loophole.

An eye-glass mounted on the butt of a gun made for
King Frederick of Denmark is perhaps one of
the earliest optical sights.

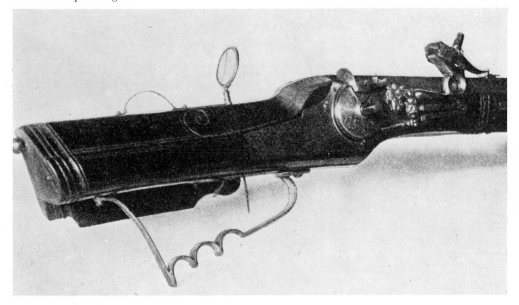

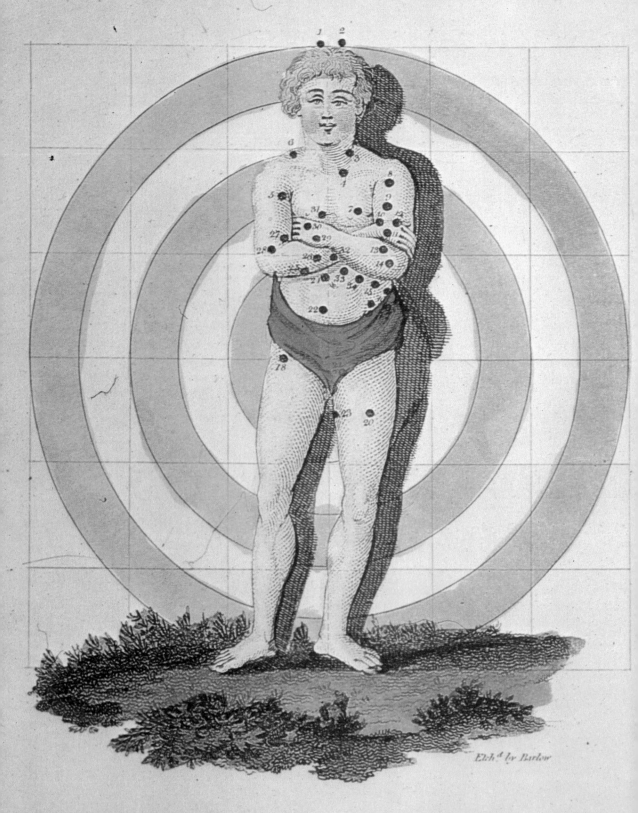

Rifle Made and Shot by Ezekiel Baker.

Opposite page
Ezekiel Baker's target
on which he registered
34 shots at 100 yards
with a rifle made
by himself (1821)

Two of the hunting
targets used by the
German Sporting Association

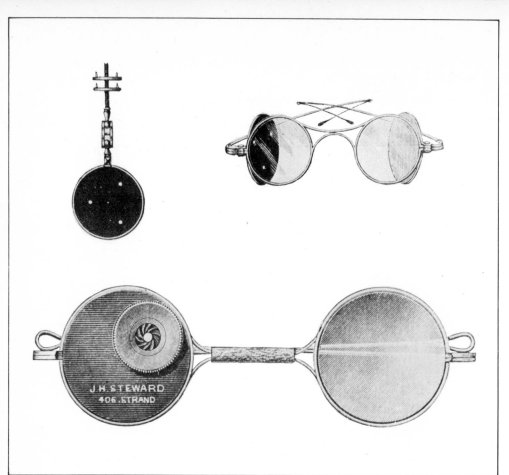

Optical aids

Opposite page top
A British army
rifle of World
War I equipped
with telescopic
sight

Bottom
Telescopic sight of
1904. (Zeiss 2)

Eventually, as in most wars, the British learned the lesson, but they never quite matched the Jägers at this murderous game, largely because they never had enough private rifles and telescopic sights, but had to rely on the ·303 Pattern '14 or Ross (Canadian service) rifle, of which too few were fitted with telescopic sights.

After 1918 there was in all armies less emphasis on accurate marksmanship and more on automatic weapons. Like most keen riflemen, I think this was a pity. I was shocked, in the 1939–45 war, by the poor rifle-shooting on both sides, and remain convinced that, even now, when every infantry soldier carries a semi-automatic rifle which is virtually a machine-gun, the training of a few expert individuals to meticulous, single-shot accuracy would be well worth while. Nobody who has seen a good rifleman at work, firing shot after shot into a 15-inch bull at 600 yards, can doubt this.

There are five basic positions, each with many variations, for rifle shooting: lying on the stomach, lying on the back, kneeling, sitting, and standing. The favourite position for English target riflemen, the one at which they practise most, almost to the exclusion of other positions, is lying on the stomach, known in military jargon as the 'prone position' and on the Continent as the 'English position'. This is rather strange, for English marksmanship in Victorian times was essentially

amateur-military in character, being a product of the Volunteer movement; and in the early years of the National Rifle Association soldiers, whether in the 'thin red line' or the British square, usually fired standing or kneeling, ready if necessary to use their bayonets – not lying down. Indeed the prone position was seldom used until improvements in firearms made it really rather dangerous to stand up in battle. One likes to think that these Dundreary-whiskered enthusiasts, preparing themselves every Saturday for the Battle of Dorking Gap, had a sounder idea of military realities than had the Duke of Cambridge. The truth, however, is probably that their style of shooting was based, consciously or not, on deer-stalking in the highlands, in which most shots are taken from the prone position.

In this the rifleman lies flat on his stomach, his body more or less oblique to the line of fire with the left shoulder forward. Reason suggests that the body is steadier if the legs are wide apart, providing a broader base: but some riflemen lie with the legs together, some even with the legs crossed. In the classic prone position, as taught by musketry instructors in the nineteenth century, the left elbow is directly

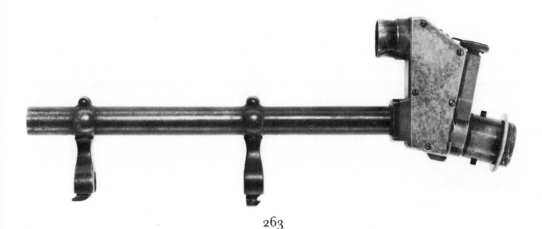

263

Long barrels lend accuracy

The long eastern rifle
with its bipod stand

under the rifle, the left hand holding the fore-end as far forward as possible. Some modern marksmen spread the elbows, so that the forearms viewed from in front, form an inverted V. Snipers sometimes, to reduce the target they offer, spread the elbows so wide that the rifle is only 2 or 3 inches off the ground.

The prone position is undoubtedly the steadiest, since both elbows and the whole body are supported. It is also the safest, since it presents a small target to the enemy. But it has certain drawbacks. A soldier advancing on the enemy or a sportsman stalking through the bush loses time if, on sighting the target, he flings himself to the ground before taking a shot. You cannot easily, in the prone position, swing through a moving target. Most important, you cannot see the target over grass a few inches high.

Nearly as good for accuracy is the sitting position, with both elbows resting on the raised knees. This is a very steady position, especially useful for shooting down-hill. It is much favoured by sportsmen, especially by stalkers who generally try to get above their quarry. It is good for shooting at a moving target, and generally used by competitors in the Running Deer competition. But the British and other military authorities have strangely neglected it. Perhaps this was due to the fact that a rank, in square, of men sitting on their bottoms would not present to a charge of cavalry such a formidable hedge of bayonets as a rank of kneeling men. Colonel Fremantle suggested also that a man in this position took up too much room in close order; his bayonet got in the way, and finally, a matter of some importance, muddy ground dirtied his trousers.

The magnifying foresight was another device that was tried. After a gunmaker's catalogue of fifty years ago

More martial in appearance, but less steady for shooting, is the kneeling position, with the marksman's bottom resting on his right heel, his left elbow or upper arm supported by the raised left knee. Cavalry men never liked it, because of the risk of tearing one's breeches or impaling oneself on a spur.

There is the back position, with many variations, used for long-distance shooting, at distances over 1,000 yards, with a match rifle fitted with an orthoptic (aperture) sight fitted to the heel of the butt. The rifleman lies on his back, his eye applied to the sight, the barrel of the rifle resting on his knee or thigh: some men use the left hand to steady the rifle, others to steady their own heads.

Finally there is the controversial standing position – or, rather, positions. The orthodox version, taught in the British and other armies, is exactly the same as that used for shooting at a low bird or ground game with a shotgun – feet comfortably spread and oblique to the line of fire, weight evenly distributed between them, left shoulder forward, left elbow under the rifle with the hand holding it well forward to support its weight. It is, perhaps, a position derived from that of the arquebusier shooting with his weapon supported by a forked stick. It looks businesslike, and is well adapted for shooting at a moving target.

It is not, however, as good as it looks. In the first place the left arm which bears almost the whole weight of the rifle (which is much heavier than a shotgun) is un-

The most modern telescopic sight mounted on a double-barrelled sporting rifle

supported save by the shooter's muscular power. To remedy this some riflemen, particularly Swiss and Scandinavians who have a tradition and reputation for marksmanship, support the rifle with the left hand by holding it as far back as possible, just in front of the trigger-guard, so that the upper arm presses against and is steadied by the shooter's chest. Particularly long-armed, bony individuals can even obtain additional support by resting the elbow on the left hip, which is thus thrust forward to receive it. To facilitate this position, continental rifles were fitted with a special handle, adjustable in length, projecting downwards from the fore-end in front of the trigger-guard and terminating in a rounded disc which could be conveniently grasped by the left hand. Additional steadiness was sometimes gained by

A telescopic sight with clip mountings

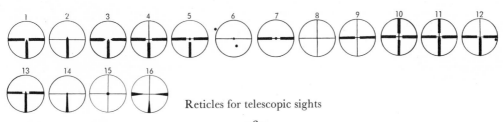

Reticles for telescopic sights

267

Preceding page
Moghul Emperor shooting lion from the back of an elephant. Note the large number of loaders with spare guns, for loading muzzle-loaders is a lengthy process. Lions were quite plentiful in India up to comparatively recently

Rear sights of (*a*) a Lancaster oval-bored percussion rifle of 1854, (*b*) experimental sight on an 1854 Brunswick, and (*c*) a Lee-Enfield No. 1 of 1933

projections from the heel and toe of the butt which fitted like a crutch around the right upper arm close to the shoulder.

English marksmen, and many Americans, deprecated any deviation from orthodoxy which the 'foreign position' encouraged – 'irregular devices for obtaining additional steadiness, such as padding the chest out under the coat, supporting the rifle under the trigger-guard with the tips of the fingers etc. They are difficult to prevent, but quite undesirable, but they are freely resorted to, both on the Continent and elsewhere, where the conditions allow.' At Wimbledon and Bisley the conditions did not allow these: National Rifle Association rules laid down that the whole of the left hand must be in front of the trigger-guard. In *The Royal Rifle Match*, by a Dr Scoffern, written about 1860, a Swiss competitor at Wimbledon is thus described:

'The anxious moments of firing are now come round. See how the Switzer employs them. He begins by planting his legs wide apart; left leg foremost. He tries the ground under him for a moment or so, to find whether it be soft; and if he can wriggle out two little graves, one for each foot, the better. Should you have turned away your eye for a moment, and then direct your glance at the Switzer again, you will have found him half as big again as he was when you last saw him. He has puffed himself out with a deep breathing, like the frog who aspired to become a bull. By this deep inspiration, the Switzer has stiffened himself, just after the way one takes the limpness out of a Macintosh cushion – by filling it full of wind. The Switzer is firm planted and rigid now; he could no more bend from side to side than a hard-rammed sausage. If he were obliged to hold his wind as long as we take to tell our tale, it would be bad for him. He would burst outright, like an overcharged rifle. Well! with legs apart – like a little Rhodian Colossus, and bated breath – the Switzer shoulders his piece. At the end of the stock is a boss, which he tucks between the right arm and right ribs. Gathering his two hands close together, he rests his rifle on the left hand, placed close in front of the trigger guard; pressing his left elbow, not on the left knee, indeed – but upon the left hip. Lot's wife could hardly be more rigid. Limited power of motion, nevertheless, the Switzer has. Heavenward you see his rifle pointing, and if you observe the Switzer's nose – that organ, only given for ornament, as some affirm – it is turned to a purpose of utility. The Switzer is steadying the butt end of his rifle against it. His nose is a lateral rest. By this time that nose is red on the tip, the face turgid, the eyes projecting. The Switzer's whole position is decidedly not graceful – one very suggestive of extrusion. Heavenward you see the rifle pointing. Gradually down and down it droops. The blank is seen, the trigger pressed. Rifle crack and Switzer's grunt follow on the heels of each other. He could not hold his breath for ever. Picket and imprisoned breath both fly off together. Behold him now panting and puffing like a Cinghalese pearl-diver, fresh from the worrying of a ground-shark.'

The sling, originally intended only to help carry the musket, was found to have other uses. Volunteers preparing to resist Napoleon's invasion found that when the marksman lay on his back to shoot, he could put his foot through the sling, thus rendering innocuous the Baker rifle's heavy recoil. In the standing position some daring experimenters supported the rifle's weight by twining the sling round their necks; others steadied the rifle by standing on the sling. Modern practice is to twist

Buffalo hunting
on the Great Plains,
from a water-colour
by William Hind

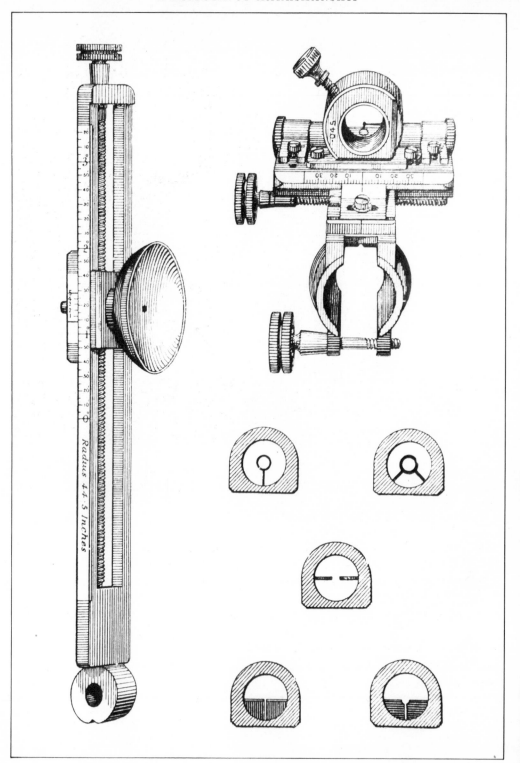

Opposite page
The early modern
aperture sight

Vertical and lateral
drums for the No. 4
rifle

the sling tightly round the left forearm and upper-arm. Properly adjusted, it fairly clamps the weapon in place, and adds perhaps 15 per cent to one's score.

In the opinion of the Island Race, which rather fancied its marksmanship, any form of 'off-hand' shooting* was to be deprecated, and the 'foreign position' was the worst of all, since it was of little use for quick snap-shots and for shooting at a moving target. God intended man to shoot either lying on his tummy or sitting on his bum, as Queen Victoria's volunteers proceeded in the latter part of her reign to show.

In America and on the Continent marksmanship was the by-product of big-game hunting. The American sharpshooter and the German sniper were, essentially, hunters who applied their talents and experience to war. In Britain there is very little for the rifleman to hunt, and rifle-marksmanship was clearly linked to the Volunteer movement. During the Napoleonic Wars, scores of rifle units were formed, composed mainly of middle-class patriots who experimented enthusiastically, and largely at their own expense, with various versions of the Baker rifle. After the peace, many of these units survived as Rifle Clubs: and in 1859, under the spur of a new French

* The American term for shooting from a standing position.

275

Shooting wild boar
by J. Vetz. Using
muzzle-loaders,
the shooters required
spare rifles

invasion threat, the Volunteer spirit revived, and with it a renewed interest in marksmanship. In 1860 there was held at Wimbledon the first annual meeting of the National Rifle Association. Swiss marksmen, then the acknowledged experts at the game, attended as guests; and the opening round was fired by Queen Victoria herself, with a long silken cord, from a Whitworth rifle secured in a vice and steadied by enormous weights.

The renewed interest in rifle-shooting came at a time when the rifle was improving rapidly in accuracy.

A rifleman of 1800, armed with a weapon rather more accurate than the service Baker rifle, could shoot consistently into a 12-inch circle at 150 yards and into an 18-inch circle at 200 yards. The Minié conical bullet and its successors enabled mid-century marksmen to shoot far more accurately. Lancaster, the well-known gunmaker, 'shot a match last year [1845] for Mr Graham at 300 yards, firing from the shoulder without a rest, he backing me to hit a bull's-eye 8 inches diameter six time out of nine. I hit it six times following, and averaged three bull's-eyes in five shots during the last forty-five rounds. In fact, I have done more at 300 yards with the cone than I ever did or saw done at 200 yards with the spherical ball.'

Several types of target marksmanship developed during the nineteenth century and are still practised.

First, there are competitions confined to the ordinary military rifle as issued to the ordinary soldier. Depending on military practices of the day, the sights may be open or aperture, fixed or capable of lateral adjustment for wind; a sling may or may not be used. The point is that the practices should as nearly as possible approximate to the conditions of contemporary warfare. Standing, kneeling, and prone positions are all used, the range may be from 200 to 600 yards, or whatever is currently considered to be the maximum effective range of the rifle in war. Fire and movement may be combined, the rifleman shooting one practice at, say, 300 yards

General Fulton's position

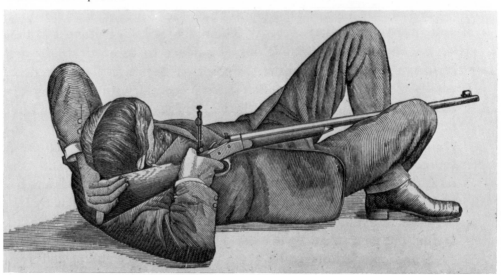

The Parker Hale
5E aperture sight

and then doubling forward to shoot another at 200 yards. Practices may be application, rapid, snap, or a combination of all three. The competitor is generally allowed two sighting-shots.

In an application practice, the competitor simply fires a certain number of rounds, commonly seven or ten, in his own time, at a stationary target. The value and position of each shot is marked, so that he can if necessary adjust his sights or his aim for the next one. It is the easiest practice. With, say, a 4-inch bull at 200 yards, open sights and no sling (the conditions for service rifle (b) competitions at Bisley in the 1930s) any score over 90 per cent would be regarded as pretty good.

In snap-shooting competitions the target, generally the size and shape of a man, head and shoulders or from the waist up, stays in position for a fixed time, say three seconds, and then disappears. There are commonly seven or ten exposures, and a shot must be taken at each exposure. Hits are generally not indicated, so the firer has no idea whether or not he has made the right allowance for wind, unless he is clever at judging his shots from the earth they throw up on the butts.

Finally, and always rated very high in the British Army, is the rapid practice. Details naturally vary according to the type of rifle in use. With the ·303 Lee-Enfield which, modified from time to time in minor details, was the British Army rifle for some sixty years, the standard rapid practice was fifteen aimed rounds a minute. An expert could fire nearly twice as many – his rifle remaining at the shoulders, in the aim, his right hand working the bolt with the regularity of a fast-moving machine.

279

Shooting pigeon from a hide

In the rapid practice, scores tend to be slightly lower than in the application: snap-shooting scores are generally a bit higher, because of the larger bull or the figure target. In both rapid and snap practices the shooter is at a disadvantage because, individual hits not being indicated, he may make a close group of shots, all to one side of the bull, with no hint that he should adjust his sights or change his point of aim.

Closer still to military reality is the field firing competition, in which figure targets, fixed or disappearing, half-concealed or in the open, are placed at various ranges which the competitor must judge, as he must judge the wind, without sighting shots. This is a speciality of the Scandinavian countries, and in Sweden there is a sort of standardized field firing range with targets scattered over the area at eight

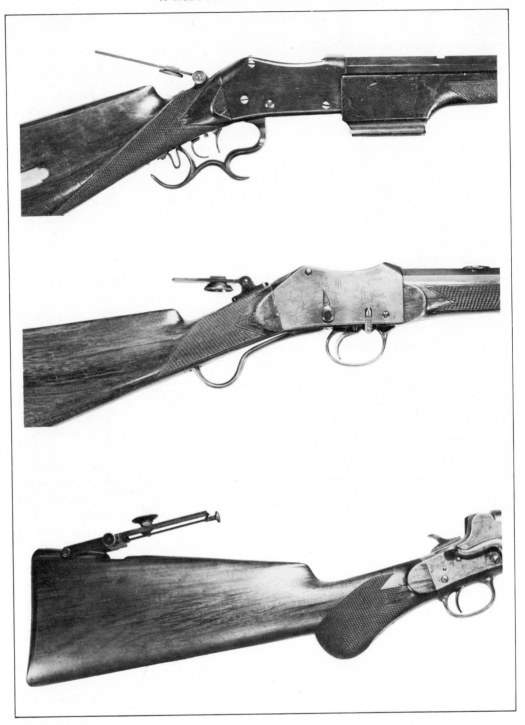

Match rifle sights

different ranges from 145 to 425 metres, giving first-class practice in military or sporting marksmanship, combined sometimes with ski-ing.

Some competitions are confined to sporting rifles, at sporting ranges (seldom more than 200 yards) and at sporting targets, representing a running deer or other animals. For a moving target the sitting position is preferred, for from it one can swing through the target, as with a shotgun.

In Britain, the Commonwealth, and the United States the most popular form of full-bore competitive shooting was with the current service rifle, or something approximating to it, assisted by a sling and an aperture sight with very fine adjustments. Now the armies of most advanced countries use automatic rifles, not markedly accurate: so in this type of shooting special heavy barrelled target or snipers' rifles are used. By National Rifle Association rules the rifle must fire the 7·62 mm cartridge and weigh not more than 11½ lbs. It may have any military type action, the Mauser being most popular, and any iron – not telescopic – sight, aperture backsights and ring foresights being generally used. The stock must not have a thumb-hole. Until recently this form of marksmanship was known in Britain as S.R.* (b), a term which for convenience will be used in subsequent pages. In these competitions only application practices are shot, from the prone position, generally at 200, 300, 500, 600, 900 and 1,000 yards. With the aid of the sling and aperture sight, with a couple of sighting-shots and a telescope to view the mirage, one should score 2 or 3 per cent more than with the ordinary service rifle: that is to say, a score of 48 out of 50 is creditable: 'possibles' are not unusual. To my mind this is the most fascinating form of target-shooting: one can achieve a very high standard of accuracy without grossly artificial aids. When I was up at Oxford my chief ambition was to win the King's Prize. I never came anywhere near it.

The term 'Match Rifle shooting' is reserved in English-speaking countries for shooting with special long-range rifles, not as a rule of government pattern, at ranges of not less than 900 yards. For some riflemen this has a sophisticated fascination which they can find in no other form of marksmanship. Any artificial aid can be used, including telescopic sights. The back position is often used, with a finely adjustable aperture backsight fixed to the heel of the butt, an aperture foresight and sometimes a built-in spirit-level to ensure that the sights are accurate, for at these long ranges canted sights would send the bullet yards off target; or the normal prone position. All these scientific aids are essential to accuracy, but the art of wind-judging, in which no scientific aids are of much use, is of capital importance, for a stray puff of wind at a long range can frustrate the most exact aim. Wind-judging is also peculiarly difficult, for the wind at the butts may be quite different from the wind near the target, and the bullet's high trajectory takes it well above the surface winds, which are shown by the mirage. Nevertheless, in good conditions very remarkable results can be obtained, such as the Victorian records of 37 successive shots in the 36-inch bull at 1,000 yards, or 18 out of 20 shots in a 12-foot × 9-foot target at 2,000. This form of shooting is of great interest to ballistic experts, who try out such inventions as streamlined bullets at these long ranges. For this reason, since 1921 in Britain Match Rifle competitions have been restricted to weapons of the current military bore.

* Service Rifle.

Goya's *3rd May 1808*

Man is the target again, but here he cannot shoot back
(from J. Callot's *Les Misères de la guerre*)

A development of great importance took place in 1854 – the grant to Sir Joseph Whitworth of a government subsidy for his experiments in improving the muzzle-loading Enfield. He reduced its bore from ·577 to ·450 inch, and gave it a longer bullet than the Enfield's, of the same weight, with spiral grooves to fit the lands of the rifling. It was, despite its high trajectory, a very accurate weapon: there are official records of it making twenty-shot groups of 6½ inches at 500 yards and 21 inches at 1,000 yards. In 1865 Victorian marksmen competed even at 2,000 yards: the target was a large one, 12 × 24 feet, and at this range fourteen hits out of twenty-five shots was thought a good score; but a generation earlier 400 yards had been about the maximum range of a rifle, and a century later 2,000 yards was still a very long shot.

This was the rifle chiefly used in the early years of the National Rifle Association in 800, 900, and 1,000 yards competitions, at a 36-inch bull, the competitor usually lying on his back to shoot. It performed better than rival muzzle-loaders, of which the best was the Rigby, and was immeasurably more accurate than the breech-loaders of the day, largely because the barrel was cleansed of powder-fouling by the action of ramming down the wad to re-load, a practice which in the early years of the N.R.A. was deprecated for breech-loading rifles because it was thought, quite rightly, that the weapon's virtue of rapidity in loading would be nullified if it was cleaned out after every shot. The new rifle raised what might be called an average winning score from about 50 per cent with the Enfield in 1861–2, to about 84 per cent with the Whitworth in 1862–73.* In the mid-seventies the Whitworth muzzle-loader was superseded as a long-range match rifle by various privately made weapons with flatter trajectories which raised the average winning score to about 92 per cent where it remains to this day, for there has been very little improvement in the long-range accuracy of match rifles: the wind is something which can neither be estimated nor circumvented by the marvels of modern science.

* All statistics in this and the following pages are compiled from the scores of winners of the principal N.R.A. individual competitions, viz. the Queen's (or King's) Prize for service rifles and the Albert for match rifles. The bull at 800–1,100 yards was 36 inches until 1936, when it was reduced to 30 inches. The bull at other ranges varied as rifles increased in accuracy. Only the size of the 200-yard bull is quoted: at 300, 500 and 600 yards it was larger roughly in proportion. Queen's (King's) Prize competitors are not concerned with the dimensions of inner, magpie, and outer.

Meanwhile at medium ranges (200–600 yards) there had been a steady improvement in accuracy as better rifles were introduced. Comparisons are easy because from the earliest years of the N.R.A. until the end of the century the bull at 200 yards was an 8-inch circle, and proportional at the longer ranges. With the Enfield muzzle-loader (1862–70) a score of 80 per cent would have a good chance of winning the Queen's Prize. But its conversion to a breech-loader, known as Snider (1871–7) raised this to about 85 per cent provided the barrel was cleaned after each shot, which was permitted in the seventies. The Martini-Henry had a longer run, from 1878 to 1896. It was a very accurate rifle up to 900 yards, but at 1,000 yards its performance was unsatisfactory so this practice was omitted from the Queen's Prize competition, which a Martini-Henry user might hope to win with a 93 per cent score.

For some time the advantages of a high-velocity rifle with a flat trajectory and smokeless powder escaped the comprehension of the British military authorities; but fourteen years after Major Rubin's historic invention of the nickel- or copper-coated bullet, the British Army received its first issue of the ·303 magazine rifle which,

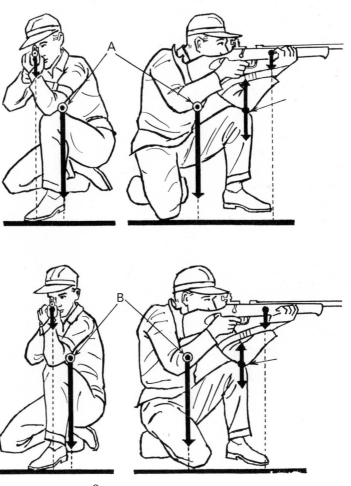

Kneeling position
and its distribution
of weight

287

Shooting deer from a high seat. Note the way the left
arm is being steadied on the frame

The kneeling position, using a sling

with minor changes, was to remain its basic infantry weapon for over half a century.

The long Lee-Enfield and the Lee-Metford were the standard rifles at Bisley from 1897 to 1914. They were very similar, except that they had a slightly different rifling; both had a V-backsight and a barleycorn foresight. On the whole the former was believed to be slightly more accurate, but there was little to choose between them.

They were considerably more accurate than the Martini-Henry, and although in 1900 the bull was reduced to 7 inches, the average winning scores rose to about 96·5 per cent.

The development of British competitive shooting has been described not because it was better than in other countries, but because for the present writer the statistics are more easily available. After the appearance of the Swiss at the early N.R.A. meetings, Victorian riflemen competed very seldom with foreign and Empire teams. From Americans in the seventies they learned the advantages of a team coach for wind-judging and of cleaning the barrel of a breech-loader after every shot, but thereafter they encountered no foreign opposition and simply assumed they were the world's best shots, except of course in the continental style of 'off-hand' shooting which they despised as of no military use and did not practise.

But in 1907 a British team competed in the United States, Canada, Australia, and New Zealand, not at off-hand shooting but in practices to which they were accustomed, and was soundly beaten, especially by the Americans. The reason, they decided, was not merely that the Americans had in the Krags Jørgensen a more accurate rifle, but that they used the aperture sight.* Very promptly this was introduced at Bisley, and though the 200-yard bull was reduced in 1907 to 6 inches,

* See pp. 196–7

The seated position at Bisley, 1970

the average winning score was raised to about 98 per cent. They were still, however, at a disadvantage competing against the Americans who used special ammunition in match-shooting and whose next service rifle, the Springfield, was the most accurate weapon of the day.

The highest accuracy was achieved in British target-shooting in the years 1911–14 with the long Lee-Enfield or Lee-Metford and the round-nosed, Mark VI ammunition. With the bull reduced to 5 inches, it still needed a score of at least 98 per cent to have much chance of winning the medium range practices for the King's Prize.

The extreme accuracy of the pre-1914 rifle is illustrated by the practice, popular in the United States, of 'making a fine target' with the aid of a solid rest for the rifle, a telescopic sight and every possible artificial aid. At 200 yards it was considered 'brilliant shooting' to place ten consecutive shots into the circle which on the standard American target scored 11 and was of 2·33 inches in diameter, and the same number in the 10 circle (3·36 inches in diameter) was 'very fine work'.

As for the rifleman, if Staff-Sergeant Wallingford, the best shot in Edward VII's army, were to bring his trusty long Lee-Enfield ·303 to Bisley or Ottawa today, he would be a formidable competitor, perfectly capable in the prone position of

putting ten consecutive shots into the bull at 200, 500, or 600 yards. For since his day rifles have not improved in accuracy. Indeed it is generally conceded that the Lee-Metford and the long Lee-Enfield, firing the round-nosed Mark VI ammunition, and the Canadian service rifle, the heavy-barrelled Ross, which were used at Bisley before 1914, were more accurate target rifles than the short Lee-Enfield and Mark VII (pointed) ammunition subsequently used. The military mind in all countries has concentrated on faster, not straighter shooting, on the 'Old Contemptible' 'mad minute' or on automatic and self-loading weapons.

Wallingford would, however, still find himself at sea, as he did in 1899, competing against continental marksmen. In that year a N.R.A. team competed for the first time in an international match on the Continent, against riflemen who shot only at one range, 300 metres, but in three positions, standing, kneeling, and prone – whereas British marksmen shot at many ranges but only in the prone position. The bull, they were pained to discover, was a mere 10 centimetres (3·9 inches) in diameter.

These foreigners used a ludicrously light trigger-pressure, instead of the 6-lb pressure enjoined by the N.R.A. The scores speak for themselves and testify to the vast superiority of the foreign methods in shooting off-hand. The best British shot

The method of holding his rifle and position adopted by the Swiss marksman (see page 271)

won the prize for shooting in the prone position: his overall score was lower than the average score in the winning team.

Name of country	Standing	Kneeling	Prone	Grand total
Switzerland	1,426	1,559·875	1,543	4,528·875*
France	1,403	1,449	1,552·175	4,404·175
Denmark	1,367·90	1,490	1,533	4,390·90
Italy	1,281	1,455·45	1,577·45	4,313·90
Holland	1,316·650	1,442·350	1,518	4,277
Norway	1,384·075	1,365·125	1,395·450	4,144·650
Great Britain	1,138·70	1,449·65	1,541	4,129·35
Belgium	1,292·700	1,360·65	1,474·525	4,127·875

The N.R.A.'s official representative wrote a rather sour report on the contest:

'Many of the other teams used for the standing position at least – most of them for all positions – fancy rifles of great weight, with "set" or "hair" triggers, which give, as compared with a heavier pull-off, a great advantage in standing and some in kneeling. These rifles were in many cases fitted with elaborate practical devices to assist the grasp of the rifle. When military rifles were used the pull-off had been specially arranged so as to require a pressure of 2 lbs. or less; the pull-off of the Lee-Metford, though reduction was effected so far as possible by extemporised means, could not be brought below 4 lbs.

'The great number of shots fired in the match, 30 sighters and 120 shots in competi-

* The decimal points are due to a peculiar system of penalizing misses.

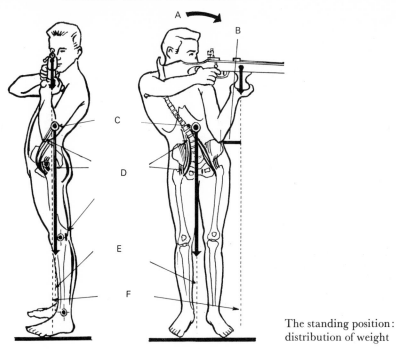

The standing position:
distribution of weight

tion per man, proved unexpectedly fatiguing, and much increased the disadvantages due to heavy pull of trigger, etc. Few of our men can give the requisite time or obtain sufficient accommodation on their ranges to accustom themselves to fire so many shots in the day with due care and deliberation.

'The only distance fired at in all the rifle competitions of the Dutch meeting was 300 metres (about 328 yards), and it appeared that one at least of the teams had not had occasion to fire all the season except at the particular distance and target used in the match.

'It must, however, be admitted, after making all these allowances, that the shooting of our team was not up to the foreign standard. Far more attention is given to the cultivation of the standing position abroad, while our system of shooting imposes upon no one the strain of firing a long series of shots standing in any important competition.

'The International Match, as at present arranged, must be considered unsatis-factory as not conforming to practical or military requirements. Thus, the innermost circle of the bull's-eye (4 inches in diameter*) and the width of the 2-inch rings into which it and the rest of the target are divided, are so minute as to be beyond the accuracy of the rifle at 300 metres. In the kneeling positions cushions and supports for leg and foot are allowed, and your delegates were only able to get the position so far restricted as that both knee and foot should touch the ground. The couches provided for lying down were narrow and placed at a steep slope to suit the crooked stocks generally used, and special permission had to be asked for the British team

* Actually 10 centimetres or 3·9 inches.

293

to shoot off the bare ground. While aperture sights were forbidden, open sights of all patterns, often with very delicate screws for adjustment, were used. The customs of shooting from under cover and at one distance only are such as would never be adopted in this country. To sum up, rifle competitions seem to be looked upon, except by Great Britain, Norway and Denmark, as a fancy sport, which is not meant to bear any particular relation to military or useful conditions.'

Colonel Fremantle commented: 'The above sufficiently shows that the chief part of the British team's failure in the match was due to the practical and military lines on which rifle-shooting has been developed in this country. It does not seem that for the sake of again competing in this match it will be worth while in any future year specially to arm and train a team under conditions which would almost certainly put them quite out of their form for shooting in our home competitions, and it is probable that until the International match is put upon lines more compatible with the use of military weapons, it will evoke no special interest in Great Britain and Ireland.'

The British Army's unhappy experiences in the Boer War seemed to confirm the utility for military purposes of shooting from the prone position at long ranges. British riflemen could not take continental marksmanship very seriously and so dropped out of international competitions, shooting mainly against Dominion and occasionally American teams who shared their ideas.

They did, however, compete in the rifle-shooting contests in the Olympics in 1908 and 1912. In the former they took second place to the United States in the English-style shooting, from 200 to 1,000 yards; but in the continental style of shooting, stubbornly using military positions and military rifles with no hair-triggers or hand-rests, they took sixth place. It was very much the same story in 1912.

The Great War of 1914–18 had, as one would expect, a ruinous effect on marksmanship. When serious shooting began again in 1921, the long Lee-Enfield, the Lee-Metford and the Mark VI ammunition were all obsolete: the highly accurate Ross rifle had been found unsuitable since it jammed when heated up by rapid fire. Instead there was the pointed Mark VII bullet and the Short Magazine Lee-Enfield with U-backsight and blade foresight. This combination, excellent on active service, especially for rapid fire, was thoroughly unsatisfactory for target-shooting and the 200-yard bull had to be increased in size, from 1921 to 1923, to 8 inches – the same size as had been used sixty years earlier. Packing the fore-end of the S.M.L.E. increased its accuracy, and in 1924 the 200-yard bull was reduced to 6 inches. The average winning score remained just over 98 per cent. In 1935 marksmen were allowed to use what was called the Pattern '14 rifle, a heavy-barrelled, accurate weapon intended for snipers but never issued in any quantity. It was a success. The 200-yard bull in 1936 was reduced to the pre-1914 size of 5 inches, the long-range bull from 36 to 30 inches, and the average winning score remained unaltered – over 98 per cent.

The last change, brought about by the change in the British service rifle, was the adoption in 1968 of the 7·62-millimetre target rifle. Unfortunately the ammunition was not, for the first three years, worthy of the rifle, so no relevant comparisons can be made.

The general pattern of international marksmanship remains the same. The British and Commonwealth marksmen generally concentrate on English-style shooting, at ranges from 200 to 1,100 yards, from the prone position. Continental

Opposite page
Volunteers firing
from rests, 1861

American marksman
shooting standing, 1848

The modern Russian stance here being used by a German competitor

marksmen, among whom the Scandinavians and Russians seem to be pre-eminent, prefer the rules of the International Shooting Union, a body formed in 1907, which stipulate a single range (300 metres) at which an equal number of shots (generally forty) are fired from the standing, kneeling, and prone (or 'English') positions. American marksmen usually do well in international contests in both styles of shooting. All sorts of aids can be used – slings, aperture sights, butt shaped to the firer's hand and handles for the left hand to grasp in the standing position. Here too the emphasis is on accuracy, meticulous accuracy with no concession to practical military and sporting requirements. The results are very remarkable, and most disconcerting to marksmen brought up to the more rough and ready British school.

Moreover these tiresome Russians, always so bent on proving that 'anything you can do, we can do better', analysing the traditional standing position, have discovered and corrected a fundamental error, and perfected a new position which Wallingford would certainly have condemned as very unsoldierly and ungainly but which is undeniably effective.

If a man stands in the aiming position without a rifle, his centre of gravity is above the centre of the bearing surfaces, his two feet. Give him, now, a heavy target rifle and his centre of gravity moves forward and to the left: to maintain an upright position and counteract the forward and downward movement of the rifle, he must brace his neck- and back-muscles and shift his centre of gravity back. This produces a strained, uncomfortable, and tiring position, inimicable to accurate shooting. Characteristically the Russians, unhampered by tradition, re-examined the standing

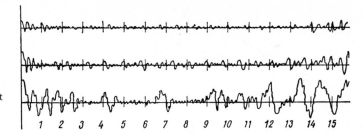

Wobble chart
for the three
positions

position *ab initio*, and developed one in which the feet are close together, the body is bent right back, so as to make the rifle's centre of gravity coincide with that of the body and minimize the muscular effort and tension. It looks awkward, it is not very good for shooting at, say, a running man or deer; but for target-shooting it has been proved over and over again to be far superior to the orthodox shooting position as taught by, say, the British Army Small Arms School.

The figures speak for themselves. The standard target of the International Shooting Union, used at Olympic, Nordic, and European competitions, has a 10-centimetre (3·9 inch bull) at 300 metres, smaller than the English bull at 200 yards. In international competitions of forty shots at each range – far more of a test than the seven-shot or ten-shot practices at Bisley – the average winning scores are about 49 per cent in the standing position, 97 per cent kneeling and 99 per cent prone. Time and time again it is American, Russian, Swedish, and Finnish marksmen who carry off the prizes: British marksmen 'also ran'.

The epitome of absolute accuracy is small-bore shooting with the ·22 rifle. At 25 yards and indoors wind has no effect on the bullet's flight: the marksman can concentrate on steady holding, exactitude of aim, a perfect trigger-pressure. The competition rifle is very heavy and curiously shaped as to butt and fore-end to fit the firer's hand; the sling clamps it like a vice to the left arm; there is a very light trigger; the sights permit the most minute adjustments. Every other attribute of a firearm is sacrificed for meticulous accuracy to enable the specialist small-bore marksman with iron self-control and nerves of glacial ice to put shot after shot into a centimetre bull.

Small-bore shooting first became popular when, in the early years of this century, the very accurate ·22 rifle with the long rim-fire cartridge was developed. It was

Breathing chart: the relative steadiness of holding and
not holding one's breath

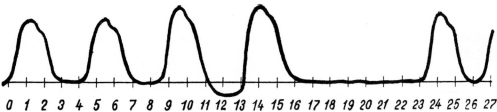

Three holds for the standing position

Opposite page
The modern match small-bore rifle with all its aids (except the sling)

cheap, comparatively silent, and could be safely practised on 25-yard ranges even in the heart of a city. So it became extremely popular: small-bore rifle clubs and marksmen proliferate all over the world: there are far more small-bore than full-bore competitions.

There is much the same difference between British and continental small-bore shooting as with the full-bore. British marksmen shoot at 25, 50, 100, and occasionally 200 yards, nearly always from the prone position: continental riflemen only at 50 metres, forty shots each in standing, kneeling, and prone positions. They achieve a very high standard of accuracy: the average winning scores in international competitions are about 94 per cent standing, 98 per cent kneeling and 99·5 per cent prone.

The most modern Russian and American ·22 target rifles have the foresight, rather than the backsight, adjustable. The marksman gets his butt, cheek-piece, handgrips, etc. either made to measure or adjusted for the greatest comfort, and thus with his sling clamps himself and rifle into a position in which movement is almost impossible. The backsight must be always in the same position relative to the eye: it must not be moved by so much as a couple of centimetres, so all vertical and lateral adjustments must be to the foresight.

In this prone position, with modern rifles and ammunition, aperture backsight and foresight, the accuracy achieved is extraordinary, as is indicated by the size of the central ring in which a shot scores 10. At 50 yards it is 0·9 inch, at 100 yards 2 inches, and 200 yards 7·20 inches. At these distances wind is a variable, inconstant factor which cannot be entirely eliminated. At 25 yards, the usual range in this country, the 10-ring has a diameter of only 0·25 inch – that is to say, 0·03 inch larger than the bullet: since 1966 the 'outward gauge' has been used at this range, which means that if the outer edge of a bullet hole touches the 10-ring, the shot scores only 9. To score 10, it must be absolutely central. The full-bore marksman, putting a 7·62-millimetre bullet into even a 10-centimetre (3·9-inch) circle at 300 metres is, in a sense shooting into an area, albeit a small one; there is a margin for error, he can make a shot which is not dead accurate without being penalized. But the small-bore marksman, putting a 0·22-inch bullet into a 0·25-inch circle, is shooting at a point: the margin of error is precisely 0·015 inch, which means in fact that there is none. Any deviation from accuracy carries a penalty. Yet 'possibles' are commonplace.

This is the ultimate in accuracy, the end of the road: from here there is nowhere

The 'drilling' that gives the shotgun a rifle barrel for occasional use

to go, and the small-bore enthusiast in his eternal search for perfection finds himself rather frustrated, which is why many are turning to the pistol instead of the rifle.

Of course, the ·22 rifle will always be used in other roles – training young shots before they use the full-bore, or for shooting purposes at rabbits, pigeon, even roe-deer. But as a target rifle it is losing its appeal for the paradoxical reason that it is too good, and perfection, attained too frequently, can be boring.

The target rifleman has certain characteristics of the White Knight, particularly a penchant for eccentric clothing and gadgets: he is unable to resist buying anything which he thinks, or the gun-dealer assures him, may add a point to his score.

Observe a prime specimen waiting at his firing-point on Bisley's Century Range. He wears a hat with a wide brim to keep the sun off his aperture sight, embellished perhaps by a selection of regimental, club, or national badges. (If he is a real zealot, of the trans-Atlantic variety, he may in the prone position proclaim his allegiance by badges sewn to the back of his coat or the broad seat of his trousers.) His ancient coat is frayed, padded, stiffened and leather-patched at elbow and shoulder. Over one shoulder is slung his rifle, the sights protected by covers lest at any time he knock them against a stone. Over the other is slung a telescope with its tripod and a capacious, well-filled haversack or gadget-bag. This contains his ammunition, a scorebook and a small bottle of blacking for his sights, lest the sun's reflections dazzle him. Perhaps he has also a pair of large ear-protectors, lest the noise of his neighbours' rifles disturb his concentration.

Apart, of course, from the ammunition, the most important thing in his bag is the scorebook. On every page is a scale diagram of the target, at different ranges. It is marked off in vertical and horizontal lines, the distance between each line representing one minute of angle, subtended by four 'clicks' on his aperture sight. There are also tables showing the wind-flags and appropriate wind-allowances, and space for recording the weather, the value of each shot fired, every change in his sights, and any miscellaneous information. A scorebook, properly used, is of enormous value in an application shoot.

His turn comes to shoot. He adjusts his protectors over his ears; has a friendly word with the neighbour who shares his target, firing alternate shots; then lowers his bulky person on to the ground sheet. The telescope is adjusted and focused, close to his left eye; the haversack and its contents are conveniently arranged. He spreads wide his legs, straddles his elbows and takes a couple of snaps with an empty rifle to satisfy himself that his holding and trigger-pressure are, after last night's session at the club, all they should be. The range is 500 yards. He makes sure that his aperture sight is set at the reading he last used for 500. His notebook reminds him that last time it was a dull day: now it is fine. 'Lights up, sights up' says the ancient rifleman's adage: should he add a click or two to his elevation? He decides to wait and see. The flags indicate a light, intermittent breeze from between ten and eleven o'clock: four clicks, or one minute left should give enough wind-allowance. He studies the mirage carefully through his telescope, trying to memorize its pace as a basis for further comparisons. His target is up and he is ready for his first sighting-shot.

It is a good shot: he is satisfied with his aim and with his trigger-pressure. The target goes down, the frame comes up signalling an inner. The target rises with a white patch just outside the bull at five o'clock. While his neighbour fires, he enters it in his scorebook, marking the shot on the diagram. Should he raise his sights a little? If he is wise he will do nothing of the kind until he has fired his second sighter.

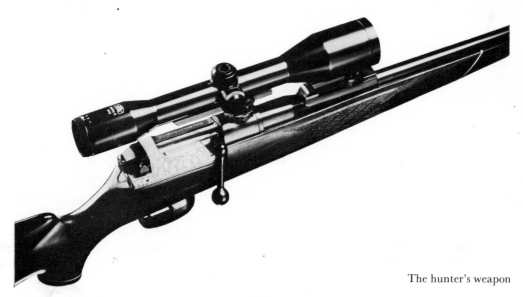

The hunter's weapon

Shooting deer from a forest stance

It is his turn again. He takes a last look at the mirage: no change. It is, so far as he can tell, another good shot. This time it is just inside the bull, at four o'clock. Now it is time to alter his sights, not just chasing his last shot but taking into account both sighters. He estimates on the diagram that the mean between them is one and a half minutes to the right of centre, and turns his wind-gauge six clicks left. It is also about the same distance below. This is rather puzzling: the light should not make all that difference: perhaps he did take rather a fine sight after all. However, he gives three clicks more elevation.

The result is an inner at twelve o'clock. He makes an observation appropriate to the occasion. But don't panic, don't panic! He was not quite satisfied with his aim that time: he may have taken rather a full sight, and there is no use chasing loose shots all over the target. He fires again, scoring a bull this time, but also a little high. So he brings his sight two clicks down, and scores two more bulls.

As he is on the point of firing his fifth shot he feels on his right cheek-bone a cold warning that the wind has changed. He relaxes the first pressure, lowers the rifle and peers through his telescope. Yes, the mirage is now 'boiling' or even moving from right to left: the flags, flapping gently from one o'clock, tell the same story. This is rather tricky. Has the wind really changed, or is this just a stray, flighty puff? Glancing down the long butts, he sees several inners and even one or two disastrous magpies. He cannot wait forever: his neighbour will be justly aggrieved. He takes

302

the plunge, boldly moving his wind-gauge from ten clicks left to two clicks right, and is rewarded by two more bulls.

The last three have, however, all been a trifle low and there seems to be a tendency for each shot to drop a little. His scorebook tells him that this often happens towards the end of a shoot, perhaps because his rifle barrel warms and expands. For his last shot he moves the sight one click up, and shoots quickly, before the wind can change again. Bull! And the white disc is bang in the centre. Clap i' the clout! 34 out of a possible 35. It is not a winning score, but if he does as well at 600 yards, it should put him in the money.

Increasing accuracy in rifles made it necessary to give far more attention to sights. The fundamental difficulty in aiming a rifle is that the eye must bring into line and, so far as possible, focus simultaneously three points at different distances – the backsight, the foresight, and the target. It cannot be done: it is an optical impossibility. But it certainly helps if one must try to focus only two – the foresight and the target. This can be achieved by the aperture or orthoptic sight, a small hole, placed near the eye, which cuts off the rays which would otherwise pass through the outer part of the eye-lens, enabling the foresight and target to be brought into far better focus. The principle was known as early as the sixteenth century, when crossbows were fitted with a form of adjustable peep-sight, a vertical blade pierced by several holes for use at different distances. Early rifles were

Shooting bear from a high seat in Czechoslovakia

sometimes fitted with a backsight in the form of a tube, 2 or 3 inches long, or a plain aperture. However, the muzzle-loading rifle, firing a spherical ball, did not group close enough to necessitate a really accurate sight for the ranges at which it was used: a plain V or U backsight was quite good enough, so long as it was wide enough to enable the target to be clearly seen, but narrow enough for errors in elevation to be obvious. Since such rifles had a low velocity and a high trajectory, the sight had to be adjustable for different ranges, and this was usually done by providing two or three leaf-backsights; the rifleman simply flipped up the one appropriate for the range at which he was shooting.

As rifles improved in range and accuracy, riflemen needed a sight that was more accurate and more easily focused. The aperture sight was the answer. It greatly simplifies aiming, not merely because it facilitates focusing the foresight and the target, but because the marksman need not consciously centre the tip of the foresight and the target in the middle of the aperture: the eye does this automatically, since the middle of the hole is clear, its surroundings blurred. It is a common error to suppose that one can obtain greater accuracy with a smaller aperture. This is not so. Within reason, whether the aperture be large or small, the tip of the foresight and the aiming mark are still automatically centred within it.

With an ordinary open backsight, the closer it is to the foresight, the easier both can be brought into focus. At the same time, the closer the two sights are to one another, the greater the effect of errors in aiming. With an aperture sight these

The stalker

The awkward moment when your quarry comes up on
you from behind

considerations do not apply: it is best placed as close to the eye as possible, always
bearing in mind the rifle's recoil. In military bolt-action rifles it is generally fixed to
the bridge over the bolt. The Lyman aperture sight, on sporting rifles, is fixed to the
small of the butt, just in front of the right hand.

Wind became an important factor, as it had been for the bowman. A light,
elongated bullet is far more affected by a cross-wind than a heavy, spherical ball;
and, of course, the longer the range, the further a bullet of any shape and any
velocity is blown off course. Fremantle instances the 1894 N.R.A. meeting at Bisley
when for several days the wind blew so steadily and so strongly as to necessitate an
'aim-off' of 22 feet at 900 yards. By a happy coincidence this was the exact distance
from one target to the next, so no sight-adjustment was necessary: each competitor
simply aimed at the bull of the man on his right. (But what happened to the unlucky
right-hand man?) But a backsight, open or aperture, which could be adjusted
laterally to make allowance for a cross-wind was obviously more satisfactory than
aiming-off.

So by the early twentieth century aperture backsights, adjustable both vertically
and laterally, were used for any competition in which they were permitted. These
are still in use: they are capable of very fine adjustments, making as small a difference
as one inch at 200 yards.

There is a conflict between the requirements of target-shooting and field shooting, whether in hunting or war. In target-shooting the mark is easily seen, easily

A walking-stick makes a good rifle rest

identified: so long as one does not shoot on the wrong target, all that is required of the sights is that they should promote extreme accuracy by making obvious any error in the aim. An aperture backsight, as already explained, is best for this purpose: and, provided the aiming-mark is round, an aperture or ring-foresight too: errors in aiming are far easier to see with a ring-foresight than with a blade or bead. It is, therefore, generally used where the rules allow, especially in ·22 competitions when the round black aiming mark should be fitted into the ring of the foresight with a symmetrical band of white all around it.

But for hunting or war a ring-foresight is thoroughly impracticable, because it blacks out the area round the target, so making target identification more difficult. For these purposes a bead or blade is much better.

For similar reasons military authorities for many years deprecated the use of aperture backsights: the types used for target-shooting blacked out too much of the area around the target. Then from America came a form of large aperture sight known as the Lyman sight which covers less of the target area than an open backsight. It became very popular among sportsmen, and by 1939, in the form of a 'battle-sight', had been adopted by the British and other armies as the standard sight for the service rifle and most automatic weapons as well.

More recently, however, a robust, low-powered telescopic sight is beginning to find favour for military and sporting weapons. There are no focusing problems: the whole target area can be kept in view, and indeed magnified and clarified, even in a bad light. Undoubtedly it is the best sight, for all purposes, provided it is not knocked about.

There is another way, recently invented, of solving the problem of focus. The basic difficulty in aiming, as has already been mentioned, is that the eye cannot focus simultaneously on three objects at different ranges – backsight, foresight, and target. The aperture sight eliminates the need to focus on the backsight, but there are still two objects, a long distance apart, on which to focus, so in aiming one is bound to be blurred, and the eye tires (especially in continental forty-round practices) from focusing first on one, then on another. The difficulty in this double focusing is due to the fact that the rays coming from the distant target to the eye are more nearly parallel than the rays from the foresight, which are more nearly parallel than the rays from the backsight. If somehow the rays from backsight and foresight can be converted into rays as parallel as those from the target, all three can be brought simultaneously into focus, with great advantage to the marksman.

This is what the Reuss mirror-sight does. In place of the backsight is a small black triangle: in place of the foresight is a parabolic mirror, that is to say a mirror with a curved surface. The triangle is reflected by the mirror back to the shooter's eye, with the curved mirror surface making the rays as parallel as those from the target. Both triangle and target are thus in sharp focus, and all the marksman need do is to align the tip of the triangle (which is at the top edge of the mirror) with the bull's eye. Aim is taken with both eyes open, the left eye focused only on the target. This 'single-point' or mirror sighting system is so effective that in Germany it has been banned from competition shooting as unfair. It would seem to be impracticable for military or sporting use, as the slightest knock would upset the delicate adjustment of triangle and mirror.

Sportsmen and soldiers have always sought a good night-sight, and until recently have not found one. A torch clamped to the rifle may serve the sportsman sitting up for tiger, lion, or leopard over a kill, but would be suicidal for the soldier. A luminous foresight is useful only at a very short range; a luminous backsight, also possible in theory, is not in fact practicable, for if both sights are clearly visible, they dazzle the eye and the target then cannot be discerned. Until recently night-shooting, except at close range in clear moonlight, was mainly a matter of luck. In the last twenty-five years, however, some progress has been made in developing infra-red night-sights which are generally too expensive and bulky for use on sporting rifles. Recently Messrs Holland and Holland (and, no doubt, other firms) have applied to night-shooting the principle of the single-point aim.

The Holland Singlepoint night-sight looks like a small telescopic sight. At the front of this scope is a phosphorescent light-point, rays from which are directed to the shooter's eye in a parallel beam. All the shooter has to do is, with both eyes open, to 'put this white dot on the target' (both are in focus) and fire. With this, it is claimed, a man-size target can be hit consistently up to 300 yards – provided, of course, it can itself be seen. This is something far in advance of all previous night-sights.

Given a high standard of aiming, holding and trigger-pressure, and steady nerves, such as may be assumed at a national rifle meeting, it is not too much to say that at ranges over 500 yards wind-judging and the lateral adjustment of sights is the match-winning factor. Both the strength and the direction of the wind must be taken into account: a wind blowing from one o'clock will have less effect on a bullet's flight than a wind of the same strength blowing from three o'clock. Most ranges are provided with flags at regular distances from which the strength and direction of the wind can be estimated: a flag flying at, say, forty-five degrees indicates a stronger wind than one at an angle of only 15 degrees. Tables have been worked out, and are easily obtainable, showing the appropriate allowance for wind as indicated by these flags. Complications arise when the flags near the firing point are behaving differently from those near the butts; or when there is a shifting, variable wind. In the latter circumstances last-minute adjustments to the sights are unsettling and inimicable to accuracy: it may be better to aim-off; and the man accustomed to aim and shoot quickly will have a great advantage.

Another, and generally better, method of wind-judging on a fine day is by the movement of the mirage, as seen through a telescope on a tripod directed at the target, conveniently placed for the firer to look through it with his left eye without changing his position. For example, a gentle wind from three o'clock and a moderate wind from one o'clock have the same effect on the bullet and appear to make the mirage, as seen through a telescope, move across the target at the same pace. There are, of course, no tables for calculating the lateral adjustment necessary for the first sighting-shot when using this method of wind-judging: only practice can help in this. But one can very soon learn to judge the comparative pace of the mirage, to say to oneself: 'A bit slower than for the last shot: one click less on the wind-gauge.' Most competition riflemen, when the weather is suitable, use the mirage rather than the flags, or perhaps a combination of both. The mirage shows only the wind at ground level, which may be quite different from the wind at the top of a bullet's flight at long range.

Of course, in war there are no flags available and, except perhaps for snipers, no telescopes either: wind-judging is very much a matter of luck, which partially accounts for the very small proportion of 'hits' to rounds fired. In big-game shooting the range is generally too short for a cross-wind to be of any importance.

Big-game shooting is as different from military and target shooting as chalk from butter and cheese. The buffalo, elephant, or big cat does not shoot back. Except at very close quarters, he is quite innocuous: but at very close quarters a large animal is more dangerous than a man since it takes more to knock him down. Wounds make him more, not less dangerous. In war it is as effective to wound an enemy as to kill him: indeed it may be more effective, for a wounded man has to be carried off by stretcher bearers and ambulance drivers, treated by surgeons and then nursed perhaps for months: while a dead man needs only to be buried. But prudence and humanity alike make wounding an animal the worst crime a sportsman can commit.

The end of a deer stalk

So the sportsman should never take a shot over 200 yards, which in war or target shooting is a very short range: for large, dangerous animals he must get much closer, to make sure of killing or disabling with his first shot. A light bullet, hitting him almost anywhere, will put a man out of action: but for a dangerous animal only a heavy bullet, or a light one very accurately placed, will suffice: a misplaced light bullet may simply provoke a charge.

In very general terms, therefore, the big-game hunter must suit his rifle to his quarry. If he is hunting mountain or plains game, such as ibex or oryx, which are very wary, harmless, and comparatively small targets, he will find it difficult to approach within 150 yards, but will probably, if his first shot does not kill, get the chance of a second. A heavy bullet is unnecessary: what he needs is a high-velocity rifle with as flat a trajectory as possible, so that he can take the same aim for any distance up to about 200 yards. If he is hunting medium-sized game – lion, say, or kudu – in bush country, a flat trajectory is not so necessary, for he will seldom take a shot over 100 yards: but he needs a heavier bullet which will knock his quarry down, for if it gets away wounded in such country, he may lose it and the animal

309

Shooting seal from a kayak

may die a lingering death with a broken leg or a bullet in the guts. For heavy, dangerous game, which is generally found in thick country, he will probably take his shot at under 50 yards: what he needs is the heaviest rifle he can conveniently carry, packing a punch which will turn a charging elephant or buffalo even if it does not kill. (The matter is not quite so simple as this or so uncontroversial, and we shall return to it later.)

Successive developments in sporting rifles have altered one's ideas on what constitutes a high velocity or a heavy bullet. In the days of the muzzle-loading rifle, anything under ·5 inch calibre would be regarded as a light rifle, suitable for deer stalking and other forms of hunting which generally involved long shots at non-dangerous game. But with the development in the latter part of the century of breech-loading 'Express' rifles, with muzzle velocities over 1,600 feet per second, the whole picture altered.

To take some examples, the pre-Express ·577 rifle was considered a medium-weight rifle, much lighter than the 8-bore (·835) or the ponderous 4-bore (1·052) elephant rifles. At 200 yards its conical bullet dropped 32 inches and its spherical ball 49 inches from the line of sight. But a typical medium-weight Express rifle, the ·450, could be zeroed for 150 yards and the bullet would not, up to 200 yards, rise or fall more than 4·82 inches. It could, at 150 yards, make a 5-inch group. Later, at the turn of the century, came the 'accelerated Express' or high-velocity rifles, with muzzle velocities over 2,400 feet per second, still flatter trajectories, and still closer grouping: the bullet of the high-velocity ·450 had a rise and fall of less than half that of the Express.

A high-velocity rifle with a flat trajectory is not merely a more accurate but a more deadly weapon than the Express or pre-Express rifle of the same calibre. The killing power of a rifle, provided a suitable bullet is used, depends on its 'striking

energy' at any given range, and striking energy is a product of the bullet's weight and velocity at that range. As, therefore, the velocity of rifles increased, so smaller calibres could be used with no loss in striking energy. For example, a ·450 high-velocity rifle, firing a bullet of 480 grains, has a striking energy at 150 yards of 4,020 lb, while the ·500 Express has at the same range a striking energy of only 1,934 lb.

The high-velocity sporting rifle has not developed much during the last sixty or seventy years, largely because it is so deadly against animals that any further development would make it unsporting, since big-game shooting would then be too easy. (Many people think that point has already been passed.) Subsequent remarks about sporting rifles may be taken as applying, more or less, to any decade in the twentieth century.

For plains and mountain game the ideal rifle has a calibre between ·240 inch and ·300 inch. There are several rifles in this category, all with trajectories so flat that with the sights zeroed for 150 yards one should, without varying the aim, be able to put a bullet in the shoulder of an animal at any distance up to 200 yards, which is about as far as a true sportsman will shoot (except to stop an animal getting away wounded). The right bullet must, however, be used. A pointed bullet may be deflected by a bone instead of smashing it: a solid bullet will go straight through a medium-sized animal unless it happens to hit a large bone, making only a small wound and wasting half its force on empty air. What is needed is a soft-nosed or expanding bullet which should, ideally, go through the body without coming out on the far side. There is rather a vogue, nowadays, for high-velocity ·22 magnum rifles. In my opinion these should not be used for any quarry larger than a small gazelle: their bullet is too light and breaks up if it hits a bone.

The other extreme of big-game shooting is the large, dangerous animal – an elephant, say, or a buffalo – in forest or jungle. There it is easy and highly desirable to take the first shot at a very close range, not more than 50 yards, to make sure of it. If the animal goes away wounded, he must at all costs, at all risks and however hard it is, be followed up and killed. To leave a dangerous wounded animal, who will probably attack the next person he sees, without making every possible effort to finish him off, is absolutely unforgivable. For this type of hunting you need the heaviest rifle you can comfortably carry – not less than a ·450 and probably, because of its sheer weight, not more than a ·500 unless you are a veritable Hercules. (You should, of course, always carry your own rifle.)

Again the choice of bullet is important. For soft-skinned game (lion, tiger, or leopard) you need soft-nosed bullets. For elephant you undoubtedly need solid bullets: soft-nosed bullets will not smash the shoulder-blade or penetrate the honey-comb-like skull to reach the brain. For rhino or buffalo it is debatable: a solid may go straight through without doing much damage: a soft-nosed may be stopped by a heavy bone without breaking it. Personally I used solids.

For medium-sized game such as kudu in fairly open bush you need a medium-weight, medium-velocity rifle – something between ·318, perhaps, and ·375.

Should you use a magazine rifle or a double? Here again experts differ: a lot depends on your purse and physique. A magazine rifle is cheaper and lighter than a double. If an animal goes away wounded, you may be able to fire three or more shots before he is out of range. On the other hand, you cannot get off the second shot from a magazine nearly as quickly as you can from a double. On the whole the best course, if you can afford it, is to have a heavy double for dangerous game in thick country, and a magazine rifle for other purposes.

The development of the high-velocity rifle has given rise to a controversy, particularly about elephant-shooting, which has rumbled on for some sixty years. Some hunters, of whom the most experienced, expert and articulate was the famous professional, 'Karamoja' Bell, maintain that every kind of big game, even elephants, are best hunted with a light, high-velocity rifle. Their argument goes like this:

'The alleged knock-down power of the heavy rifle is illusory against elephant. Unless the aim be true, it is not the elephant who will be knocked down by the bullet, but the hunter by the recoil. The biggest bull elephant in Africa will drop to a tiny ·256 bullet provided it is correctly placed, in the heart or the brain. At the end of a long hunt in a tropical country the man carrying a heavy double will be in no condition to place its bullet correctly, while the man carrying a light magazine rifle will be comparatively fresh. The proper weapon, the safest weapon for the elephant hunter is, therefore, something like a ·275 high-velocity magazine rifle firing solid bullets.'

To this advocates of the heavy rifle reply: 'A ·475 bullet fired into the forehead or chest of a charging bull elephant will deflect even if it does not kill him. A ·275 bullet will not. Karamoja Bell was a professional, a hunting genius, a dead shot in all circumstances, who had killed hundreds of elephants and knew exactly where to put his bullet from any angle. Moreover, he hunted generally in country more open than that in which large tuskers can usually be found nowadays. Elephants in his day were so numerous, and so unafraid of man, that he could pick his shots. The day of the professional ivory hunter is over. The modern hunter is either a sportsman who will probably not shoot a dozen tuskers in his lifetime, or a white hunter or game warden who has the unenviable task of finishing off the truculent bull that someone else has wounded, or moving a troublesome herd out of a cultivated area which they raid at night. The sportsman can never gain the experience to use a light rifle with certainty; and the conditions in which a white hunter or game warden operates, generally in thick bush, often at night, in high crops or in the middle of a herd, are such as to make a light rifle wholly inappropriate.'

The argument continues, but on the whole the advocates of the heavy rifle prevail. I personally know many game wardens and white hunters, but not one who would willingly go after elephant with anything less than a ·450 double. In many countries it is specified on the licence that the shooting of elephants with a rifle less powerful than the ·375 magnum is illegal.

Is there, for the man who cannot afford two or three rifles, a general-purpose weapon? Well, no, not really: such a weapon must be something of a compromise, not as powerful as one would like for an elephant and buffalo, or as flat in trajectory as one would like for ibex or chamois. Having said this, I must add that I used to be both impecunious and a dedicated big-game hunter,* and shot many varieties of animal, varying from *Ovis ammon* and Tibetan antelope to tiger, buffalo, and elephant all with one weapon – the Holland and Holland ·375 magnum magazine rifle. This is certainly the nearest thing there is to the general-purpose rifle, because it fires three different bullets of 235, 270, and 300 grains, for use against different types of game.

Its performance is very remarkable, as the following figures show:

Some ballistics of the ·375 magnum rifle

Bullet weight	Muzzle velocity	Ideally zeroed for	Rise of bullet above line of sight	Striking energy
300 gr.	2,500 ft per sec.	175 yd	2·4 in.	3,530 lb at 100 yd
270 gr.	2,650 ft per sec.	175 yd	2·0 in.	3,550 lb at 100 yd
235 gr.	2,800 ft per sec.	200 yd	2·4 in.	2,600 lb at 200 yd

From these it is clear that the ·375 magnum is a reasonably good weapon against heavy game at close range with the 300-grain bullet; a very good weapon against medium game at medium ranges with the 270-grain bullet; and extremely deadly against mountain game at long ranges, for with sights set at 200 yards, the bullet will never rise more than 2·4 inches above the line of sight, and at 300 yards has dropped only 4 inches.

As most sporting shots are taken at much less than 200 yards, and the vital point

* I am still impecunious, but have long outgrown the wish to shoot anything bigger than a pheasant.

is considerably bigger than the 5-inch Bisley bull at that range, the sights of a sporting rifle need not be such as to promote extreme accuracy. A target aperture sight, or a small V or U backsight would, indeed, be quite unsuitable because they would tend to obscure the quarry, especially if it were barely visible in thick bush, and would not facilitate a quick snap-shot at a running beast. If an open backsight is used, it should be a wide, shallow V. If an aperture sight is used, it should be a rather large Lyman sight. In either case the foresight should be clearly visible in a poor light: an ivory bead is good, or a silver or white-metal disc tilted to reflect the light of the sky. The foresight at least must be protected. Sir Frank Messervy, the distinguished war-time general who introduced me to Himalayan shooting, once trekked for three weeks from Srinagar to the furthest corner of Changchenmo without ever taking his rifle out of its case. When, on reaching Tibetan antelope country, he did so, he made the disconcerting discovery that the foresight was missing. All he could do was to trek back, without firing a shot.

I have never used a telescopic sight, holding that a man with normal eyesight should never shoot at a range longer than that at which he can aim perfectly well with open Lyman sights. I am probably wrong. The real value of the telescopic sight is that with it one can pick out a target in a bad light – the head of a leopard, say, just before dusk.

The point of aim on a big-game animal is another vexed question. Let us first dispose of the elephant, which is a special case. A shot in the brain will drop him dead, one which just misses the brain will probably give him no more than a severe headache for a few hours. A shot in the heart or the great arteries entering it will drop him within a few hundred yards, but one which misses these may result in his dying after several days' agony, or recovering to wreak his vengeance on mankind. Much the same applies to a lung-shot, though he will run much further before he drops. A heavy bullet in the shoulder-blade will smash it and immobilize him; but a light bullet will not. If you are sure of your shooting, the brain-shot is the most deadly and the most humane. From the side, at a ninety-degree angle, you should shoot slap-bang through the ear-hole: this is the easiest shot in the book. From the front the brain-shot is much more difficult, since the point of aim is hard to identify and depends largely on the angle at which he is carrying his head. If he is at rest and you are shooting on the same level, you should aim at the shallow, saucer-like depression just below the centre of his forehead. The trouble with the brain-shot is that the brain is very small, and is partially surrounded by an impenetrable, honeycomb-like skull structure: unless the bullet takes the correct route, it will not reach the brain. So if you are standing at an oblique angle, or the elephant's head is carried high, or low, then you must aim at a different point, and much experience is needed in picking this.

The heart-shot is easier, since the heart is bigger than the brain, and a bullet through the main arteries will be as fatal as one actually through the heart. The point of aim, from a ninety-degree angle, is easy to identify – directly above the elbow joint, one third of the way up the body. If the bullet is placed too far forward, it should smash the shoulder-blade: if too high and far back, it should penetrate the lungs. One should not, however, deliberately aim for the lungs.

A charging elephant can generally be turned, and eventually killed, by a bullet in the chest, provided you can get a clear shot at it. Failing that, take a shot at the base of his trunk, if his head is held high, and run for it. If you have to run, run downwind.

. Karamoja Bell, shooting from astern, dropped many an elephant with a bullet in the spine just above the tail, or in the base of the skull. I have never met anyone who tried these shots, and I should certainly never do so myself.

With all other animals the neck shot is the best, the most deadly and the most sporting, since it nearly always results in a clean kill or a clean miss, very seldom in a wounded animal. I do not like the heart-shot, since it is all too easy to aim too far back and put a bullet in the stomach. In theory a high-velocity bullet in the stomach has an explosive effect which is as deadly as one through the heart: in practice it too often results in the unfortunate animal running off, stumbling over his own intestines. So if, as not infrequently happens, I doubt my ability to hit him in the neck, I aim at the shoulder; or, rather, at a point between the two shoulders. If the bullet hits a shoulder-blade, it would drop him on the spot: if it is 6 inches too far back, it will go through his heart; and if it is too far forward, it will miss him altogether. A raking shot, at the chest or the root of the tail, will drop any animal dead, except an elephant. A brain-shot is very inadvisable, especially from the front. It will probably glance off the boss of a buffalo or the horn of a rhino, and even from the sharply sloping head of lion or tiger.

Stopping a charge presents special problems. If it is one of the big cats, he is probably moving very fast and his chest is covered by his head. In theory the best shot is over his head, between his shoulder-blades: in practice you just blaze off into his face and hope it turns him. A buffalo carries his head high until the last moment, so exposing his chest; but if it is the last moment, and he has lowered his head to toss you, it is no use shooting at his boss: a bullet there will have no more effect than from a pea-shooter. You must either dodge and let him have one in the ribs as he thunders past; or, if you are a good enough shot with steady enough nerves, wait until he is almost on you, then put a bullet between his shoulder-blades, to break his spine. To be honest, I have never done it. Fortunately a charge is rare unless an animal is surrounded or has already been wounded. Moral: get in as close as you can: then get in 5 yards closer, to make sure of the first shot.

This chapter would not be complete without some observation on the ethics of big-game hunting, of shooting animals for sport. I have done it, and enjoyed it. I no longer do it, and would not now enjoy it. But, with certain provisos, I cannot see that it is any more wicked than slaughtering sheep and cattle because you like eating them. If one is wrong, so is the other: we could get on perfectly well without it, but we kill domestic animals because we *like* their flesh. So, I say, the enjoyment of big-game hunting is perfectly permissible provided the hunted animal is in no danger of extinction; provided every effort is made to kill him clean and not leave him wounded; provided not too many, and only males, are killed; and provided the odds are not too heavily on the side of the hunter. The last proviso is vital. Any weapon more deadly than the high-velocity rifle, and too free use of vehicles and planes, would make big-game shooting no longer a sport. Perhaps they have already done so.

As for the enjoyment, no one who has not experienced it can belittle the tense excitement of creeping up to within 20 yards of a great bull elephant, tracking a lion through thorn-scrub, or waiting in a bush for a tiger to return to his kill. There is a different kind of thrill in the long hunt, with many disappointments, before at last one sees within easy range some desperately wary and elusive animal such as a bull bongo. Best of all, to my mind, is the long, long trek – two or three weeks of it – to hunt the wild sheep and goats which inhabit the great mountains of the world – *Ovis ammon*, markhor, ibex, Barbary sheep and others: the slow careful scanning through a telescope of the distant cliff or hillside; the anxious testing of the wind, the panting, lung-searing climb to reach a vantage-point in the rocks above that ram with the great, curling horns.

I have loved it all, and though I never want to do it again, I am not in the least ashamed of having done it.

Now I hunt with a camera. It is not nearly so exciting, and it is, I think, much safer and easier: but it has certain advantages over shooting which need not here be listed.

I think, if I were twenty years younger, I would take to hunting with the bow.

INDEX

Acerbi, Joseph, *88*
Agincourt, Battle of, 61
American weapons, Civil War, 71
239, 256; War of Independence,
203, 205
Anna Comnena, 46
Arabs, 43
arbalete, arbalister, 47 ff, *58*, *59*.
See also crossbow
archers, mounted, 37, 41, 42, 43
archery, 77 ff, *78*, *79*, *84*, *85*, *86*, *93*,
94, *95*, *96*, *97*, *108–9*; aiming, 69,
85–6; in America, 89; butts, 66,
70; clout-shooting, 88, 91; clubs
and societies, 77–8, 89, *83*; competitions, 89; drawing, 36, 67–8,
80–1, 84–5, *39*; field-archery,
91; hunting, 92–3; loosing, 36,
67–8, 80–1, 86–8; modern, 79 ff;
nocking, 83; popinjay-shooting,
91, *74*, *98*, *125*; stance, 83, *72*;
Swiss, 98; target, 90; target-
shyness (freezing), 89; effect of
wind, 9, 69–70
arquebus, 105, 109, 111, *113*, *116*,
125
arrow, 23 ff; flight-arrow, 70;
longbowman's, 64–5; metal, 80;
sheaf-arrow, 70; throwing
arrows, *23*; arrow-nock, 37
Ascham, Roger, 67–9, 87
assegai, 17
Assyrians, 37, *34*, *38*
Australia, aboriginal weapons, 10,
13, 14, 17, 18, 19, *36*

Bacon, Roger, 103
Baker, Ezekiel, 206
ballista (siege-engine), 46
Bannockburn, Battle of, 61, 75
Barne, Harman, 125
battue, 141, 142, 154
Bayeux Tapestry, 46
Beaumont, Battle of, 58
Belisarius, 17, 39
Bell, Karamoja, 312, 315
big-game shooting, 308 ff
bird-shooting, birding, birding-
piece, 118, 121, 125, 126–7,
130 ff, 143 ff

Bisley, 279, 289, 300, 305
Black Prince, 76
blow-pipe, 19, 20
blunderbuss, 179
Boer War, 251, 253
bola, 15
boomerang, 19, *16*, *20*
bow, 23 ff, *24*, *27*, *29*, *32*, *40*, *46–7*,
56, *82*, *92*, *93*; centre-shot, 27;
composite, 34, 35, 37, 75, *31*,
45, *48*; Holmegaard, 25, 29, 82,
77; modern, 80, 82; nocked, 28;
recurved, reflex, 33, 34, 35, 37,
39, 75, *30*, *41*, *45*, *48*; self-bow,
29, 33, 34, 39, 43, 82; bow-sight
84–5; stringing, 35, *38*. *See also*
crossbow, longbow
bowstring, 24
de Braose, William, 59
Breckinridge, Judge, 236
breech-loader, 109, 151, 154, 193,
202, *210*, *212*
British Army, 120–1, 195–8, 222,
253–6, 279, 287, 294–5
de la Brocquière, Sieur Bertrandon, 75, 76
Brown Bess, 195–6, 206
buffalo, 94–5, 210–13, 311 ff,
272–3
bullet, 220, 251, 310 ff; jet-
propelled, *250*; Minié, 222, 278
von Bülow, Marconay, 258
Bushman weapons, 29, *31*, 36, *40*
Byzantine Empire, 39, 43

caliver, 107, 111
cannon, 103, 112
carbine, 111, *198*
cartridges, 163
Catlin, George, 210
cave-paintings, 19, 25, 34
chakra, 21
Chandos, Sir John, 76
Charles II, *73*
Chinese weapons, 43, 75, *61*, *82*, *89*
Churchill, Jack, 91–2
clay pigeons, 174 ff, *138*, *150–1*,
170, *187*, *188*
club, *16*
Colt, Samuel, 239

Corbett, Jim, 13
Cowper, H. S., 13
Cox, Nicholas, 126
crannequin, crannikin, 54, *54*, *57*
Crécy, Battle of, 61
de Crescentis, Pietro, 20
Cripps, H., 125
crossbow, 43 ff, 73–5, *50*, *51*, *55*, *57*,
60, *61*, *66*, *67*, *70*, *90*, *99*, *102*;
Bollinger, 98; siege, 55; for
tranquillizing darts, 99 ff; Winseler, 98
crossbowmen, *52*, *53*, *60*, *88*, *89*, *90*
Crusaders, Crusades, 43, 46, 50,
51, 59, 75, 76
Cumming, Rowaleyn Gordon,
213

Damietta, Battle of, 75
Danes, 58
David, 15, *16*, *17*
deer shooting, *113*, *288*, *302*
Dickson of Edinburgh, 213
Dixon, J. I., 91
Drake, Harry, 91
driving, 143, 163, 166
duck-shooting, *111*, *114*, *147*, *155*,
176
duelling, duels, 226 ff, *238*, *239*
Dunkirk, 91
Dunois, Sieur, 76
Dyrrachium, Battle of, 43

Earp, Wyatt, 241
Edward II, 75
Egyptians, Egyptian weapons, 38,
22, *33*
ejector, non-ejector, 163, *174*, *175*
elephant-hunting, 95–6, 210,
213 ff, 311 ff
English longbowmen, 58 ff, 75–6;
English arrows, 64–5
Erpingham, Sir Thomas, 76

Falkirk, Battle of, 61, 75
Fiedler, August, 256
flighting, 163, 166–7
flint-lock, 111, 120, 134, 135, 140,
134, *145*, *199*, *202*, *210*, *214*
Flodden, Battle of, 72

Ford, Horace Arthur, 71, 78–9, 82, 87, 91, *92*
Forsythe, Reverend Alexander, 135, 138–9
fowling-piece, 123
Fox, Charles James, 143
Franks, 43
Fremantle, Colonel T. F., 254, 266, 294

Game Laws, 128
German Army, 258–9; Jägers, 199, 204, 206, 255–6, 259, 262; weapons, 193, 202, 204, 258, 259, *198, 199*
Giraldus Cambrensis, 59, 65, 67
goat's-foot lever, 54, *51*
Greek weapons, 10, 16, 21, 34, *31, 32*
Grimley, Gordon, 29
grouse shooting, *157*
de Guesclin, Bertrand, 76
gun, *see* pistol, revolver, rifle, *etc.*
gunpowder, 103, 105, 129
gunsmiths, 125, 126, 129–30
Gunsmiths Company, 126

handgun, 103, 112, 113, *102, 104, 132–3, 136–7*
Hanger, Colonel George, 135, 203
harpoon, *18, 19*
Harold, King of England, 43
Hastings, Battle of, 43, 46, 58
Hawker, Peter, 135
Heath, E. G., 88
Henry III, 59
Henry VII, 105
Henry VIII, 70, 72, 109, 116–17
Herbert, Thomas, 41
Hill, Howard, 75, 94–8
Hodgkin, A. E., 86
Holinshed, Ralph, 73
Holland and Holland, 129, 307
holster, 242, 247
Hood, Robin, 59, 72
Hundred Years War, 63, 72
Huns, 37, 39

Iliad, 10, 18, 34, 35
International Shooting Union, 296, 297

Japanese marksmanship, weapons, 126, *23, 29, 128*
javelin, 17, 18, *14*
jezail, 209

Kappel, Battle of, 10, *10*
King, Dr John, 99–101
knob-kiris, knobkerrie, 13, *11*
Kollner, Gaspard, 107
Kotter, Augustus, 107

Lafauchaux, 151
Lana, Father Francesco, 256
Lancaster, Earl of, 76
Lancaster (gunmaker), 278
Latimer, Bishop, 68, 84
longbow, 27, 31, 35, 57 ff, 75–6, 82–3, 114, *42*

Manton, Joe, 227
Markham, Gervase, 121, 123–4
de Marolles, Magné, 134
Martin, Samuel, 227, 229–35
Martinez de Espinar, Alonso, 195
Masai weapons, 17, *11*
matchlock, 103–4, 110–11, 219, *106, 115, 117, 121, 140, 204, 257*
Matthews, R. D., 91
Minié, Captain, 222
Mongols, 37, 43
Montluc, 112
Moore, William, 213
Moors, 43
moulinet, 54
musket, 107, 112, 114, 120–1, 193 ff, *144, 148–9, 156*; Tower musket, 195–7
muzzle-loader, 139, 141, 151, 154, 193, *221, 265, 268–9, 276–7*

National Rifle Association, 262, 271, 278, 283, 286–7, 289, 291–2, 305
Nicols, Richard, 68
Normans, 43, 46

Olympic Games, 294, *87*
ownep, *12*

Paine, Ira, 241
Parthians, 43
Paulus Jovius, 72
Payne-Gallwey, Sir Ralph, 35
pea-shooter, 20
Pepys, Samuel, 126
percussion-lock, 135, 138–41, 151
Persia, Persians, 37, 41, 74; Persian weapons, 17, 41
petronel, *120*
pigeon shooting, *139, 160, 179, 280*
pistol, 226 ff, *234, 235, 248, 249, 250*; automatic, 242–5; flint-lock, *232, 233, 236, 237*; wheel-lock, *227, 228–9, 230*
poaching, 125
Poitiers, Battle of, 43, 61
Pope, Major B. H., 35
Pope, Saxton, 32, 65, 70
Prince of Wales ('Prinny'), 135, 143
proof-firing, 126
Purdey, James, 135

quivers, *29, 50*

Red Indian weapons, 31, 32, 33, *81*
repeater, 225
revolver, 109–11, 225, 238 ff; Adams, 239; Colt, 239, 241, 245; Webley, 239, 241, 244
Richard II, 57
Richard Cœur de Lion, 50–1
rifle, 193 ff, 226, *123, 200, 253*; air rifle, *209*; Baker, 206–7, 271, 275; Brunswick, 222; Dickson, 215; Enfield, 222, 286–7; Express, 310–11; Ferguson, 204–5; Holland and Holland, 313; Kentucky, 201, 205, 207; Krags Jørgensen, 299; Lee-Enfield, 279, 290–1, 295; Lee-Metford, 290–2, 295; Mannlicher, 259; Martini, 225; Martini-Henry, 251, 287, 289; Mauser, 225; modern, 251 ff; Purdey, 213, *200*; Rigby, 286; Ross, 262, 291, 295; small-bore, *299*; Springfield, 290; Tula, 206; wheel-lock, *119, 123*; Whitworth, 256, 278, 286; Winchester, 225
Rifle Brigade, 207
rifling, 107–8
Romans, Roman weapons, 17, 43, *50*
Rubin, Major, 251, 287
Russian marksmen, 296–7, *244, 296*; Russian weapons, 206

sampit (Sunda Islands), 21
Sancerre, Battle of, 16
Schwartz, Bertold, 103
Scoffern, Dr, 271
Scythians, 37, *38*
seal shooting, *310–11*
serpentine, 104–5
shooting competitions, 105–8, 207–9, 249, 278 ff, *124*; shooting galleries, *220*; guilds, 105, 107
shooting flying, flighting, shooting technique, 126 ff, 166–7, 170, *127, 129*
shooting, legislation for, 115–17, 128
shooting positions, 262 ff, *271, 278, 289, 290–1, 292* ff
shooting signals, *161*
shotgun, sawn-off, *179*
sight, 193, *203, 259, 263, 282*; aperture, 303–4, *274, 279*, backsight, 55; collimator, 98; foresight, *119, 266*; Holland Singlepoint, 307; leaf sight, *254, 255, 256*; Lyman, 305, 306; rear sight,

*120, 196, 197, 200, 201, 205, 208,
211–14, 270*; Reuss, *307, 246, 247,
249*; telescopic, 256–8, *250, 262,
267*; tunnel, *120, 136–7*
sling, 14–16, 18, *15, 37*
slingers (*petraboli*), 16
snaphaunce lock, 118–20
sniping, 254–5, 265, *258*
Spanish weapons, 105, 115
spear, 9, 16, *16, 40*; spear-thrower,
17–18, *13, 16, 28, 36*
stalking, *304, 309*; stalking horse,
stalking ox, 124, *64, 65, 118, 119,
122*
Stone Age weapons, 18, 19, 24,
31–3, 24, 30
stone-throwing, 9, 10, 12, 13, *10,
102*

target, 195, *241, 260, 261*; target-
shooting, 249, *108–9*
Tatars, 37
Tenchebrai, Battle of, 58
Thompson, Maurice, 71, 94
Thompson, Will, 94
throwing-spear, 17. *See also*
javelin
throwing-stick, 13, 14, 17, *33*
thumb-ring, *39*
Truelocke, 126
Turks, Turkish bow, 35, 37, 41,
43, 50–1, 74–6, 91, *46–7*
von Turnov, Eugen, 258

Upton, William, 125

Vikings, 43, 58

Wales, Welsh bowmen, 59
Wallingford, Staff-Sergeant, 290–
1
walking-up, 143, 163
Wellington, Duke of, 144, 146
wheel-lock, 110–11, 118, 226, *254*
Whitworth, Sir Joseph, 286
wild boar, 96–8, *276–7*
wildfowling, 124, *110, 142, 154,
178, 180, 181, 184, 186, 192*
Wilkes, John, 227, 229–35
William Rufus, 50
Williams, Sir Roger, 112–15
wind-judging, 283, 289, 305, 308

Zahn, Johannus, 256